CULTURAL TOURISM AND POVERTY ALLEVIATION

THE ASIA-PACIFIC PERSPECTIVE

WORLD TOURISM ORGANIZATION
Madrid, Spain
2005

**Cultural Tourism and Poverty Alleviation:
The Asia-Pacific Perspective**

ISBN 92-844-0810-5

Published and printed by the World Tourism Organization, Madrid, Spain
First printing in 2005

World Tourism Organization
Calle Capitán Haya, 42
28020 Madrid, Spain
Tel.: (+34) 915 678 100
Fax: (+34) 915 713 733
Web site: www.world-tourism.org
Email: omt@world-tourism.org

TECHNICAL SEMINAR ON CULTURAL TOURISM AND POVERTY ALLEVIATION

Siem Reap, Cambodia

8 June 2004

ACKNOWLEDGEMENTS

Cultural tourism forms an important component of international tourism in our world today, and the demand for it grows with each passing year. It has a high potential for contributing to the reduction of poverty in poor and remote communities, which are rich in intangible cultural resources, such as customs and folklore and are often located near famous heritage sites. The *Technical Seminar on Cultural Tourism and Poverty Alleviation* and the *Ministerial Conference* on the same subject were organised with the main objective of capitalising on the vast rich cultural resources Asia is endowed with, to support one of the UN's top Millennium Development Goals, i.e. the eradication of extreme poverty.

The World Tourism Organization wishes to express its heartfelt gratitude to the Royal Government of Cambodia and the Socialist Republic of Vietnam, for graciously hosting these two important meetings in the culturally rich cities of Siem Reap and Hue respectively. The warm reception and hospitality extended to all the participants are very much appreciated. WTO would also like to thank all the speakers for their instructive and thought-provoking inputs which contributed in no small way to the success of the meetings. Last but not least, we thank all participants, including Ministers of Tourism, tourism decision makers, researchers and private sector stakeholders for their valuable contribution to the discussions and deliberations, which formed the basis upon which the *Hue Declaration on Cultural Tourism and Poverty Alleviation* was drawn.

This publication has been compiled by the Regional Representation for Asia and the Pacific of the World Tourism Organization.

TABLE OF CONTENTS

1. INTRODUCTION

This report provides an overview of the technical seminar on cultural tourism and poverty alleviation that was held 8th June 2004, Siem Reap, Cambodia. The seminar was part of the forty – first (41st) meeting of the WTO Commission for East Asia and the Pacific that took place from 7-9 June 2004.

The seminar was organised by the World Tourism Organization in close cooperation with the Ministry of Tourism of the Royal Kingdom of Cambodia.

2. BACKGROUND

Cultural tourism forms an important component of international tourism in our world today. It represents movements of people motivated by cultural intents such as study tours, performing arts, festivals, cultural events, visits to sites and monuments, as well as travel for pilgrimages. Cultural tourism is also about immersion in and enjoyment of the lifestyle of the local people, the local area and what constitutes its identity and character.

International tourist arrivals are forecast to top 1 billion in 2010 and over 1.6 billion in 2020. Among the segments of tourism, cultural tourism stands out owing to its growth in popularity, which is faster than most other segments and certainly, faster than the rate of growth of tourism worldwide.

Asia is richly endowed with some of the world's most outstanding and grandest monuments such as Angkor Wat, Borobudur, the Great Wall, and the Taj Mahal. In addition, the continent boasts an impressive number of less known cultural assets, tangible as well as intangible, that could progressively be converted into a vibrant tourism supply. In fact, many of the Asia-Pacific countries have been successful in utilising their cultural resources as the main product of tourism. In order to encourage this aspect of tourism development, a special international conference on cultural tourism was organised by WTO in 2000 to address the very issue of culture and its relationship with tourism development. At this conference a wide-range of case studies were presented from all over the world to discuss the impacts of tourism on the preservation and conservation of cultural heritage, policies and guidelines for cultural tourism development and its marketing techniques.

Using culture as a vehicle for sustainable tourism development is now becoming an important item in the priorities of public policy planners. Apart from the socio-economic benefits that cultural tourism can generate for the well being of countries, the World Tourism Organization endeavors to explore the possibilities of using cultural tourism as a potential tool in fighting against poverty. As is known to all, many poor and remote communities are rich in intangible cultural resources such as customs and folklore and are often located near famous heritage sites. If well combined and integrated into tourism products, these two cultural resources, intangible and tangible, can become a powerful and perhaps the only tool for reducing poverty levels of such communities.

Through cultural tourism it is hoped that the remarkable growth rate projected and the higher expenditure profile of cultural tourists will help to generate economic growth, investment and employment and consequently, make an important contribution to poverty reduction – a top priority among the UN Millennium Development Goals and an ethical obligation of public and private decision makers.

3.   OBJECTIVES

- To examine ways in which cultural tourism can be channelled effectively to achieve poverty alleviation in Asia

- To identify policies that governments could adopt to increase their share of the cultural tourism market and increase its contribution to poverty alleviation

- To identify the roles that local authorities can play in cultural tourism management to ensure that socio-economic benefits are fairly distributed among the local poor

4.   ORGANIZATION AND STRUCTURE OF THE SEMINAR

The technical seminar on cultural tourism and poverty alleviation was inaugurated by his Excellency Mr. Veng Sereyvuth, Minister of Tourism of the Royal Kingdom of Cambodia, his Excellency Mr. Frangialli, Secretary General of the World Tourism Organization and his Excellency the Prime Minister Samdech Hun Sen of the Royal Kingdom of Cambodia.

The actual seminar began with a brief introduction on the aim and structure of the seminar. Two keynote presentations by WTO gave an in depth analysis of the principles, challenges and opportunities that cultural tourism provides in relation to poverty alleviation. Also an overview of opportunities for community involvement in cultural tourism was presented. In addition the Sustainable Tourism for Eliminating Poverty (ST-EP) programme was presented by WTO and further elaborated by Mr. Beong Heok Yoo, Director of International Tourism Division of the Ministry of Culture and Tourism of the Republic of Korea.

During the main part of the technical seminar different case studies from different countries in East Asia were presented. This part of the seminar was concluded with an overview of the common themes and issues that had emerged from the case study presentations. The main recommendations were put forward for discussion during the Ministerial Conference held 11-12 June 2004 in Hue, Viet Nam.

The seminar was concluded by Mr. Francesco Frangialli who pointed out that there is a need to balance the interests of the private and public sector and the need to exploit more cultural sites that have the potential to be developed. Also the social impacts of tourism must be addressed in relation to cultural tourism, not only from the macro point of view but also at the micro level, especially in reducing leakages.
Finally, culture is not only about archaeological sites but is also very much about making crafts, songs and oral traditions.

Mr. Veng Sereyvuth stressed the need to link the local suppliers to the hotel sector and the tour operators. He also urged for regional cooperation among Asian countries, especially with respect to cross border issues such as the issuing of visa. In line with the ethic code of conduct it is important to balance the need of the tourists and the living local culture.

5. CONCLUSIONS AND RECOMMENDATIONS

Due to time constraints there was little time for the participants to discuss the conclusions and recommendations. The most important observation was made in respect to point 11, as not to limit government policies and actions to the national level but also to include regional and especially local authorities.

General:

1. Important target groups for poverty alleviation are communities and (individual) poor people. Tackling the issue of poverty is difficult, especially in reaching the poorest of the poor.

2. Poverty alleviation is about a different approach to tourism development and marketing, it is not always about creating new and different products.

3. There is a need to gain more insight into the economic and social-cultural benefits for the poor and for communities. Indicators to measure and monitor these benefits should be developed and mechanism should be put in place to share the gathered data.

Tourism related products:

4. To create tourism packages (in the surroundings of cultural sites) that focus on traditional village life. Such products will add extra value to the visitors experience and will also extend their stay at the destination and reach more poor people.

5. The production and selling of crafts provides direct benefits to the makers. It is essential to produce quality crafts in accordance with market demand and to create professional outlets at different levels.

Conditions for success:

6. To have tourism policies and general management plans in place at the local and regional level, and at the destination as a whole.

7. To create public awareness on the issue of poverty reduction in relation to tourism.

8. To increase access to capital for the development of micro enterprises.

9. To support entrepreneurial skills among poor people and communities.

10. For community projects the critical issues are marketing, (hospitality) training, support from outsiders, gradual exposure to tourism, quality standards for tourism products and strong commitment of the community.

Stakeholders:

11. Government policies need to be adjusted towards the poor in general and communities specifically. Government action needs to be well coordinated and integrated.

12. It is essential to create synergy between tourism development programmes and other (inter) national development programmes carried out by national governments, non-governmental organizations and UN bodies.

13. Guidelines for hotels, tour operators and other private sector companies need to be formulated to integrate elements of poverty alleviation in their daily business operations and supply chains.

14. Close cooperation between the private sector and communities should be encouraged, especially in terms of developing (new) tourism products, crafts and (joint) marketing.

Opening Speeches

WELCOMING ADDRESS BY THE MINISTER OF TOURISM OF THE ROYAL KINGDOM OF CAMBODIA[1]

Samdech Hun Sen, Prime Minister of the Royal Government of Cambodia
H.E. Mr. **Francesco Frangialli**, Secretary-General of the World Tourism Organization
Excellencies, Distinguished Delegates, Ladies and Gentlemen,

First of all, please allow me, on behalf of the leaders and officials of the Ministry of Tourism, the Private Sector and all seminar delegates, to express my highest esteem to Samdech **Hun Sen**, Prime Minister of the Royal Government of Cambodia who as we know regards the tourism industry as one of the most vital industries to assist in the rehabilitation and economic development of our State. Moreover, Samdech Hun Sen is dedicated to stimulating and advocating appropriate tourism projects and activities, which translates to creating a healthy and vibrant environment for tourism development. More honorably, he has taken his valuable time from his busy schedule to preside over this important seminar on Cultural Tourism and Poverty Alleviation that is being organized jointly by the Ministry of Tourism and the World Tourism Organization.

May I take this opportunity also to extend my thanks to H.E. Mr. **Francesco Frangialli**, Secretary-General of the World Tourism Organization for allocating Cambodia with the honor to host this seminar on Cultural Tourism and Poverty Alleviation in the Asia-Pacific region. This seminar runs in conjunction with the 41st Meeting of the WTO Commission for East Asia and the Pacific that was conducted fruitfully and successfully yesterday.

I would like to extend a very warm welcome to honored national and international guests, diplomatic corps, WTO delegates, the delegates of the WTO Commission for East Asia and the Pacific, delegates of the WTO Commission for South Asia and delegates from the Royal Government institutions, provincial authorities, international organizations, NGOs, tourism universities and the tourism industry private sector that, added together, numbers approximately 200 participants attending this seminar today.

- Honorable Samdech Hun Sen, Prime Minister of the Royal Government of Cambodia
- H.E. Mr. Francesco Fangialli, Secretary-General of the World Tourism Organization
- Delegates

Siem Reap Angkor is the National Historical Cultural Tourism Center (NHCTC). By complying with the sound policy of the Royal Government of Cambodia, this Tourism Center has progressed rapidly as can be observed in the quality of infrastructures such as the airport, roads, electricity and other tourism-related development.

Approximately 57% of international visitor arrivals come to Angkor Wat temple in 2003 and in 2004, the number of visitor arrivals will increase to approximately 570,000. By 2008 we estimate numbers will reach 1.3 million and by 2010, 1.9 million. Tourism revenue in this province particularly collected approximately US$100 million in 2003 and based on our forecast, it will increase to US$240 million in 2006 and

---

[1] H.E. Mr. Veng Sereyvuth

US$600 million by 2010.

In 2003, Siem Reap province had 3,000 luxury and international standard hotel-rooms and this number is expected to double by 2005. The tourism industry has helped generate more than 50,000 job opportunities for locals in this province; with the majority of work coming in the service sector such as hotels, restaurants, tour-guides, tourist transportation, airport, souvenir vendors, construction and supply services such as foodstuffs.

The Royal Government of Cambodia under the brilliant leadership of Samdech Hun Sen as Prime Minister has made great effort in tourism investment in this region with sound policy that will attract more tourists while at the same time the government is determined to ensure the preservation and sustainable development of this world famous historical, cultural site. By doing so we will improve the living standard of the local population and contribute to the alleviation of poverty.

- Honorable Samdech Hun Sen, Prime Minister of the Royal Government of Cambodia
- H.E. Mr. Francesco Frangialli, Secretary-General of the World Tourism Organization; and
- Delegates

The 41st Meeting of the WTO Commission for East Asia and the Pacific that was conducted yesterday provided a vital forum for country members of the region to hold discussions on many topics relating to the work programs of the World Tourism Organization and other current issues including the Programs of Tourism Trends in the region, the Implementation and Evaluation of General Works and the Implementation of Global Code of Ethic for Tourism.

Today, the seminar on Cultural Tourism and Poverty Alleviation will be held with many experts and noted tourism professionals in our company. This seminar will, I am sure, provide insightful discussion regarding the ways and means that cultural tourism opportunities can play a role in reducing poverty in our region as well as here in Cambodia. Through the seminar today, we hope to determine some recommendations that may contribute to decision-making on the role that local authorities can play in cooperative management of cultural tourism sites. Furthermore we seek ideas on concepts that will ensure the equal distribution of benefits amongst the people of local communities. In addition the seminar will be privileged to receive the recommendations of Samdech Hun Sen, Prime Minister of the Royal Government of Cambodia who maintains the principle that tourism development must be sustainable and contribute to the social and economic development of the people of Cambodia.

Finally, I extend to Samdech Hun Sen, Prime Minister of my highest esteem; wishes of good health, wisdom and prosperity and the continuation of his inspirational leadership of the Royal Government of Cambodia.

I also wish H.E. Mr. Francesco Frangialli, Secretary-General of the United Nations and his colleagues every success for their mission in order to achieve the United National Millennium Development Goals in the new capacity of the WTO as a Specialized

Agency of the United Nations.

Furthermore, I wish all international and national delegates a successful seminar and an enjoyable stay in this wonderful site of Angkor.

Thank you.

MESSAGE BY THE SECRETARY-GENERAL OF THE WORLD TOURISM ORGANIZATION[2]

On behalf of the World Tourism Organization (WTO), it is indeed my pleasure to welcome you all to the forty-first meeting of the WTO Commission for East Asia and the Pacific and the Technical Seminar on Cultural Tourism and Poverty Alleviation, which are being organized in Siem Reap, Cambodia from 7-9 June 2004 at the gracious invitation of the Royal Government of Cambodia.

The Asia-Pacific region has become one of the fastest developing tourism destinations of the world. For the first time in 2002, with 131 million international arrivals, the region became the second-most visited destination of the world after Europe, overtaking Americas. Although SARS had a severe impact on tourist arrivals to Asia in the first half of 2003, the region demonstrated extraordinary resiliency and capacity to recover and many destinations managed to show positive results in international tourist arrivals by the end of 2003.

The 41st Meeting of the WTO Commission for East Asia and the Pacific will provide an important platform for our Member States in the region to meet together and dwell upon a number of subjects relating to the WTO programme of work and other issues of contemporary concern. Delegates will be apprised of the performance of international tourism in 2003 through the presentation of global, regional and country-specific tourism trends.

In line with the UN Millennium Development Goals, the World Tourism Organization, as a specialized agency of the United Nations, is organizing this Seminar on Cultural Tourism and Poverty Alleviation in collaboration with the Royal Kingdom of Cambodia, with the aim to: examine ways in which cultural tourism can be channelled effectively to achieve poverty alleviation in Asia; identify policies that governments could adopt to increase their share of the cultural tourism market and increase its contribution to poverty alleviation; and identify the roles that local authorities can play in cultural tourism management to ensure that socio-economic benefits are fairly distributed among the local poor.

I must take this opportunity to thank the Royal Government of Cambodia for hosting the events which are important activities of WTO in the Asia-Pacific region. I am pleased to note that Cambodia, with its unparalleled cultural heritage and tropical ecology, is enjoying a resurgence of interest amongst foreign travellers looking to savour the essence of Indochina. At the top of any list of places to visit in Cambodia is the Angkor complex of ancient temples in the Province of Siem Reap. The most famous of these sites is Angkor Wat, the world's largest religious monument and truly one of the architectural wonders of the world.

I am convinced that the WTO Commission meeting and the Seminar would be of great benefit to all the participants. It is no coincidence that the WTO Meetings are being held in Siem Reap for the second time – a beautiful city whose authorities are playing an important role in the maintenance and preservation of Khmer culture. In

---

[2] Mr. Francesco Frangialli

Siem Reap, we will be able to appreciate the warm and gracious hospitality of the Cambodian people and their rich traditions and culture.

OPENING SPEECH BY THE PRIME MINISTER OF THE ROYAL GOVERNMENT OF CAMBODIA[3]

H.E. Mr. Francesco Frangialli, Secretary General of the World Tourism Organization; Your Excellencies, Ladies and Gentlemen;

Today, I am very pleased to participate in this *Forty-First Meeting of the WTO Commission for East Asia and the Pacific and the Technical Seminar on Cultural Tourism and Poverty Alleviation.*

On behalf of the Royal Government of people of Cambodia, may I extend my warmest welcome to all *Your Excellencies, Distinguished Delegates and Guests* from many countries in this significant international gathering on the wonderful land of Angkor, the Kingdom of Cambodia.

I am delighted to meet H.E. Francesco Frangialli for the second time since the *International Conference on Cultural Tourism*, first held in Siem Reap in late 2000. May I also express my appreciation to Mr. Frangialli ad his colleagues of the WTO who have exerted strong leadership in promoting mutual understanding, encouraging sustainable tourism development and thereby helping us all realize these shared goals.

May I also express my congratulations to the United Nations for recognizing the World Tourism Organization as a Specialized Agency of the UN since 24 December 2003.

This recognition provides the WTO with further momentum to collaborate more intensively with the UN family. It also manifests the importance of tourism development, upheld by the international community, particularly the sector's contribution to poverty alleviation, development, conservation of cultural heritage, environmental protection, strengthening of peace and mutual understanding among all nations. Indeed, the WTO's status as a specialized agency of the UN provides it not only with legitimacy in economic development cooperation, but it also attests to the significant role of tourism toward the achievement of the UN Millennium Development Goals.

Your Excellencies, Ladies and Gentlemen:

Asia is rich with diverse cultural heritages. In particular, Cambodia has many cultural and historical sites dating thousands of years back to our ancestors, the most prominent of which are the unique Angkor temples that are the greatest products of Khmer architecture, sculpture and history. During the Angkor Era, Cambodia reached its peak as a civilized nation. At that time, we employed the most modern technologies in construction, architecture, urban management, agriculture and other infrastructures. In the City of Angkor, the people, forests and temples co-existed in harmony, peace and prosperity. Even today, all who are fortunate to visit and gaze upon the Angkor monuments fall under their spell of beauty, mystery and greatness, and are forever held in thrall.

---

[3] H.E. Mr. Samdech Hun Sen

At the same time, Cambodia also has many other natural, recreational and eco-tourism sites, which we are working hard to further develop into wonderful tourism venues. These include geographic sites rich in unique cultural and natural attractions. Based on this favorable condition, the Royal Government has determined the policy of tourism development of Cambodia as a " *Cultural and Natural Tourism*" destination.

The Royal Government keenly appreciates the enormous potentials for tourism's contribution to Cambodia's socio-economic development. The Government also shares in the global recognition of tourism as a unique mechanism for trade and communication, which contributes broadly to national revenues, job creation, and improvement of living standards. Moreover, cultures, traditions and national reputations are promoted worldwide through tourism, impacting on regional and international understanding, cooperation and peace.

It is, therefore, not by accident that the Royal Government of Cambodia considers tourism as one of the six priority thrusts in its strategy to promote economic growth and poverty reduction.

Your Excellencies, Ladies and Gentlemen:

Tourism has been crucial to Cambodia's growth. In 1998-2002, the sector grew steadily, by 25%-30% annually. Unfortunately, in 2003 Cambodia's tourism sector was adversely affected by the outbreak of SARS in the region, while Cambodia itself was not affected. In 2003 visitor arrivals to Cambodia fell by 10%, lower that the fall across ASEAN of an average of 14%.

The tourism sector demonstrated its resiliency by its speedy recovery from the SARS outbreak. The collaboration and coordination among the Heads of Governments in the region, the World Tourism Organization, World Health Organization and other international development partners promoted the rapid recovery of tourism. *In Cambodia, in the first four months of 2004, international arrivals have increased 29.62% if compared to 2003!*

Your Excellencies, ladies and Gentlemen:

The Royal Government of Cambodia clearly recognizes that physical infrastructures, including roads, water, electricity, telecommunications and other services are crucial to significant and sustained growth not only of the tourism sector but the economy as a whole.

Due to the growth of tourism, Siem Reap has remarkably developed its infrastructure, including the airport, roads, traffic facilities, power, hotels, restaurants and recreational facilities. Indeed, tourism has promoted the development of all socio-economic sectors of the province, with linkages to and positive impacts on surrounding and other priority tourism destinations.

The Royal Government of Cambodia has exerted efforts to attract more tourists to the Angkor Zone, while at the same time protecting and conserving the Angkor for sustainable development. The Royal Government has formed the APSARA Authority as a Special Authority to protect and conserve the Angkor cultural area. Efforts of the

APSARA, in collaboration with the UNESCO and other international partners have moved beyond the rescue stage into a new era of conservation and development.

The Royal Government is monitoring all developments in the Angkor area to keep track of both positive as well as negative impacts, and to facilitate corrective measures. A master plan for the development of the Angkor area has been formulated with worldwide assistance and is now under implementation in terms of projects such as water and electricity supply, wastewater management and other infrastructures all toward the goal of preserving and developing the area into a sustainable cultural tourism destination that we can all be proud of.

The Royal Government of Cambodia is also focusing on the development of the areas surrounding the Angkor, particularly linked to the tourism, cultural and natural destinations of neighboring countries such as Thailand and Lao PDR. The most. The most important joint initiative between Cambodia, Lao PDR and Thailand is the Emerald Triangle Development Program. In this regard, I thank the World Tourism Organization for its conduct of appraisal on the Emerald Triangle Development Program.

Your Excellencies, Ladies and Gentlemen:

It is an honor for the Kingdom of Cambodia to be elected as Chair of the East Asia and the Pacific Commission of WTO for the 2004-2005 mandate. I appreciate the results of the 41st Meeting of the WTO Commission for East Asia and the Pacific, which discussed the details of the regional programs, including the preparation, implementation and evaluation for general programs of work, the implementation of the *Global Code of Ethics for Tourism, the Emerald Triangle Tourism Development (Cambodia- Lao PDR- Thailand) Program and the Heritage Necklace Project* initiated by Thailand.

I am convinced that the Seminar on *Cultural Tourism and Poverty Alleviation* today will examine ways in which cultural tourism can be channeled effectively to achieve poverty alleviation in Cambodia and Asia. Indeed, we should identify policies that governments may adopt to increase their share of the cultural tourism market and increase the contribution of tourism to poverty alleviation. Moreover, we should define the roles that local authorities can play in cultural tourism management to ensure that socio-economic benefits are fairly distributed among the local poor.

With our strong commitment to achievement of the Cambodia Millennium Development Goals, the Royal Government of Cambodia has launched its *2003-2005 Cambodia National Poverty Reduction Strategy* and set up the *Tourism Poverty Alleviation Working Group* chaired by the Ministry of Tourism. Such coordination will help ensure that poverty alleviation is always at the forefront of our activities, including our tourism development efforts.

Your Excellencies, Ladies and Gentlemen:

After this meeting, tomorrow you will tour the Angkor Wat monuments. The temples will offer you many rewards from our heritage and ancient civilization. We hope that during your brief stay in the Kingdom, you will appreciate that while Cambodia has a rich heritage; our nation is firmly moving forward into a brighter future, with hope and confidence in our own strong capability and commitment.

May I extend to Your Excellency Francesco Frangialli and all Your Excellencies, Ladies and Gentlemen my wishes for success in all your endeavors, good health and a pleasant and enjoyable stay in Cambodia!

Thank you for your attention!

Technical Sessions

INTRODUCTION TO THE CONFERENCE BY WTO'S REGIONAL REPRESENTATIVE FOR ASIA AND THE PACIFIC [4]

Ladies and gentlemen, let us commence the technical session of this seminar. First of all, the Secretariat would like to invite the distinguished delegates to refer to the document entitled the Technical Note for the Seminar, which specifies

- the background of the Seminar;
- the aims and the objectives of the Seminar; and
- the methodology that is used for the Seminar

This document would serve effectively the introduction of the Secretariat to this seminar.

As you are aware, cultural tourism is an important component among the segments of tourism. Many Asia-Pacific countries have been successful in utilising their cultural resources as the main product of tourism. Using culture as a vehicle for sustainable tourism development is now becoming an important item in the priorities of public policy planners.

However, how to use cultural tourism as a potential tool in fighting against poverty is what the World Tourism Organization endeavours to explore at this Seminar. As is known to all, many poor and remote communities are rich in cultural resources such as customs and folklore and are often located near famous heritage sites. If well combined and integrated into tourism products, these two cultural resources, intangible and tangible, can become a powerful and perhaps the only tool for reducing poverty levels of such communities.

Against this background and in collaboration with the Royal Kingdom of Cambodia, the World Tourism Organization is organizing this Seminar on the subject for the first time in Asia with the following objectives:

- to examine ways in which cultural tourism can be channelled effectively to achieve poverty alleviation in Asia

- to identify policies that governments could adopt to increase their share of the cultural tourism market and increase its contribution to poverty alleviation

- to identify the roles that local authorities can play in cultural tourism management to ensure that socio-economic benefits are fairly distributed among the local poor

Ladies and gentlemen, today we have got with us a galaxy of high-profile senior officials and professionals who will deliver various presentations from different perspectives, global, regional or local. We shall start with two keynote presentations by WTO on the international scenario of cultural tourism and its contribution to poverty reduction. The main technical presentations will be followed by special WTO case studies and country presentations with the aim to analyse the methodologies and

---

[4] Mr. Xu Jing

guidelines for successful cultural tourism development at national and local level as a tool for poverty elimination. Two special remarks on the WTO ST-EP Programme (Sustainable Tourism – Eliminating Poverty) will also be made, one by the WTO Secretary-General and one by the delegation of the Republic of Korea.

The Seminar will conclude with a summary of its proceedings with conclusions and recommendations that will be reported further to the forthcoming Ministerial Conference on Cultural Tourism and Poverty Alleviation in the city of Hue, Vietnam.

Ladies and gentlemen, let us first invite Mr. Eugenio Yunis, Chief of WTO Sustainable Development of Tourism to make the first presentation.

WTO KEYNOTE PRESENTATION ON
CULTURAL TOURISM AND POVERTY ALLEVIATION[5]

Introduction

An important and still current trend in international tourist movements is the diversification of destinations that has taken place during the last 30 years or so. While in 1950 fifteen countries, all of them from Europe plus USA and Canada, accounted for over 90% of total international tourist arrivals, in 2002, their share of the market had fallen to around 60%. In parallel, many developing countries saw their tourist arrivals increase significantly. In 2002, three Asian destinations appeared among the top 15, as shown in the table below.

World's Top Tourism Destinations by International Tourist Arrivals

Rank	1950	World Share	1970	World Share	1990	World Share	2002	World Share
1	United States		Italy		France		France	
2	Canada		Canada		United States		Spain	
3	Italy	71%	France	43%	Spain	38%	United States	35%
4	France		Spain		Italy		Italy	
5	Switzerland		United States		Hungary		China	
6	Ireland		Austria		Austria		United Kingdom	
7	Austria		Germany		United Kingdom		Canada	
8	Spain	17%	Switzerland	22%	Mexico	19%	Mexico	14%
9	Germany		Yugoslavia		Germany		Austria	
10	United Kingdom		United Kingdom		Canada		Germany	
11	Norway		Hungary		Switzerland		Hong Kong (China)	
12	Argentina		Czechoslovakia		Greece		Hungary	
13	Mexico	9%	Belgium	10%	Portugal	10%	Greece	11%
14	Netherlands		Bulgaria		Malaysia		Poland	
15	Denmark		Romania		Croatia		Malaysia	
	Others	3%	Others	25%	Others	33%	Others	40%
Total		**25 million**		**166 million**		**456 million**		**703 million**

Source: World Tourism Organization (WTO) ©   (Data as collected by WTO September 2003)

Furthermore, some of the least developed countries in Asia with a small inbound tourism market in 1990, like **Cambodia, Lao** and **Vietnam,** witnessed an impressive growth between 1990 and 2002: international tourist arrivals were multiplied by 46 in Cambodia, by 15 in Lao, and by 6 in Vietnam[6]. In addition, several other countries also registered strong growth rates:

- **China** (which still counts with wide poor regions): nearly **37 million** of ITA in 2002 and an average annual growth of **9%** between 1995 and 2002
- **Malaysia**: more than **13 million** of ITA in 2002 and an average annual growth of **5%** between 1990 and 2002

---

[5] Mr. Eugenio Yunis, Chief, Sustainable Development of Tourism, WTO
[1] Between 1990 and 2001

- **Thailand**: nearly **11 million** of ITA in 2002 and an average annual growth of **6%** between 1990 and 2002
- **Indonesia**: more than **5 million** of ITA and an average annual growth of **7%** between 1990 and 2002

Note: World average annual growth (1990-2002): 3.7%

The rich and varied cultural offer that characterises Asian countries is one of the main reasons that explain these good results. Indeed, the profusion of heritage assets and cultural events act like catalysts of tourist demand; such attractions, combined with the other facets of the Asian tourism offer (beaches, nature, business, shopping, etc), serve to significantly increase the attractiveness of all these destinations in the international tourism market.

At the same time, Asia is host to 65 per cent of the world's poor, as defined by the World Bank. This means 712 million people living with less than one dollar per day. There is, therefore, an ethical obligation for the tourism sector in the region to find practical ways in which this activity, particularly when it is motivated by cultural attractions, could more effectively contribute to alleviate the poverty situation. In addition to fulfilling an ethical imperative of our times, helping to reduce poverty is a key element for the long term sustainability of tourism development in Asia, since tourism cannot eventually survive under extreme poverty conditions, since it becomes unsafe, risky and somehow anachronistic in the eyes of many visitors.

Can tourism contribute to reduce poverty?

Looking at the location of poverty in the world, and then at tourism flows, two key points emerge. Firstly, tourism is increasingly playing a major part in the economy of poor countries. In 2001, international tourism receipts accruing to developing countries amounted to US$ 142,306 million worldwide, of which 31 per cent correspond to Asian developing nations (i.e. US$ 44,380 million). Tourism is the principal export in a third of all developing countries and, amongst the 49 Least Developed Countries (LDCs), it is the primary source of foreign exchange earnings. In some countries it plays a major part in their sustainable development strategy. In Africa for example, it was tourism that enabled Botswana to cease to be an LDC back in 1994.

International tourism receipts in Asian Countries, $millions

	1990	2002	% change 1990-2002
Low income countries	3,165	10,413	229
Lower middle income countries	7,965	18,002	366.3
Upper middle income countries	1,674	1,606	332.3
High income countries	19,552	20,464	112.3
Asia Total	**32,356**	**140,762**	**335**
World Total	*265,316*	*457,890*	*72.6*

World Tourism Organization; World Development Report 2003 (World Bank)

Secondly, tourism is growing much faster in developing countries than in developed countries. The graph below shows the relative growth of international tourist arrivals in low-middle- and high-income countries of Asia in recent years.

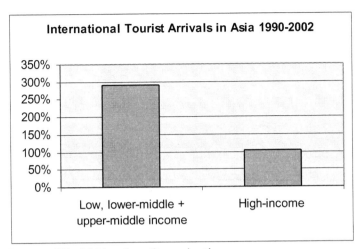

International Tourist Arrivals in Asia 1990-2002

Source: World Tourism Organization

In line with this, a predicted growth rate of around 5.9% per annum between 2000 and 2020 for South Asia, which is home (with Africa) to most of the world's poorest people, is considerably greater than for the world as a whole; and much of such growth will be motivated by the continuous incorporation of more and more cultural attractions into the tourism offer of these countries.

However, it is not purely a question of market growth. Some other reasons serve to explain why cultural tourism is particularly well placed to meet the needs of the poor. These include:

- The fact that tourism is one of the few industries in which many developing countries actually have a comparative advantage over developed countries in terms of cultural heritage, particularly considering cultural assets and traditions that are very different and less known to the current main generating markets of Europe and North America.
- The attractiveness of some interesting cultural heritage sites located in remote rural areas, accompanied by the living cultural traditions of the corresponding rural communities. This point is particularly important, since three quarters of people in extreme poverty live in rural areas.
- The opportunity to support, through cultural tourism, traditional activities such as ancient rice cultivations, tea growing, collecting and roasting, and a wide range of traditional handicrafts. It can also offer an opportunity to maintain traditional building methods for the construction of tourist lodges or for the restoration of monuments.
- The fact that tourism is a labour intensive and a diversified industry, which can provide jobs for women and young people within and around cultural heritage sites, ranging from basic tourist services in hotels and restaurants that require little training, to jobs in artistic performances, festival and other cultural events.
- It is also an industry where entry barriers to establishing new small businesses can be quite low, or can be easily lowered to allow poor people to establish new activities or to formalise existing micro-ventures.
- And leaving aside economics, it can bring non-material benefits such as pride in local culture and a valorisation of the surrounding natural environment and cultural landscapes in the eyes of local communities. Besides, since cultural tourism can

23

positively contribute to the fame and renown of a place, it can help to attract new companies and investors, which would like to associate their name with its image.

Having revisited the advantages of cultural tourism and having looked at the international policy context, we identify a short set of overarching principles that should be borne in mind when seeking to address poverty through tourism in general, and cultural tourism in particular. These are:

- **Mainstreaming:** Ensuring that sustainable development of all segments of tourism, including the cultural one, is included in general poverty elimination programmes. And, conversely, including poverty elimination measures within overall strategies for the sustainable development of all segments of tourism. In parallel, programmes linking culture and poverty have to be envisaged, like the Dutch-supported initiative "Learning and Research on Culture and Poverty" lead by the World Bank and aiming at improving poverty reduction efforts by mobilizing cultural strengths and assets.
- **Partnership:** Developing partnerships between public and private sector bodies, with a common aim of poverty alleviation. In addition, since culture and tourism cannot be considered like competitors but rather as collaborators, partnerships have to be established between tourism administrations and tourism companies on the one hand, and cultural authorities and cultural site managers on the other, with a view to examine ways in which the local poor could be trained and employed at sites to help serve the tourists' requirements.
- **Integration:** Adopting an integrated approach with other sectors and avoiding over-dependence on tourism. And within the tourism sector, linking the cultural tourism offer with other tourism segments (nature, beach, and especially business tourism, etc).
- **Equitable distribution:** Ensuring that development strategies of cultural tourism focus on achieving a more equitable distribution of wealth and services, since growth alone is not enough. This contributes also to raise the awareness among local populations about the fact that cultural assets have to be protected, since they provide them with additional income and job opportunities.
- **Acting locally:** Focusing action at a local destination level (a village, a site or a city), within the context of supportive national policies. And establishing partnerships between tourism and cultural authorities at the local level too.
- **Retention:** Reducing leakages from the local economy and building linkages within it, focussing on the very long tourism supply chain.
- **Viability:** Maintaining sound financial discipline in tourism enterprises and assessing the commercial viability of all actions taken.
- **Empowerment:** Creating conditions to empower and enable the poor to have access to information and to influence and take decisions, and provide them suitable training to continue and strengthen their involvement in cultural tourism activities.
- **Human rights:** Removing all forms of discrimination against people working, or seeking to work, in tourism and eliminating any exploitation, particularly against women and children. Indeed, in many communities women are the guarantors for traditional continuity and must be included in the decision-making process regarding cultural tourism activities. The corollary is also valid; tourism development must consider the right to self-determination and cultural sovereignty of indigenous communities, including their protected, sensitive and sacred sites as well as their traditional knowledge.

24

- **Commitment:** Planning action and the application of resources for the long term.
- **Monitoring:** Developing simple indicators and systems to measure the impact of cultural tourism on poverty, as well as the impacts of tourism on the cultural assets and values. It regards, among others, increases in revenues, employment statistics, possible physical deterioration of assets (caused by tourists or not), the dependence of communities living close to the sites on the tourism resources, their loss of control over cultural properties, leakages, etc.

The above principles need to be taken into account, bearing in mind that the best strategy for a country or region to conserve its comparative advantage in the tourism market is to maintain and develop its combination of cultural assets, traditions and arts that make up its uniqueness. Yet, for this to occur in a sustainable manner, it is necessary to achieve a mutually beneficial relationship between tourism and cultural heritage. This requires:

- Understanding by the tourism sector of the holistic nature of culture, and reciprocally, understanding, by the cultural heritage specialists and conservation professionals in general, the importance of tourism and the needs and legitimate desires of the tourist.
- Preparing a tourism master plan or a site management plan for the heritage object and its surrounding areas.
- Applying modern planning and monitoring techniques and methodologies (e.g. environmental impact assessment, carrying capacity, the definition of sustainability indicators).
- Responding differently to the needs and preferences of cultural travellers and of other categories of visitors.
- Interpreting the heritage sites for the visitors, including the living cultural elements around them.
- Setting up a marketing strategy and a pricing policy for tourism at heritage sites, and establishing appropriate mechanisms for ensuring that a significant proportion of tourism earnings revert to conservation purposes.

The 7 approaches for poverty reduction through cultural tourism

The above evidence and principles regarding tourism and poverty have pushed WTO to initiate specific research about the various forms and conditions in which tourism does contribute to reduce poverty in different countries and in different segments of the tourism industry. In a recent publication *Tourism and Poverty Alleviation: Recommendations for action*, WTO has presented the results of such research, identifying seven different ways of addressing poverty through tourism. These can be applied in almost every country, provided a number of issues are suitably addressed. I will attempt today to adapt these 7 approaches to cultural tourism and to Asia in particular.

The first way is simply through **the employment of the poor in tourism companies, but also in cultural enterprises** (as a guide or a guardian in a heritage site, for example) within or outside cultural sites or monuments. This can occur in small as well as large enterprises and in rural and urban areas. In Asia there are already many large hotel establishments catering for cultural tourists, and they could be encouraged to gradually replace foreign staff with local people, strengthening at the same time the local cultural image of the destinations; but policies and laws that encourage the employment of local people, such as those recently approved in the Maldives for example, are more likely to open up opportunities for the poor.

The advantage of addressing poverty through existing tourism enterprises is that it enables the poor to benefit from the entrepreneurial skills and market access of others, and can potentially reach quite large numbers of people. Many issues need to be addressed in Asian companies in order to secure potential advantages for the poor through tourism employment, such as:

- Having proper contracts and fair pay conditions.
- Providing part time work, enabling poor people also to attend to other commitments, and also helping in this way to reach more people.
- Disseminating the flows of tourists towards less visited cultural assets close to famous sites, in order to create job opportunities for even more people and in a wider radius.
- Addressing the question of how and where job opportunities are promoted and advertised.
- Looking at seasonality issues, if any, and the need to provide more year round opportunities, which in the case of cultural tourism should be easier, since tourists are not motivated by, or dependent on climate conditions.
- The choice of location of new developments, giving greater importance to sites or monuments surrounded by poor populations, and to living cultural expressions of poor communities.

The second way is through **the supply of goods and services to tourism enterprises by the poor.** This can happen at various points in the tourism supply chain, including the choice of products featured by tour operators as well as goods and services provided to hotels, such as food and textile furnishings, especially if these are is produced with traditional techniques, thus doubly enhancing the cultural experience of visitors, handicrafts and decorations, building services at the construction stage (including heritage restoration works), and so on. The advantage in the supply-chain approach is that this can make use of existing skills in poor communities and of the existing hotel and other tourism infrastructure, encouraging it to examine its supply chain and to strive to use locally supplied goods and services instead of imports. The two main issues to address are:

- How to encourage and help enterprises to identify new sources of supply.
- Working with poor communities to enable them to provide an assurance of quality and reliability.

A practical approach is to take small steps, making a few carefully selected linkages, where success seems most likely, and then building on this. NTAs can help in establishing the linkages between the hotel and catering sector and the local manufacturers of different goods.

The third way is through **direct sales of goods and services to visitors by the poor.** This is about the informal economy, and includes stalls selling food and handicrafts, portering, some forms of transport, and informal accommodation. The informal sector is hugely important in many developing countries and this can be one of the most direct ways of getting visitor spending into the hands of the poor. However it is characterised by chaotic trading conditions, congestion in the site access and over-supply. Issues here include:

- providing some order and quality control, which may include licensing or training (for example, in the framework of a cultural visit, it requires a good knowledge from the guides to provide tourists with a high-quality experience),

- giving some reassurance to visitors as potential purchasers. However, it is important still to maintain the ease of access to such trading by poor people, which is the main advantage of the informal economy.

Example for the 2 approaches above: Pakistan's largest inbound tour operator, Travel Walji's Limited (TWL), is the first tour operator to organize tours to Karimbad, a village that constitutes the cultural center of Hunza in the Karakorum region, where it supports local entrepreneurs. There are now 27 shops selling handicrafts, trekking equipment, food, postcards etc. and more than 70 small family-owned hotels provide income for local people.[2]

Fourthly, there is the process of supporting the **establishment of tourism enterprises by the poor.** These may be micro, small and medium sized enterprises (MSMEs), or community based enterprises. Compared with working in the informal economy, this is about helping poor communities develop something for the longer term, and about placing power and control in their hands. In the case of cultural tourism, the corresponding authorities can grant technical, financial or simply marketing support poor communities to produce traditional shows, performances, and even improve their traditional handicrafts in order to complement and diversify the cultural tourism offer.

The challenges are many, including:
- access to capital, and the forthcoming International Year of Microcredit might be a suitable opportunity to address this issue,
- acquisition of skills, confidence and motivation,
- property rights and legal recognition, and especially
- securing access to tourism markets.

Example: A Bedouin Craft programme in the Sinai Peninsula, Egypt, assists women in preserving, developing and marketing their traditional skills and in generating additional income. Currently, about 400 women are involved in a Bedouin-owned company, Fansina, established and officially registered to produce and market craft items for tourists.[3]

The fifth way in which tourism can address poverty is through a **tax or levy on tourism income or profits with proceeds benefiting poverty reduction programmes.** This has the advantage of enabling resources to be channelled to the most needy people and communities without requiring their involvement in tourism activity either directly or indirectly. The approach can be at a national level, or at a local level. There are a number of examples showing how this can work quite well at a local level – such as negotiating concessions with tourism enterprises involving a proportion of income per

---

[2] Tour Operators Initiative, 2003
[3] Sustainable Development of Ecotourism: A Compilation of Good Practices (WTO, 2003)

bed night being given to the local community. Fiscal income can also be perceived on monuments or sites as entry fees, one part being affected to conservation purposes, the other part to poverty alleviation programmes. However, approaches involving taxes and charges have to be treated with caution in order not to deter investment and income flows in the long term.

The sixth way has some similarities with the previous one but here it is about **voluntary giving by tourism enterprises and tourists.** This may include payments into general charities and programmes, such as HIV/AIDS programmes, by tourists and tour operators, or more specific support for projects in destinations visited. Many tourism enterprises are engaged in supporting social programmes in their neighbouring communities. Funds from tourists may be collected in the country of origin or in the destination, through voluntary supplements or invitations to donate. During the visit of a cultural asset, the guide could be the "spokesperson" of the surrounding poor communities and raise awareness among visitors about the role they could voluntarily play in helping them financially to undertake specific improvements in the village, etc. Although these approaches can generate worthwhile resources that can be directed to needy causes, it is important to be sensitive in promoting this type of activity and to avoid token gestures.

Finally, poor communities can benefit from **investment in infrastructure stimulated by tourism.** This is about the provision of roads, energy supplies, sanitation, clean water and telecommunications, on the back of tourism investment. Careful planning in such situations is clearly very important and local communities should be involved from an early stage.

WTO has also identified a certain number of common themes that keep recurring across all these methods. These include:

- Understanding the nature of poverty and its link with the cultural assets (particularly religious ones) in an area and how engagement in tourism will complement and support other livelihood options.
- The whole issue of capacity building and training.
- Trying to introduce simple processes of quality control, if necessary in cooperation with cultural site managers or with cultural authorities that supervise art performances, etc.
- Raising consumer awareness: providing visitors with better information to direct their purchasing.
- Creative, realistic and viable cultural product development and marketing, and
- Adopting an integrated approach to planning and management at a local destination level.

It is also important to provide a framework for action by the different stakeholders, and I will refer to them in the remaining of this presentation.

International Development Agencies should pay more attention to supporting cultural tourism as a form of sustainable development. They have considerable influence and can require that specific measures be in place to address poverty. There is greater scope for them to work together and with WTO and they should look to support capacity building and marketing rather than just capital programmes.

Example: In Lao PDR, the Luang Prabang (WHS) Provincial Tourism Office, in collaboration with the Dutch Development Agencies (SNV), has developed a programme outline for community-based sustainable tourism. This programme, I quote, "addresses the need for new community-based tourism products, more equitable distribution of tourism benefits, and more tourism related income and jobs in the Province of Luang Prabang." [4]

National governments should pay more attention to cultural tourism in their poverty reduction strategies and in trade negotiations, where they should ensure that sustainability and poverty issues are considered alongside export promotion. Governments are often in a position to influence the location and nature of new tourism development and should seek to benefit poor communities in so doing. Other relevant instruments include legislation affecting employment and credit. Governments can also support capacity building, appropriate marketing and undertake monitoring of the impact of tourism on poverty. They are also very important in contributing to heritage conservation and supporting appropriate cultural product development and marketing. Finally, they can stimulate cooperation among cultural and tourism authorities in a common effort to fight poverty.

Intra-regional bodies can play an important role in supporting the development and marketing of appropriate tourism, including tourism based on cultural assets and traditions and cultural routes through developing countries, which may lack the scale or resources to make an impact on their own. They could encourage a joint approach to poverty issues across the region, including the sharing of good practice.

NGOs have a particularly valuable role to play in networking and forging relevant linkages, in representing and championing the poor, in capacity building and in identifying social programmes that can be supported through cultural tourism income.

Destination management organisations, which may be local authorities, private public partnerships or possibly protected area bodies, have a critical role to play in issues such as developing local supply chains and improving the relationship between the informal economy and sites visitors.

Tourism enterprises, including international tour operators, incoming operators and tourism service providers, must be central to any strategy to tackle poverty through cultural tourism. They should include concern for poverty as part of their commitment to corporate social responsibility. This should be reflected in employment policies, supply chain management and support for local communities. They also have a critical role to play in providing relevant information to their guests, especially in respect of local cultures and styles of life.

Looking back over these six types of organisation, it is very important that they should not feel that they have to take action in isolation. Joint action is needed. One suggestion is the establishment of joint committees for tourism and poverty (some of these committees can focus on cultural tourism and poverty) at a destination level, which seek to engage all stakeholders.

---

[4] Sustainable Tourism Development in Nepal, Vietnam and Lao PDR: Experiences of SNV and partner organisations (2003)

So, and to conclude, this is a considerable challenge. It requires purposeful, well-directed action. Tourism in general, and cultural tourism in particular, will not address poverty automatically. It also requires commitment and political will, making poverty alleviation a primary objective of tourism policies and development plans.

Fighting poverty on the one hand, and facilitating inter-cultural understanding through cultural tourism on the other, are the main pillars to establish more stability, more security and more peace in our world at a time of international tensions.

Thank you

WTO KEYNOTE PRESENTATION ON THE INVOLVEMENT OF LOCAL COMMUNITIES IN CULTURAL TOURISM[6]

Involvement of local communities in the (inter) national tourism sector in developing countries is relatively new. It was only since the late eighties that communities in developing countries were faced with tourism developments on a large scale. Previously, tourism tended to be enclaved in small areas or in sea-sun-beach resorts and concentrated in only a few developing countries that had emerged as important destinations. Interaction with local communities was limited to brief encounters on the beach where entrepreneurs tried to sell crafts, food or other items. Tourists were also exposed to local communities during shorts excursions to nearby villages.

However, the development of long haul travel in the main source markets in Europe and North America during the late eighties and nineties changed the tourism sector in many developing countries. Tourists wanted to 'explore' unknown areas, visit new cultures and experience real local life. Local communities and indigenous peoples were often confronted with tourism development that turned their culture, traditions and natural environment into a tourism product that was to be sold on the new emerging markets. But also the traditional sea-sun-beach destinations were expanded rapidly exposing (small) coastal communities and the nearby inland villages to mainly western tourists.

The expansion of the tourism sector had positive impacts on local communities: cash, income, employment opportunities and upgrading of local infrastructure. But it also led to the loss of land, economic dependency, conflicts and cultural disruption. Growing recognition of rights and ownership of local resources by local communities and the need to involve them from the perspective of sustainable development paved the way to develop new concepts and opportunities for community involvement in tourism development. This was clearly stated, among other matters, in the Quebec Declaration on Ecotourism.

I will try to provide a general overview of these concepts and illustrate them with practical cases from different continents in different cultural settings. Some of these concepts heavily relate to nature-based tourism, an area in which the concept of community tourism was initially developed. Others are typical for culture-based tourism whereas an increasing number combine both forms of tourism. Some concepts are simple and straightforward and within easy reach. Others are complicated and require long-term efforts. However, they all have in common that different stakeholders within the tourism sector need to cooperate and join forces.

The best way to explore the options for community involvement in cultural tourism is to go on an imaginary trip to one of the many cultural sites that are found worldwide. We are, in contrast to the real tourist, not faced with the dilemma of selecting a specific cultural site. The options for community involvement around the ruins of Machu Picchu in Peru are essentially the same as for the ruins of Angkor Wat in Cambodia.

Before we set out on our journey, two final remarks. The word "community" is used in different contexts and is therefore the subject of academic debate. For the purpose of this presentation a community is defined as '*a mutually supportive, geographically*

---

[6] Mr. Ruud Klep, WTO Consultant

specific, social unit such as a village or tribe where people identify themselves as community members and where there is some form of communal decision-making' [1]. The advantage of this definition is that it is not limited to farmers and fishermen living in a typical rural setting but also includes communities in urban areas.

Secondly, the concept of community-based tourism is different to the idea to involve communities in (cultural) tourism from the point of view of poverty alleviation. The key elements of community-based tourism are empowerment, local control and communal decision-making. Although local communities and its individual members are often classified as poor, an important difference between pro-poor tourism initiatives and community-based tourism is that the former puts poor people at the heart of tourism developments, which does not necessarily imply to involve a community[2].

A visit to the cultural heritage site

Labour

We begin our journey at the cultural site itself. Here, direct employment opportunities for the poor are obvious. Labour is needed for maintenance of the ruins or other cultural assets, to manage the supporting facilities and to provide different types of services to the visitor. From a pro-poor point of view, the most important aspect is acceptable working conditions and fair wages as advocated by the Fair Trade in Tourism Movement, and as stated in the Global Code of Ethics for Tourism.

Porters, cooks and guides in Nepal are often paid poor wages, required to carry enormous loads, allowed to climb in unsuitable equipment, and given little or no medical assistance. When injured, they do not get paid and often have no contract, job security or regular wage. To address these conditions, Specialist Trekking Co-operative (STC) pays staff double their previous wages, provides clothing for adequate protection, limits the loads they can carry, adequately insures staff, and retains many throughout the year to provide security of income[3].

Guides

To fully appreciate the site we hire a local guide. This type of job is not easily accessible by poor people. Knowledgeable as they are on the local region, it is difficult for the poor to meet (inter) national standards to qualify as an officially licensed guide. Formal education and on the job training are possible solutions to this problem. Some countries have created a special status for local or community guides, which implies that less stringent requirements have to be met to officially qualify as community guide.

Crafts

Just before we finish our tour we visit the local craft market that has been set up next to the entrance of the cultural site. The production and selling of crafts provides excellent opportunities to link poor communities to the cultural tourist.

Traditional and authentic crafts are true expressions of the living, local culture; but there are more reasons to stimulate production and selling of crafts. Production can often be organised within communities in such a way that it does not interfere with traditional

---

[1] The good alternative Travel Guide, Mark Mann 2002
[2] Source: *Pro-Poor Tourism Strategies: Making Tourism Work For The Poor. A review of experience.* Caroline Ashley, Dilys Roe, Harold Goodwin. ODI, IIED, and CRT, April 2001
[3] Source: Tearfund - *Tourism Putting Ethics into Practice*

livelihoods. Crafts can be produced during times of the year when the normal daily activities are less intense or when labour is needed to work on the land or to carry out other subsistence activities. Skills to produce traditional crafts are in many cases already present within the community. Many of the blouses, cloths and carpets that are sold in Guatemala are produced using traditional methods.

Another advantage is that the craft item is the commodity itself and not the culture, and does therefore not directly impact the living culture of the local community. Finally, when developing crafts it is essential not to rely entirely on the (internal) tourism market. Tourism development should be the engine to start a craft business but once it is up and running other markets, both national and international, should be penetrated to avoid over reliance on the tourism sector.

The Bushmen in Southern Africa are a group of disadvantaged indigenous peoples that live as hunters and gatherers in small communities in remote desert areas. Part of their tradition is the production of beadwork and crafts that are made out of ostrich egg shelves and local wood. These crafts are produced by both men and women in between daily activities such as gathering of foods or hunting. The crafts are sold directly to tourists that stay on nearby campsites or to tourists that visit the village. Crafts of excellent quality are bought by an intermediate not-for-profit organisation and sold to national crafts shops or to overseas galleries.

In the villages of Roka and Preahdak in the Banteay Srey district in Cambodia a project was started aimed at providing opportunities for out-of-school youth to receive non-formal education and to practice craftwork as a way of income generation. The main activities of the project included providing second level literacy to one hundred youth and conduct training of basketry to those one hundred youth. The trainees also learned skills on running small business, marketing and promotion. An exhibition that was set up has shown that in a short lapse of time, the quantity and diversity of the products made are impressive, revealing the potential of basketwork in these two areas.

The main lessons to be learnt are the need for training, to improve the quality of the crafts and to meet the needs of the market by drawing on the private sector. Also different outlets and (inter)national distribution channels need to be created.

A place to stay
After a long day at the cultural site it is time to relax and find a hotel. The overnight facilities offer a whole range of opportunities for community benefits:

Sharing of benefits
Voluntary sharing of benefits by hotels for the community is a concept that is frequently used by accommodations that have been established near or even on community ground long before the issue of community participation was raised. The benefits can be financial, such as a bed levy (fixed amount per person per night) or a percentage of turnover of the annual profit. But hotels can also provide capital (loans), materials and labour for community based enterprises, or support community activities in general by providing transportation for community meetings. Although community involvement is still rather passive in this approach, community structures need to be in place to ensure transparency in the amount of money that is donated to the community. Also the process of decision-making needs guidance, especially with regards to selecting community

projects or activities on which the money will be spent. Finally, it is essential to keep communication and cooperation ongoing between the local community and the hotel.

Direct employment of poor people in hotels is one of the most effective ways to address the issue of poverty. It is evident that the issue of fair wages and proper working conditions is also relevant for the entire hotel and accommodation sector. The importance of creating outlets for local crafts has already been mentioned. But there is more. Making the entire supply chain more local is another approach in to contribute to combat local poverty. Farmers produce crops and fruits that could be incorporated in the supply chain. Cooperatives of carpenters or workers can sell their furniture to the hotel and giving it an extra local touch. The laundry service in the hotel makes good business for local women. In near all cases training is needed to ensure that the quality of the (food) items meet the international tourism standards.

Partnerships and joint ventures
Partnerships between local communities and representatives of the private sector have proven to be successful in many countries. The reason for their success is a combination of the best of two worlds. The private sector has access to capital, insight in the dynamics of the main generating tourism markets and hands-on experience and knowledge in running a top class hotel or lodge. The community can contribute to the venture through the provision of labour, in some cases land and most important through its local and living culture.

In Southern Africa, Wilderness Safaris, which operates lodges in partnership with local communities, has a local employment policy that means that all staff except management are recruited from the local area. Also, a fixed percentage of the turnover is transferred to a community fund that is used for projects identified by the community itself. The company also has a training program that enables local people to advance in the company. As well as benefiting the local community, Wilderness Safaris benefits from low staff turnover (most local staff remain in their jobs until they are forced to leave)[4].

Success however is not easy. Partnerships require time and efforts and can therefore be too costly for the private sector. Communities need clear guidance from non-profit organisations during the negotiation process. Local and national governments must have a clear policy on land rights for local communities or offer the possibility of long-term leases that are attractive to the private sector.

Community owned enterprises
In this type of approach the tourism operation is owned and operated by the local community or individuals within the community. In most cases the accommodation is simple and basic. Typical examples are campsites, guesthouses and restaurants.

At Bai Chay, Ha Long Bay in Vietnam, almost a dozen local families run private hotels, but local involvement in tourism spreads far beyond this, to an estimated 70–80% of the population. Apart from those with jobs in the hotels and restaurants, local women share the running of six noodle stalls, many women and children are ambulant vendors, and anyone with a boat or motorbike hires them out to tourists.

---

[4] Source: *Pro-Poor Tourism Strategies: Making Tourism Work For The Poor. A review of experience.* Caroline Ashley, Dilys Roe, Harold Goodwin. ODI, IIED, and CRT, April 2001

Namda Lama, a single mother at Yalbang was abandoned by her husband and forced to find a way to support herself. She used a loan she received from the religious leader in the village to start her own business. At first she ran a tea stall with no building, but in time she built a small 'hotel' on school land beside the tourist campsite. She now runs a thriving hotel serving local beer and alcohol, Chinese imported alcohol, tea, Nepali food and snacks to local people and beer and coke to tourists. Although she is dependent on loans to start the business each season in April, she makes enough profit (c. Rs 15,000 or USD 250 per 6-7 months) to repay the loan and support herself and her two daughters through the winter[5].

From the perspective of cultural tourism, home stays are of particular interest. The concept of home stay is built on staying and interacting with a local family as this provides a real cultural experience.

In the mountainous regions of Central Asia and in the Himalayas good examples can be found of home stays. In Kyrgyzstan an association of service providers was set up to deal with the growing tourism in the country and to manage its growth in a sustainable way. Among the activities organized are yurta building (a traditional Kyrgyz and Central Asian felt dwelling) and sharing local Kyrgyz hospitality in nomads' houses. Similar activities are carried out in Tajikistan and Kazakhstan.

The Baima people in China offer home stays to tourist on the way to Panda reserves The home stays provide alternative income after all logging activities were officially banned in the region.

To further develop the potential of cultural tourism, the existence of upmarket tourism lodges and resorts is also interesting. In Bolivia, the Chalalan Lodge offers tourists the chance to experience the culture of the community of San Jose Uchupiamonas in a natural setting. Facilities are well developed, meals are of excellent quality and short walks in the surroundings provide insight in the true meaning of living in harmony with nature. The entire operation is owned and managed by the local community.

The Cree Village Lodge in Canada is a community house used by the local Cree people for community purposes. It was also built to accommodate tourists during the summer season. This combination has created a unique place where tourists can catch a glimpse of Cree Village life (marriages take place in the community house) and a place for the Cree people to meet, and thus preserve their culture.

Non-governmental organizations often advocate that community owned enterprises are the best scenario to empower communities and to combat poverty. There is a direct link to the local community and a high level of skills is required when it comes to management, cooperation and decision-making. However, community owned enterprises often lack knowledge on tourism issues and the latest trends in developments. They also fail to market their business and the lack of (individual) incentives also hampers their success.

A trip into the surroundings

---

[5] Source: *Pro-Poor Tourism Strategies: Making Tourism Work For The Poor. A review of experience.* Caroline Ashley, Dilys Roe, Harold Goodwin. ODI, IIED, and CRT, April 2001

We have decided not to limit our visit to the cultural heritage site but also want to explore its surroundings and the people living in it. This type of tourism, that is more curious about ways of local life and their contemporary manifestations, is increasing rapidly. Let look closer at some examples.

In Tanzania tourists are offered guided tours through the mountains and forests, experiencing the daily life and farming methods of Wasamba farmers. They get the chance to accompany a village group collecting medicinal herbs and all the profits are used to assist local primary schools in the area[6]. Near Longido tourists can participate in a walking safari guided by local Masaai. During the walk the local village or Boma is visited and at the end of the trip the women have prepared a lunch. The money is distributed according to the input of the guides and the women.

In Ecuador the community of Agua Blanca hosts groups up to 16 people in their village during a 3-day visit that is entirely organised by the community. The visitors are shown around the archaeological site near the village and are introduced to the crops that are grown. For diner and breakfast the group breaks up in small groups of 2-3 people and have their meals with individual families. All revenues are distributed according to the labour provided.

Local guides
In Namibia the local community members have set up an association of guides. They offer their services to visitors that visit Twijfelfontein, one of the most important cultural sites of rock carvings in Southern Africa. The system for selecting the guide is based on rotation. This ensures that all guides get an equal chance to show tourists around. The price for a guided tour is not fixed but a general sign indicates what prices are regarded as fair. In addition, one of the local breweries has supported the association of guides by sponsoring displays that explain the history of the site and describe the flora and fauna that can be found.

Traditional villages
One of the challenges of visiting a community is to find the right balance between accommodating the wishes of tourists that want to experience 'real community life' and the intrusion into the privacy of individual community members. The establishment of traditional villages has proven to be a successful answer to this problem. Apart from providing direct employment and revenues the traditional villages also ensure that cultural practices are passed on to future generations or that practices that were nearly lost, are revived.

The performance of cultural groups adds extra dimension to the visit. And although some tourists will complain that these performances are artificial, they do provide opportunities for groups and individuals to conserve traditional dances and rituals that otherwise would have been lost.
Summary and lessons learnt

To conclude this presentation, let us have an overview of the most potential areas for community involvement in cultural tourism:
1. The production and selling of crafts

---

[6] Source: Tearfund - *Tourism Putting Ethics into Practice*

2. The creation of cultural packages around village life and the surroundings where local communities live
3. The establishment of (micro) enterprises by communities or in close cooperation with the private sector

From a community perspective the following issues are of crucial importance:
To increase understanding of the (cultural) tourism industry
To explore pro and cons of tourism, at both the level of the community and the individual household
To strengthen community organization (management, negotiation and representation)
To maintain realistic expectations on tourism developments through constant communication and information
To explore options to convert cultural traditions into tourism products that respect local traditions and that do not interfere with the cultural or spiritual values of the traditions
To develop skills for small enterprises.

Thank you for your attention.

Presentation by
WTO Deputy Secretary-General[7]

ST-EP Sustainable Tourism Eliminating Poverty

- WTO is poised to make an important contribution to the global challenge of poverty reduction. Our position as the UN Tourism Agency gives our industry a seat at the decision making table for the first time ever.[1]

- ST-EP announced at the Johannesburg Earth Summit 2002. To link Sustainable Tourism ~ Eliminating Poverty. And to link the UN Millennium Development Goals to halve extreme Poverty by 2015 and WTO's Global Code of Ethics.

- WTO led .... with other global, regional and national partners.

- ST-EP will focus on long-term social, economic and ecological projects to encourage sustainable tourism that alleviate poverty, bringing jobs and development to the world's poorest countries and regions that have tourism potential. Itt will provide a leadership program for the sector itself and flagship for governments, the private sector & civil society worldwide

- Goal is to seek New Funds: New Research. New Projects

- With a funding patrimony target of $20 million by 2010 and a delivery target of 5000 projects by 2015.

- WTO held 18 month worldwide Stakeholder consultation and widespread support

- Approved by WTO Assembly Beijing October 2003
  The General Assembly Referring to the plan of action of the World Summit on Sustainable Development. & the contribution tourism can bring to poverty alleviation
  Having considered the report on the ST-EP initiative
  Notes with appreciation the efforts devoted & actions taken
  Welcomes the partnership established with UNCTAD
  Approves the plan submitted for the completion of the initiative
  Concurs with the proposal for a ST-EP Forum
  Agrees to establishing a ST-EP Foundation
  Entrusts the Secretary-General to secure the necessary funding
  Requests him to report progress at its sixteenth session (2005)

---

[1] Manifest by the UN Millennium Declaration on Poverty Reduction, the Doha Summit on Trade and Development, The Monterrey Summit on Debt Financing and the WSSD Johannesburg on Sustainability

GHL / Status April 2004

ST-EP Sustainable Tourism Eliminating Poverty

- Highlighted by UN Secretary General Kofi Annan January 2004 in a letter to WTO Secretary General

  "The WTO's activities, such as the "Sustainable Tourism – Eliminating Poverty" programme, will contribute to strengthening collaboration within the United Nations system to promote socially, economically & ecologically sustainable tourism, aimed at alleviating poverty and bringing jobs to people in developing countries.....these objectives are fully consistent with the outcome of the World Summit on Sustainable Development and the goals set out in the Millennium Declaration".

- ST-EP will have Four Components:
  - An International Foundation to attract new dedicated sustainable financing from business, philanthropy and government sources
  - A Research Base that identifies linkages, principles and model applications – demonstrating how to turn theory into better practice
  - An Operating Framework that both promotes and provides incentives for "good practices" among companies, consumers and communities.
  - An annual Forum to bring together stakeholders from public, private and civil society sources for information exchange and buy-in.

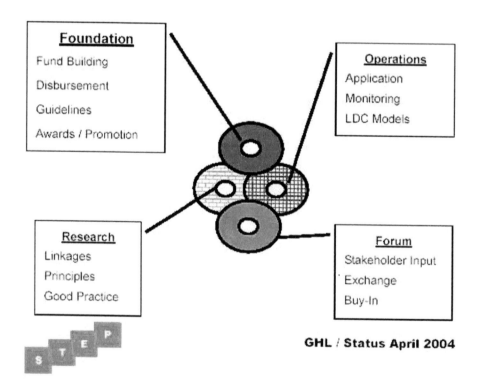

 **ST-EP Sustainable Tourism Eliminating Poverty**

- All preparatory work on the four components has been completed. The key to the exercise is the launch of the Foundation and its Financial Patrimony, which will ensure effective implementation of the program.
- The ST-EP Foundation will:
  - Establish the **ST-EP Council** of distinguished international leaders from industry, government, sport and entertainment, who will direct its activities. It is forseen that her Majesty the Queen of Jordan will be the initial Chair the Council. It will have a focused annual high profile Council Assembly, keynoted with a lecture by a top-level global leader and the premium Annual ST-EP Awards
  - Secure & maintain funding from new sources for ST-EP. With a target of $20 million by 2010 and $100 million by 2015
  - Disburse interest on such funds annually for ST-EP Research and Operations – with a goal of 5000 projects by 2015.

- **To date the Government of Korea has pledged $5 million to Headquarter the Foundation in Seoul and the Governments of France, Germany and Italy are working to mobilise a matching amount from Europe. The Secretary General of WTO has committed $500,000 for ST-EP Projects subject to Executive Council endorsement.**

- The Foundation will be a non-profit entity under Korean laws, fully compatible with relevant international laws, and established with the capacity to stand alone while retaining links with the WTO. It will have regional operating nodes in Europe, North America and other locations.

- The Foundation will seek funding from private sector sources directly & indirectly linked to tourism, from individual, corporate & institutional philanthropy & public-sector funds already budgeted for entrepreneurship: agricultural transformation, service capacity building, tourism education, ecological protection etc

The long-range goal of the entire ST-EP endeavor, by helping to alleviative deep poverty through sustainable tourism development, is also to contribute to world peace by promoting beneficial exchange, friendship and understanding between cultures, bringing the world closer together.

GHL / Status April 2004

STEP

Sustainable Tourism-Eliminating Poverty

Ministry of Culture and Tourism
Republic of Korea

01_Background

Importance of ST

○ Closely linked with Environmental, Social and Cultural Resources
○ Economic Benefits are Anticipated
○ Achieve the Ideal Climate for the Interests of Tourists, Local Residents and Environment
○ Needs proposed at the UN Conference on Environment and Development (UNCED) in 1992

▶

Increase International Society's Interests in ST

○ "Sustainable development should have the highest priority in government policy and international cooperation" (UN Assembly, 1987)
○ "Tourism can contribute towards economic advancement, poverty alleviation, environmental protection and cultural and socio-economical development" (LDCs, 2001)
○ Presenting new concept linking sustainable tourism and elimination of poverty" (WSSD, 2002)

▶

Poverty Elimination through ST

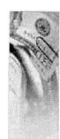

▶

ST-EP Foundation(Korea)

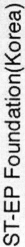

⊙ 2003 ——▶ ⊙ 2004 ——▶ ⊙ March 2004 ——▶

2003
Approval of ST-EP Foundation
(WTO General Assembly, Beijing)

2004
Reaffirm UN Secretary General's Support

March 2004
ST-EP Forum
(Sign MOU between WTO and MCT, Exchange Opinion about the Establishment of the ST-EP Foundation in Korea)

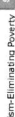

Sustainable Tourism-Eliminating Poverty

02_Mission

ST-EP in Korea

- Share Development Experience with International Society
- Support by Korean Government
- Apply the Best IT Infrastructure

Foundation

S T E P

- Strengthen International Cooperation
- Research on ST-EP
- Provide Tourism Development Roadmap and Support for Developing Areas

- Implementation and Management of ST Project
- Create Jobs and Increase Income of Developing Areas

- Poverty Elimination through Sustainable Tourism

03_Target Areas

Classification of Target Areas

■ **Least Developed Country**
49 countries designated by UN, identified as such through their weak human assets and economic vulnerability

■ **Developing Country**
Countries not included in LDCs and its population under the poverty line is more than 35%, similar to LDCs

■ **Impoverished Area**
Areas of countries in similar condition compared with LDCs

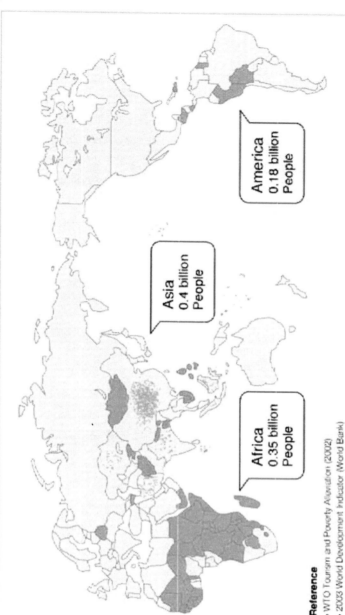

Asia
0.4 billion
People

Africa
0.35 billion
People

America
0.18 billion
People

Reference
• WTO Tourism and Poverty Alleviation (2002)
• 2003 World Development Indicator (World Bank)
• World Population Report (2002)

Most of the developing countries are located in Africa(37 countries) and Asia(11 countries). In terms of population, Asia is 0.4 billion, America is 0.18 billion and Africa is 0.35 billion. ST-EP project should be addressed in a balanced and broad approach to resolve problems efficiently.

4_4 Securing Funds

ST-EP in Korea

Active Support from Korean Government ($5 million scheduled) with WTO's Support ($0.5 million scheduled)

Fast Growing Asian Tourism Market

2004
WTO
KOREA

S T E P
Foundation

ST Project

Patrimony
2015 **$100** million

Fund Raising

Self-Sufficing

Return of Funding

Event

Branding

Donors (Governments/ Corporations)

05_Expected Result

Establish Worldwide Network for ST-EP
2

Support Developing Countries by ST-EP
4

Increase Worldwide Interest in ST-EP
1

Promote Research and Development Projects on ST-EP
3

STEP

Sustainable Tourism-Eliminating Poverty

Ministry of Culture and Tourism
Republic of Korea

51

CULTURAL TOURISM AND POVERTY ALLEVIATION

The case of Siem Reap-Angkor Cambodia

TITH CHANTHA (MA)
Deputy
Director General

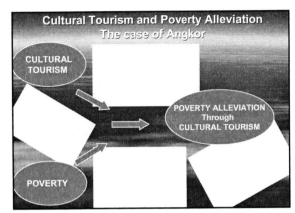

Cultural Tourism and Poverty Alleviation

- ▮
- ▮
- ▮

INTRODUCTION

➢ Tourism and Poverty:

➢ Tourism, economy, environment, society and culture are interdependent.

➢ Tourism has a multiplicity of backward and forward linkages into community, has social, Cultural and environmental impacts, crucially affects the wider economic milieu, and has major implications for government (e.g policy, regulatory, provision of infrastructure,…).

➢ Tourism is an economic sector and tourism revenue is a direct injection into the country's economy. E.g 2002 there were US$475 billion receipts from international tourism (WTO)

➢ Tourism is the world's growing service sector for more than 30% of all service exports. 1990- 2002, International arrivals grew about 54% and reached at 700 million (WTO).

POVERTY

➢ Regarding Poverty, up to 1.2 billion people still live in extreme consumption poverty, and 2/3 of them are in Asia (WTO). 24% lived on less than US$ 1 per day in the late 1990's (WB).

➢ Millennium Development Goals: (Un)
  - Eradicate extreme poverty and hunger
  - Halve, between 1993-2015, the proportion of people whose income is less than the national poverty line.
  - Decreasing the proportion of people whose income less than national poverty line from 39% in 1993 to 19.5% in 2015.

➢ Cambodia: Tourism has been recognized as a significant tool in the fight against poverty and can help achieve the above goals. This is mentioned in a National Strategy for poverty alleviation (2003-2005).

➢ This can be seen in the following case study of cultural tourism of Angkor

---

CULTURAL TOURISM

❑ World Situation :
  - Cultural Tourism shares a significant part of tourism and is growing faster than other segments of world

❑ Cambodia:
  - Cultural Tourism plays very vital roles in tourism development, and culture is a main tourist attraction
  - It accounted for about 70% of Cambodian tourism and is the main generator for country's income from tourism.
  - From 1993 to 2003, international arrivals grew by about 25%, and Angkor was the main cultural attraction.

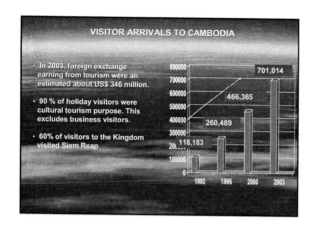

VISITOR ARRIVALS TO CAMBODIA

- In 2003, foreign exchange earning from tourism were an estimated about US$ 346 million.
- 90 % of holiday visitors were cultural tourism purpose. This excludes business visitors.
- 60% of visitors to the Kingdom visited Siem Reap

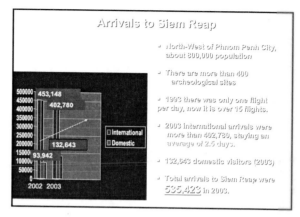

Arrivals to Siem Reap

- North-West of Phnom Penh City, about 800,000 population
- There are more than 400 archeological sites
- 1993 there was only one flight per day, now it is over 15 flights.
- 2003 international arrivals were more than 402,780, staying an average of 2.5 days.
- 132,643 domestic visitors (2003)
- Total arrivals to Siem Reap were 535,423 in 2003.

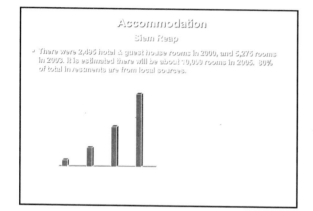

Accommodation

Siem Reap

- There were 2,495 hotel & guest house rooms in 2000, and 5,275 rooms in 2003. It is estimated there will be about 10,000 rooms in 2005. 80% of total investments are from local sources.

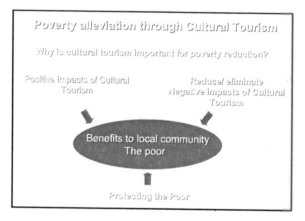

Poverty alleviation through Cultural Tourism

Why is cultural tourism important for poverty reduction?

Positive Impacts of Cultural Tourism

Reduce/ eliminate Negative Impacts of Cultural Tourism

Benefits to local community
The poor

Protecting the Poor

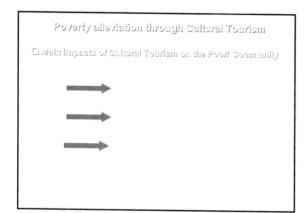

Poverty alleviation through Cultural Tourism

☐ Main Impacts of Cultural Tourism on the Poor/ Community

ECONOMIC IMPACTS OF THE CULTURAL TOURISM
The case of Angkor

- Tourism revenue in Siem Reap represents a major injection of new money into the local economy, stimulating a variety of economic activities
- Foreign exchange earning from tourism has a strong impact upon GDP, value added, and thus upon incomes.
- As Siem Reap has a high propensity to consume, little savings and tourist dollars are spent and re-spent.

ECONOMIC IMPACTS OF THE CULTURAL TOURISM
The case of Angkor

❖ Support the increasing of the SMEs in the area.

❖ According to our research, a foreign visitor to Siem Reap stay around 2.5 days, and spent about US$ 97.2 per days.

❖ in 2003, Siem Reap generated about **US$ 100 million** from foreign visitors and around US$ 4 million from local visitors.

❖ Multiplier = 1/ Proportion of Leakage
Leakage = Imports + Savings + Taxes

❖ Because most investments and employment is local, leakages from the local economy in the way of profits have been low.

❖ Based upon the free market economic activity, the Multiplier of tourism revenue estimated at 1.52 (David McEwen)

MAIN JOBS CREATED BY TOURISM
The case of Angkor

❖ Four main types of job are produced by tourism and related business (WTO): Direct, Indirect and Induced employments and construction workers.

❖ Based upon the study, conducted in May 2004 in Siem Reap, There are 6 main jobs created by cultural tourism at Siem Reap:

  · Employees in the hospitality industry:
    an estimated 3,000 with an average
    income US$ 50-300 per month

  · Tour guides: 1,200, average income
    US$100-200 per month

  · Souvenir shops and other shops:
    720 families, average revenues
    US$ 45 – 200 per month

MAIN JOBS CREATED BY TOURISM
The case of Angkor

· Transport providers, e.g.
  chauffeurs, taxis, motorcycle-
  taxis 1,500, average income
  US$ 50- 150 per month..

· Construction workers:
  5,000 -7000, US$ 35- 60
  per month.

· Other related jobs: e.g. employees
  in tourist resorts, classical and traditional dancers

TOTAL Jobs estimated about 50,000, around 25% of Siem Reap
  town's population (about 200,000).

❖ The study also found that:
  · 80% said their main income is from jobs related to tourism

  · 23% noted that tourism is their extra job.

  · 65% earn between US$ 100 to US$ 300 monthly.

  · 74% shown that at least 2 persons of their family are in tourism-
    related jobs,
    while 59% work directly in
    the hospitality industry.

  · 36% have moved to Siem Reap
    from other parts of the country.
  · 95% mentioned that their standard
    of living increase because of
    the development of tourism.

Socio-Cultural impacts of tourism
The case of Angkor

➢ Tourism revenue provides an economic incentive for social
  development (e.g. infrastructure) and cultural resources
  conservation.

➢ The case of Angkor, Royal Government, especially APSARA
  Authority, UNESCO and other donor countries/ organizations, e.g.
  JICA, ADB, have played very significant roles in conserving and
  developing the area:
    · Constructed new roads and renovated existing roads linking
      tourist destinations in the area.
    · Power supply, clean water and waste water management projects.
    · Conserving and managing
      of cultural heritages both
      tangible and intangible.

➢ Developments in infrastructure
  and facilities in the area benefit
  tourists and local communities.

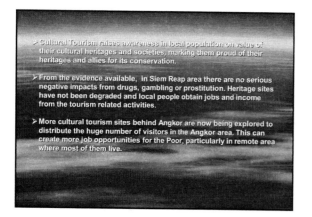

> Cultural Tourism raises awareness in local population on value of their cultural heritages and societies, marking them proud of their heritages and allies for its conservation.

> From the evidence available, in Siem Reap area there are no serious negative impacts from drugs, gambling or prostitution. Heritage sites have not been degraded and local people obtain jobs and income from the tourism related activities.

> More cultural tourism sites behind Angkor are now being explored to distribute the huge number of visitors in the Angkor area. This can create more job opportunities for the Poor, particularly in remote area where most of them live.

Environmental impacts
The case of Angkor

> Tourism and the environment can co-exist harmoniously or may conflict

> Tourism may fund for environmental protection and preservation. Local communities benefit from an unspoiled environment

> Through tourism, people become aware of their potential environment, and become more interested in (and willing to protect and conserve) their valuable heritage. Consequently, local communities are more likely to want to be involved in tourism.

> It is important that in Siem Reap the environment is suitable managed in such way that it is sustainable.

> Royal Government of Cambodia through APSARA Authority, Ministry of Environment, Ministry of Tourism has developed plans in environmental management to avoid environmental problems in Siem Reap.

> However, the increase in the number of hotels, restaurants and other establishments can create negative impacts on environment in the future.

> Problems of pollution from sewerage and the inadequate supply of potable water can mean that local people may suffer health problems, arising from tourism.

> To solve this problem, several Government projects, supported by international donors have been implemented in the area, for example; ADB's "Mekong Tourism Development Project" invested around US$ 3.5 million for waste water management in Siem Reap. A JICA project on the clean water has also prepared.

> APSARA Authority has a important plan for clean water and waste water systems that can reduce the need for industry and local people to obtain water from underground sources.

> Visitors to destination will be required to pay for the above systems to cover the costs of environmental management and operation.

> Local communities, particularly the poor, will pay less, or obtain benefits without charge. In this way, tourism contributes to local people's poverty reduction.

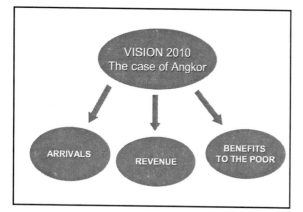

VISION 2010
Visitor Arrivals

Based upon:

❖ The previous growth rate (25%), internal economic and political stabilities, incentive government's policies on tourism development (e.g. open sky, land and water policy, visa on arrivals), marketing strategies and international cooperation.

❖ Geographical location of Cambodia, situated in the heart of a tourism developing zone (between Thailand and Vietnam, over 10 million arrivals yearly).

❖ Potential attraction of new and unique tourism products, especially associated with Angkor, the world wonder.

❖ The supporting of infrastructure improvement and development, liking to tourist destinations through out the country

❖ The number of international visitor arrivals to Cambodia, particularly Siem Reap, will increase, although major external problems can still have a negative influence (e.g. terrorism, SARS, oil price).

❖ Domestic visitors play a key role in developing tourism.

❖ With good infrastructure, political stability and safety, the number of domestic visitors to Angkor will shoot up sharply.

❖ It is forecast that total visitors (international and domestic) to Angkor will be 1 million by 2006 and reach at around 2.5 million in 2010.

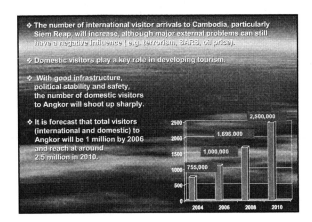

VISION 2010
Tourism Revenue

➢ According to the previous data of 2.5 days (average visitor length of stay) and US$ 97.2 per day average foreign tourist expenditure and US$ 30 per trip of a domestic tourist.

➢ It is estimated that Siem Reap can generate about US$ 240 million and US$ 600 million in 2006 and 2010 respectively.

➢ However, we have to think about the carrying capacity, management and the impacts of tourism on the Angkor area.

How can the benefits reach the poor ?

➢ The growth of the tourism revenue is not enough. The most important question is how can the local population benefit from the tourism revenue ?

➢ Understanding this, the Royal Government of Cambodia has issued major policies, regulations, plans, strategies and mechanisms for developing tourism in a sustainable way and maximizing the tourism's benefits to the local communities.

➢ These include : National Tourism Development Plan (5 years), which focused on poverty reduction through tourism, National Tourism Law, which more concerned on administration and management, Strategic Development Plan, and a National Working Group on Poverty Alleviation through Tourism.

➢ Furthermore, the plans and strategies need to be implemented properly in targeted areas and they should be linked to the WTO's initiatives on the ways in which the poor can benefit from tourism.

➢ According to WTO, There are 7 important ways that the poor can benefit directly or indirectly from tourism:

1- Employment of the poor in tourism enterprises
2- Supply of goods and services to tourism enterprises by the poor or by enterprises employing the poor
3- Direct sales of goods and services to visitors by the poor
4- Establishment and running of tourism enterprises (SMEs) by the poor
5- Tax or levy on tourism income or profits with proceeds benefiting the poor
6- Voluntary giving/support by tourism enterprises and tourists
7- Investment in infrastructure stimulated by tourism also benefiting the poor in the locality, directly or through support to other sectors.

CONCLUSION
Siem Reap- Angkor 2010

❖ In order to achieve the goals, the commitment of the government, private sector participation and the involvement of local communities are necessarily needed.

❖ Tourism is a driving force for other sectors development, including the increasing of population. It is estimated that Siem Reap's population will be around 1 million by 2010, and about 25% of them estimated to work in the tourism industry and related business.

❖ With the tourism revenue of US$ 600 million, Siem Reap's population will generally benefit US$ 600 per capita from tourism. This figure will be additional to general GDP/capita.

❖ Thus, Siem Reap will likely be removed from the list of the poor areas of the country, and cultural tourism will be seen to be an effective tool for poverty alleviation.

THANK YOU

Special WTO Case Study
Presentations

HERITAGE CONSERVATION FOR POVERTY ALLEVIATION – RAGHURAJPUR, A CASE STUDY[10]

An Abstract

Since its inception, INTACH has become one of the pioneer organisations in the country to identify and conserve its unprotected heritage, both built and natural. Another major initiative undertaken by the organisation is to make conservation movement community-centric, where local community is involved both in decision-taking and implementation process of a particular conservation proposal. In taking up Projects involving the community at the grass root level the primary consideration has been to link conservation of cultural heritage with poverty alleviation, employment generated programmes through a holistic approach. The objective of such an exercise is not only to improve the quality of life but to provide fresh opportunities for better standard of living on a sustainable basis. Raghurajpur village in Puri district, Orissa, is one such village. It has been the centre of attraction because of its centuries old crafts and dance traditions. INTACH's conservation centre in Bhubaneshwar, supported by NORAD, a Norwegian organisation, undertook a major conservation initiative in reviving the extinct mural painting tradition in the year 2001. As a follow up in order to promote heritage tourism INTACH prepared an Integrated Development Plan (IDP) for the village. A village heritage committee was established to ensure the participation of the community in decision-making. A crafts centre is being developed to provide training. The existing crafts tradition are also being upgraded. Marketing facilities are being arranged with necessary tie ups. For visitors, an interpretation centre, a small restaurant and a tourist lodge are nearing completion. Since the village has a classical dance tradition an amphitheatre has been built for such performances. All these activities will be income generating on a sustainable basis particularly with training programmes also being organised simultaneously for different activities. All these activities have also led to an increase in the number of visitors to the village. This in turn has generated a new enthusiasm amongst the villagers who can now look forward to a better and brighter future. The project is having a spin off effect on neighbouring villages – Raghurajpur, we are hopeful, will act as a catalyst for cultural heritage and poverty alleviation in the rural areas.

---

[10] S.K. Misra, Chairman, INTACH, New Delhi

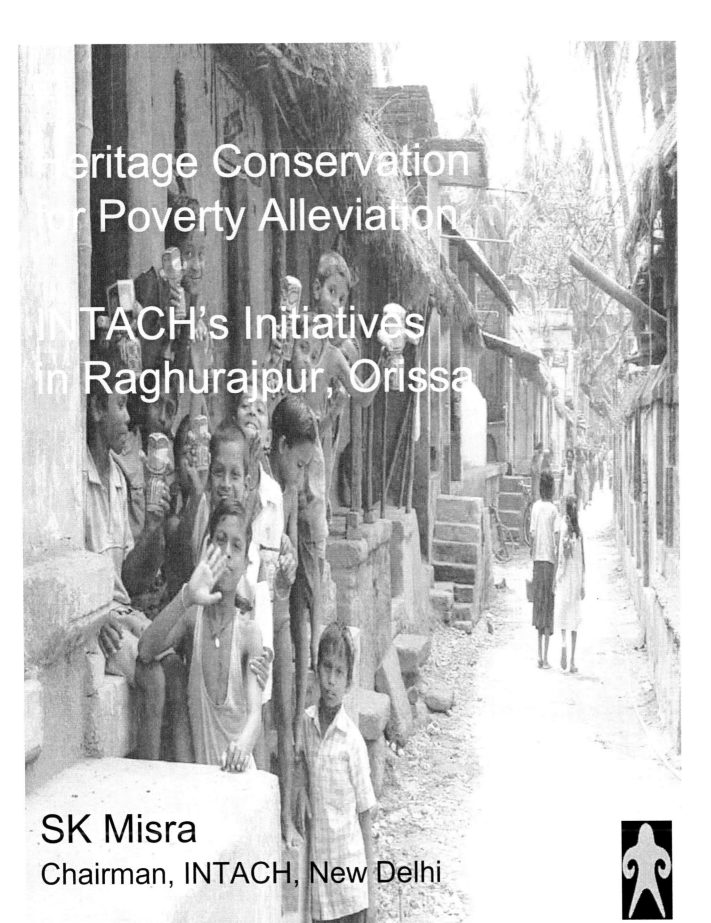

Heritage Conservation
for Poverty Alleviation

INTACH's Initiatives
in Raghurajpur, Orissa

SK Misra
Chairman, INTACH, New Delhi

Heritage Conservation for Poverty Alleviation

INTACH's Initiatives in Raghurajpur, Orissa

SK Misra
Chairman, INTACH, New Delhi

INTACH
Indian National Trust for Art and Cultural Heritage

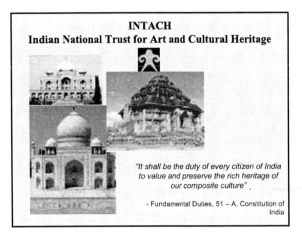

"It shall be the duty of every citizen of India to value and preserve the rich heritage of our composite culture" .

- Fundamental Duties, 51 – A, Constitution of India

INTACH
Indian National Trust for Art and Cultural Heritage

Committed to this cause, INTACH was established in 1984 as an Autonomous body with the mandate to identify and catalyse the protection of India's unprotected built, natural and art heritage. INTACH has 140 chapters in the country.

Indian National Trust for Art and Cultural Heritage

OUR MISSION

TO PROTECT INDIA's VAST UNPROTECTED MONUMENTS AND HERITAGE SITES

TO SENSITISE PUBLIC THROUGH AWARENESS PROGRAMMES, WORKSHOPS, SEMINARS AND PUBLICAITONS

TO ENCOURAGE CAPACITY BUILDING AND COMMUNITY MOBILISATION RELATED TO COMMUNITY UPLIFTMENT AND CONSERVATION OF LOCAL HERITAGE WITH A VIEW TO POVERTY ALLEVIATION

Indian National Trust for Art and Cultural Heritage

OUR MISSION

TO ACT AS ADVISORY BODY ON POLICY FORMULATION REGARDING OUR ARCHITECTURAL, NATURAL AND CULTURAL HERITAGE

TO PROVIDE TECHNICAL ASSISTANCE IN RESTORATION AND CONSERVATION PROJECTS

CONSERVATION OF WATER RESOURCES, AWARENESS EDUCATION PROGRAMMES, RURAL HERITAGE PROGRAMMES

TO UNDERTAKE EMERGENCY RESPONSE MEASURES DURING NATURAL OR MAN-MADE DISASTERS

INTACH has now launched..

SUSTAINABLE HERITAGE: VILLAGE DEVELOPMENT PROJECTS

WITH A VIEW TO SOCIAL UPLIFTMENT AND POVERTY ALLEVIATION

PROJECTS THAT LEAD TO A HIGHER STANDARD OF LIVING AND BETTER QUALITY OF LIFE, WHILE PRESERVING THE UNIQUE CHARACTER AND HERITAGE OF THE VILLAGE

TWO PILOT PROJECTS BEING UNDERTAKEN BY INTACH:

RAGHURAJPUR, ORISSA AND PRAGPUR, HIMACHAL PRADESH

RAGHURAJPUR VILLAGE

APPROX. 50 KILOMETRES FROM BHUBANESHWAR; 10 KILOMETRES FROM PURI

POPULATION APPROX. 700 PERSONS;

A LINEAR VILLAGE WITH 2 ROWS OF HOUSES AND A ROW OF PUBLIC BUILDINGS WITHIN;

MOST PEOPLE PRACTICE CRAFTS WITHIN THE VILLAGE

Fig. Above: A view of the village;
Fig. below: Details of a row of houses

VERNACULAR ARCHITECTURE

STONE AND THATCH ROOF CONSTRUCTION SYSTEM

MOST HOUSES FACE THE VILLAGE STREET

PUBLIC STRUCTURES LIKE TEMPLES ARE IN THE MIDDLE OF THE VILLAGE

Fig. Above: Row of houses;
Fig. below: Temple structure in the middle of the vilage

NATURAL FEATURES

VILLAGE FAMOUS FOR:

BETEL LEAF PLANTATION;

WATER BODIES;

COCONUT GROVES

Fig. Above: Betel leaf plantation;
Fig. below: Water body within coconut grove

A day in the life of the villagers

Regular village meetings..

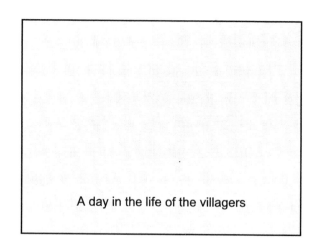

Women's meetings within the village..

Fairs and festivals..

Periodic ritual of free meal to children..

Arts and Crafts..

Arts and Crafts..

A village with 108 households with a majority of them being crafts persons

Most craftsmen belong to the Chitrakara caste, one of the lowest castes comprising depressed community and below poverty line

Village replete with intangible forms of [living] heritage – art, crafts and dance traditions but had suffered neglect over the years for various reasons

Despite the fact that the village can boast of a number of national awardees: 1 Padma Vibhushana (second highest civilian award in the country), 1 Padma Shree and 6 National craft Award winners

Arts and Crafts..

A variety of crafts practiced in the village – Pattachitra, Papier Machie, Stone and wooden sculptures, Palm leaf manuscripts, etc.

Almost every house an artist's 'studio'

Gotipua – the dance tradition still followed in the typical *Guru-Shishya Parampara*

Pattachitra Paintings..

69

Palm leaf manuscripts..

Papier Machie products..

Wooden religious figures..

Paintings on coconut kernel..

Stone sculptures..

Extension of the artist's studio..

70

Gotipua Dance Tradition..

INTACH's initiatives in Raghurajpur..

Wall Paintings revival programme
Integrated Development Plan

Wall paintings revival programme..

INTACH's Painting/Crafts revival programme – What did it do?

• Sustenance of the people depended on mural painting tradition and crafts skills. Over the years painting traditionally gradually faded into insignificance. Painters taken to agriculture, etc.;

•INTACH has now:

• Revived the mural painting tradition;

• Provided training for artists and masons;

• Artists encouraged to learn the traditional forms of paintings, and also allowed adaptations;

• prepared a comprehensive documentation of the programme

Mural Paintings Programme

INTACH Has published pamphlets to encourage the business houses, local hotels, private individuals, etc. to…

"..commission these artisans to come and make a painting in your living or work place. Through these paintings you can attract visitors, showcase your history, express your faith, or simply tell a story."

Outcome of the Revival Programme

• Employment for everyone

•Most craftsmen feel the improved working conditions in the village and increased opportunities to work

• Most craftsmen being commissioned to do work during lean tourist period thus increasing their income

• Women working along with men and engaged in activities like preparation of colour, canvas, etc.

• Most craftsmen had earlier left practicing the crafts, but have now returned to practice

Research into the wall paintings theme..

Preparation of lime mortar using traditional methods..

Villagers lime plastering their walls – readying them for paintings..

Preparation of colour pigments by villagers themselves..

Village elders painting on lime plastered walls..

Training the village youth..

Village girls participating in the revival programme..

Examples of wall paintings..

Catching the attention of the media..

Dissemination of the knowledge (Training programmes)..

Integrated Development Plan..

Objectives of the Integrated Development Plan (IDP) to generate further employment opportunities through increased tourism by strengthening infrastructure and other facilities and sale and marketing of local products.

Sustenance and Development of the rich Crafts tradition of the village; Provision of a Women's Craft Centre; Training programmes for crafts persons for revival and design innovations in each crafts category; Creating self help groups; Marketing infrastructure; Generation of employment opportunities for both men and women

Objectives of the Integrated Development Plan (IDP)

Showcase village for **rural/heritage tourism**; popular with both domestic and foreign tourists and has potential for further growth. Facilities created for benefit of tourists:

Heritage Interpretation Centre
Small restaurant for visitors - to be managed by local community only
Tourist Lodge (Gram Kutir) - to be managed by local community only
Street Signage
Open Air Theatre
Nature walks
All construction keeping local vernacular traditions in mind,

Improvement of infrastructure within the village: Widening of roads; Concreting of streets within the village; Drinking water supply to each household; Provision of toilets for each household (UNICEF); Village storm water and waste water drainage; Rain water harvesting; Co-ordination with various government agencies

Develop an **architectural vocabulary** that blends with the local environment and provides a **rural imagery** - Guidelines for new construction and **protection** of natural features;

Ensure **community participation** at all levels;

Employment Opportunities: Marketing and tie-ups with outlets outside the village

The work should be completed by the end of this year (2004)

Improvement of village streets..

Restaurant block..

Open Air Theatre..

Tourist Lodge

Gurukul (School building for Gotipua dance)

Establishing a Crafts Centre

Raghurajpur initiative went far beyond its objectives!!

• Raghurajpur portrays Orissa!!

"To feel India, come to Orissa. To feel Orissa, come to Raghurajpur"

    – Department of Tourism, Government of Orissa slogan

Conclusion

Economic condition of the people, most of whom were below the poverty line, has considerably improved;

Income for most painters/craftsmen, etc. has increased;

Painters/Craftsmen getting more work orders

"INTACH has brought about 'socio-economic' changes…in simple terms, the result of this project is positive. Mural art has been successfully revived. Odissi dance has been saved from disappearing and been transformed into a lucrative economic option."

    Excerpt from a sociological report assessing INTACH's intervention in Raghurajpur

Thank you..

CASE STUDY: BOROBUDUR TEMPLE, CENTRAL JAVA – INDONESIA[11]

OVERVIEW

The World Tourism Organization has long classified heritage tourism as a sub-set of cultural tourism, which encapsulates visitors traveling for "essentially cultural motivations such as study tours, performing arts and cultural festivals, for nature, folklore, art and pilgrimages, and visits to sites and monuments," (WTO – 1985).

Over the recent decades, international tourism has come to be viewed by policymakers in many countries not only as a generator of employment and revenue but also as a way to ensure the long-term sustainability of both built and living cultures. Tourism is a potent force that already is intimately intertwined with cultural issues throughout the world and has had a dramatic impact most notably in developing countries.

From the host community's point of view, essential goals for tourism development of any kind (cultural and heritage tourism included) must be to generate higher levels of income, create new employment opportunities, and increase foreign exchange flows thereby helping raise the standard of living of the people in the communities in those areas where heritage sites are found.

In developing countries, cultural tourism involves not only reconstructing the past; it is also part of restructuring and managing the economy. Relationships between cultural tourism and the local communities living in proximity to heritage sites involves more than employment and income issues. They include questions of land ownership; competition between old and new traditions; control of the pace and scope of economic development; heritage management issues; and, in some cases, may involve relocation of communities that have lived in a place from time immemorial.

The relationship between heritage and tourism is simultaneously a symbiotic and a contradictory one as heritage always appears in a context of social and cultural values. Tourism can be a powerful tool to help sustain heritage but it needs great care and sensitivity in planning, development, management and marketing to be socially as well as economically viable. As the Borobudur Declaration (1999 - *attached*) notes: "Sites and archaeological remains should not only be considered as academic and ideological resources alone, but also as economic resources".

Using the Borobudur temple as a case study, this paper will examine policies, strategies, and programs in which efforts have been made to work with local communities regarding heritage and tourism. With good policies, professional management, and community involvement, a major heritage site can also act as a generator for new community and cultural tourism activities in the area in which it is located.

As well, the people living in proximity to heritages sites can not only benefit economically but also become empowered regarding implementation of sustainable tourism policies in their region.

---

[11] Dr. Wiendu Nuryanti, Secretary General of International Centre for Culture and Tourism

ADVANTAGES OF HERITAGE TOURISM

The advantages of heritage tourism are too well known to this audience for me to more than briefly touch on them in order to put the economic impact of tourism directed to, and inspired by, the Borobudur temple within a wider context.

To be sustainable over the long-term, heritage tourism must meet the fundamental test of enhancing the net benefits of tourism – that is, maximizing the net economic benefits while minimizing the net negative environmental or socio-cultural impacts.
Studies have shown that people drawn to cultural and heritage tourism:
Are associated with a longer length of stay;
Have higher discretionary income levels than the average tourist;
Have higher education levels and are likely to be more interested in the local customs and surroundings than typical mass tourists drawn to sea, sun, and sand.

Furthermore, there are distinct advantages of heritage tourism in that:
It exhibits lower levels of seasonality, thus spreading out the benefits throughout the year rather than only at peak seasons;
It helps create a demand for locally produced goods and services';
It has a distinct image thus helping differentiate the tourism product from other destinations, making it more memorable to market;
For domestic tourists, it adds intangible value in pride in their collective heritage and history.

CONSERVATION AND THE PUBLIC SECTOR

3.1 Policy Setting

Borobudur temple complex is a ninth century Buddhist temple which has been designated as a UNESCO World Heritage Site. It is found in central Java, Indonesia on one of the country's most densely populated islands, and it is located about 60 kms or one hour's drive from the region's major tourism gateway, Yogyakarta.

It is arguably Indonesia's most important built heritage site and may be termed to be a primary attraction: that is, Borobudur itself is a reason enough for many tourists to visit Indonesia.

From the beginning, the site was considered a major national treasure under the protection and administration of the national government. The major restoration work of Borobudur took place between 1975 and 1982, following an initial intensive study and preparatory activities in the five years before.

The format of the restoration was an Indonesian national project, supported by international technical assistance, and coordinated by UNESCO. Since then, the maintenance of Borobudur as an archaeological monument and a source of scientific data has been the responsibility of the Directorate General for Culture under the Ministry of Education and Culture.

3.2 Protection and Designation

A five-year Master Plan was introduced in 1989 to try to ensure an integrated and comprehensive program to balance both conservation and development. In 1992, a zoning system was established to set up an archaeological park around the Borobudur monument site. The zoning system is as follows:

Zone I: Sanctuary Zone – no new buildings or construction, only grass and trees permitted. This zone is under the direct responsibility of the Directorate General for Culture.

Zone II: Archaeological Park Zone - construction is permitted within limits to facilitate access to and appreciation of the monument (such as a car park, ticket booths, souvenir shops). As well, construction is allowed to facilitate research on the site such as scientific monitoring. Zone II visitor facilities are executed and managed by the Directorate General of Tourism.

Zone III – land use regulated zone

Zone IV – historical scenery preservation zone

3.3 Management and Interpretation

In 1992, along with the zoning system, the government also set up a state corporation called PT Taman Wisata Borobudur, Prambanan, and Ratu Boko (*PT Taman*) recognizing the authority's management of tourist facilities in three important archaeological/ tourist sites in the region. PT Taman has the dual role of not only ensuring it generates economic benefits for the community and national government but also in cooperation with the Directorate General of Culture of preserving and protecting the site.

PT Taman is responsible for the management of Zone II tourism activities and operates under strict guidelines regarding the use of cultural property. So among its many roles are:

Regulating tourism objects within Zone II;
Collecting entry fees from visitors to the park;
Sharing responsibility for conservation and maintenance of the temple;
Utilization of the site for occasional religious ceremonies, for instance the observance of Waisak, an annual Buddhist holiday;
Utilization for educational programs and scientific research.

However, PT Taman's charter stipulates that it must operate in such a way so that nothing is done:
Contrary to the means of preservation of items of cultural property.
Simply or solely for the pursuit of profit.

Though the management structure of the site is formal and operational interpretation of the site and its visitor facilities is weak. Thus, the site does not generate its potential income even under existing regulations. There exists only poorly conceived or inadequate facilities such as a visitor centre, museum, audiovisual centre, signage, guides and so forth.

Furthermore, there is limited vision by the management to work within a comprehensive heritage management development plan to enhance Borobudur's values and benefits as a tourism and heritage destination.

Thus, the dual management responsibilities under different government departments, creates both policy and operational contradictions. There are conflict of interests among the different stakeholders in determining to what extent activities may be of benefit without damaging the integrity of this famous monument. A dynamic tension seems to exist at all times between the push to preserve and the will to maximize the Borobudur's contribution to the economic life of the region and nation.

PROFILE AND IMPACT OF TOURISM IN BOROBUDUR

As the accompanying charts will demonstrate, Borobudur's impact on the economic life of the region is considerable:

In good years, Borobudur receives over 2.5 million visitors annually, of whom the vast majority -- up to 90% -- are domestic visitors. This suggests important implications for the development of ancillary tourism activities in or around the site itself as well as in the villages in the cultural corridors that lead up to Borobudur from Yogyakarta and other major centers.

Average daily visitors to the site is about 5500 domestic visitors and 170 foreign tourists.

While the majority of visitors to Indonesia as a whole come from ASEAN countries, the top two countries that supply overseas visitors to Borobudur were in 2003 from Japan (39%) and the Netherlands (27%).

This reflects the fact that the Japanese are among the top five visitors to Indonesia as a whole and the Borobudur is especially famous in Japan as a Buddhist monument as well as an archaeological one. The Borobudur has long been used as a marketing tool to promote visits to central Java and often Japanese come as day visitors only, flying to Yogyakarta from Bali on day-trips to quickly tour major archaeological sites such as the Borobudur.

The challenge will be to encourage Japanese visitors to stay longer and to experience more of the "real" Java i.e. the villages that surround the Borobudur and help place it in a living cultural context.

It is easy to understand why the Dutch come in such numbers – after all, Holland was the colonial ruler of Indonesia for more than 300 years and so naturally Indonesia's archeological and historical treasures are well known in that country. Therefore, it is not surprising that the number of Dutch visitors to Borobudur far outnumbers their proportion as visitors to Indonesia as a whole as they tend to trace former family and colonial ties rather than just seeking out Bali's beaches.

Past studies on the economic contribution of Borobudur indicate that in terms of job creation, Borobudur is a major stimulus for the area. On average, Borobudur creates some:

Direct jobs (7000)
Indirect jobs (24,700)
Hawkers (Permanent – 2100; Temporary – 1900)

In terms of overall direct revenue to P.T. Taman, it can be seen that the more professional management of the site created by the establishment of P.T. Taman in 1992 played an important role in the increase in revenue. Overall, revenue and visitors numbers roughly parallel overall visitor numbers to Indonesia, which tumbled dramatically in 1997-98 with the economic and social crisis in Indonesia sparked by the Asian economic crisis of 1996.

Another useful indicator of Borobudur's economic impact as the anchor heritage attraction for the tourism industry in particular is the growth in both star and non-star hotels in nearby Yogyakarta, the main entry point for visitors to Borobudur. In general, most overseas visitors stay in star-rated hotels while visitors to non-star rated hotels – simple home stays, for instance – are domestic visitors.

Recent laws on regional autonomy have changed the Indonesian government system from a highly centralized government system to a more regionalized one. One of the resulting changes has been that Borobudur is now making a larger contribution directly to the district in which it is located. By law, some 25% of the revenue generated by PT Taman now goes to the district government with the balance going to the national government.

Economists have estimated that Borobudur contributes directly and indirectly more than 30% of the local income in the region.

5. COMMUNITY-BASED TOURISM AND POVERTY ALLEVIATION

The existence of Borobudur acts as a magnet to attract visitors from all over the world to central Java and Yogyakarta provinces in Indonesia. Simultaneously, it also offers an opportunity to develop other cultural tourism products to bring benefits directly to the villages in the "cultural corridors" that lead to Borobudur.

Therefore, the effort to develop cultural corridors linked to the Borobudur but physically located away from the site is attractive in that it preserves the integrity of the site while enhancing the benefits it generates to the region as a whole.

But it must be emphasized that without this major heritage attraction such as Borobudur to entice overseas visitors in the first place, these other community-based cultural tourism products could not in themselves attract visitors in substantial numbers to make an impact. Therefore, the link to Borobudur must be defined clearly.

A case study regarding developing the Candirejo village tourism corridor in the Borobudur area has been supported by the World Tourism Organization in order to optimize the economic impact of Borobudur for the local communities. Candirejo is a pilot village situated in the Borobudur area.
This case study was conducted last year (2003) for a period of about four months and involved strategic issues, cultural resource identification, policies, programs and recommendations.

5.1 Strategic Issues

Community and village entrepreneurship

A central challenge to ensure sustainable tourism is to find enough entrepreneurs at village level able to take advantage of any government subsidies, training etc. to establish the potential.

Other factors will also play a role, such as the tendency for people with the most potential to leave the village and move to larger urban areas that may offer more opportunities to them.

Cultural issues can also have a significant influence. For instance, Bali has a long history of entrepreneurship especially in the tourism sector; whereas in Javanese culture, entrepreneurs and business people do not enjoy high status within a social context

Economies of Scale

Economies of scale in this context refers to whether the net revenue from cultural tourism justifies the considerable initial start-up investment needed as well as ongoing costs (e.g. marketing, upgrading services or facilities etc.) to still ensure a meaningful economic contribution to the region as a whole.

A key question is how to ensure that the village / villages retain their "authentic" character so crucial to ensure sustainable long-term success without becoming too dependant on tourism but yet still benefit enough to make it worthwhile.

Not every village can or should try to offer every possible potential CBT activity e.g. home stays, village market, food and beverage supply, handicrafts, agro-tourism, nature walks, trekking, and so forth.

If too many activities are offered in a village, not only will it distort the village's economic and cultural base, it also risks becoming distorted into a Disney-style "tourism village". That is, a village, which only exists for - and, depends completely on - tourism and lacks authenticity, where the villagers literally are transformed into "actors". appearing on cue when visitors arrive.

As well, tourism must not distort the local village economy which is based on agricultural production – it should compliment the rhythms of the agricultural year and allow non-agricultural related alternatives to the young and those with household responsibilities.

Interpretation

Interpretation is essential to the delivery and enjoyment of the cultural landscape and natural resources that ensure visitors understand the context in which Borobudur temple was built and lasted for so many centuries.
Interpretation requires the well-trained guide, the supporting "pathfinders" within village life, signage, other media (e.g. CDs, brochures), that respond to different visitor segments.

To be truly meaningful, interpretation is not only a description of physical facts and tangible elements -it moves into the realms of spiritual truth, emotional response, deeper meaning and understanding.

d) Carrying Capacity

"Carrying capacity" in this context refers to the physical, environmental, social, cultural, and economic capacity of a village or series of villages to develop tourism within a level of acceptable change.

Communities are complex social institutions operating within a specific physical and cultural environment. Any form of modernization such as such as tourists arriving on a regular basis will have an effect on the community and village life.

Therefore, planning and monitoring carrying capacity becomes an integral part of the planning and management process.

Integration into the global tourism system

A fundamental element to economic sustainability of cultural corridors linked to heritage sites is their ability to be integrated in at least a minimal fashion in the global tourism system.

Government involvement in planning and implementation of can too often result in a supply-driven model that does not respond to the market demands of potential cultural tourists, nor is it integrated into the global tourism system of travel agents and tour operators who would send them to the villages.

It is therefore crucial to take into account market sensibility and function from the beginning in designing and implementing tourism policy regarding developing heritage-linked cultural corridors.

The challenge is to ensure that development remains not only socially sustainable and politically feasible but also economically viable in order to function within the global tourism system, which is based on profit and private enterprise.

Too many examples already exist of top-down, government designed that is not economically viable nor organically connected to the tourism system.

Institutional Framework

Community learning requires an appropriate institutional framework emphasizing empowerment, transparency and local accountability in order to ensure the sustainability and quality of the community's natural and cultural resources.

Conservation and attraction management are essential to ensure the tourism products, attractions, and services retain their distinctiveness, attractiveness and integrity over time.
Identification of the factors affecting conservation and attraction management are essential to developing an institutional framework that is culturally specific to a given community.

Lessons Learned and Policy Recommendations

Based on work done in part with the World Tourism Organization, the following are some of the lessons we would put forward in order to manage these corridors with maximize benefits for the local population to help alleviate poverty levels in the communities.

Balancing Cultural and Natural Conservation and Tourism Development

Tourism development should be balanced with cultural and natural conservation for the sake of the community as well as to preserve the long-term attractiveness of the destination.

Development should be done at a tempo and speed that allows for a community to change and adapt at its own pace.

The government should play a role as facilitator and mediating structure for villages / communities to control their own development and work with the local community to keep this balance between conservation and development.

Recommendations and Programs: :
The importance of participatory planning
Village conservation programme
Implementation of a Master Plan at the village level

B. Develop Village Tourism Corridors rather than Individual Tourism Villages

Few villages have enough products and potential in themselves to supply all tourists needs, nor keep their attention beyond a day, nor should that be the goal. Not every village is suitable for every kind of potential type development e.g. home stay, refreshment area, cultural performance, natural attractions and so forth.

By developing a cultural corridor linking different villages with each offering their own services and products, it helps to avoid negative cultural, economic, or environmental distortions. Very importantly, it also helps spread the benefits from visitor arrivals among different villages, thus reducing social friction and jealousy.

Recommendations and Programs
Tourism Resource Identification along Village Corridors
Voluntary village donation system can be implemented

C. Entrepreneurship should be a prime focus

For sustainable development, the must be linked to the tourism system as whole and respond to the changing needs and expectations of cultural tourists.

Entrepreneurs starting up, or already possessing small businesses, are needed to deliver the goods and services for tourism which also helps to support and enlarge the local economy to maximize the indirect benefits from tourist spending.
While certain benefits from tourism may be communally shared (e.g. donations to a village improvement fund) as well as certain facilities (e.g. visitor centre), the majority of goods and services will come from the private sector which requires entrepreneurs and small businesses.

Supporting entrepreneurship will help develop village-based enterprises that can link to exports as well as selling goods directly to visitors.

Recommendations and Programs
Entrepreneur training

Access to capital and resources
Programs should use "foster-parenting" to strengthen the business network

Balancing Marketing and Resource Management

Too many examples exist of government planned or micro-managed community tourism development that fail or perform poorly after the initial funding for infrastructure development and training are over.

Often the government involvement in the policy and program stage fails in the implementation stage due to a neglect of entrepreneurship within the village. Because the projects are largely supply-driven, there is insufficient private sector involvement that can respond to the needs and expectations of cultural tourists over time.

It is essential for the long-term sustainability of tourism resources that village planning and development ensure the village remains connected to and responsive to the global tourism system i.e. the system that will actually send visitors.

Therefore, from the earliest stages, policies and their implementation should take include a market approach that balance marketing with resource management/ conservation.

Recommendations and Programs
Tourism Resource Identification (TRI) & Attraction Management
Matching tourist and community expectations
Integrated marketing and promotion program

E. Interpretation should have a Central Role in Community-Based Tourism Development
Interpretation in all its forms plays a key role once attractions, products, and infrastructure are in place so that visitors understand and appreciate what they are experiencing.

Good interpretation is vital in as so much depends on what the visitor understands and if he/she can ask questions and get information on the living culture that they are seeing. Good interpretation ensures the village is accessible to visitors through elements such as local guides, signage, information distribution/ availability, visitor center, and so forth.

Interpretation must be planned and integrated into the support system for community based tourism from the outset.

Recommendations and Programs
Interpreters (guides) should come from within community
Village Interpretation Centre

Signage and Posting

F. Gender should have a key place in formulating Development Programs
It has been well established in development work that involving women is the most important element for successful, long-lasting, development work that has maximum impact on the standard of living and quality of life of the population as a whole at village and community level.

In addition, in the type of services and products typically needed in cultural tourism associated with , women dominate the chain of production for food services, cultural transmission, handicraft production and homestays.

Recommendations and Programs
Training of women should take account of their time and needs
Acknowledgement of hierarchical, patriarchal and cultural norms

CONCLUSION
The adoption of heritage tourism brings distinct economic advantages to some destinations. The spread of the tourist dollar over a wider geographical area, the attraction of wealthier and better educated tourists who spend a longer period of time all make sound economic sense.

Realistically, however, the volume of heritage tourism business will be relatively small and so cannot be expected to replace mass tourism for the major destinations. To be successful, the products must be well presented if they are to be attractive – they need proper and appropriate interpretation to enable the visitors to derive the maximum understanding and knowledge (and hence satisfaction) from its consumption.

As well, they must be properly maintained if they are to be sustained into the future and this means investment in heritage sites, visitor management, human resources, and awareness programs.

In closing, it should be remembered that developing sustainable community-based tourism is a long process precisely because the important changes are not the building of infrastructure but rather the transformation of the institutions and community structures in order to welcome, plan, control, and manage the tourism development process.

Time is a critical factor as time allows the community to adopt and adapt to developing tourism in their midst. But the ultimate goal is to give the community some measure of control over the development that affects them and to generate employment and revenue in the fight to alleviate poverty in the rural communities.

References:
WTO (1985) The state's role in protecting and promoting culture as a factor of tourism development and the proper use and exploitation of the national cultural heritage of sites and monuments for tourism. Madrid: World Tourism Organization.

GRASSROOTS CULTURAL TOURISM IN THAILAND[12]

Sawasdee-khrap and good morning distinguished delegates, ladies and gentlemen. It is a pleasure for me to address delegates of the World Tourism Organisation (WTO) on the Thai cultural tourism situation and challenges. My special thanks to WTO for organising this conference which I believe will make a positive contribution towards creating a long-term, sustainable tourism industry in the Asia-Pacific region.

Ladies and gentlemen,
Culture and tourism are very closely intertwined. To experience another country's culture is one of the primary reasons why people travel these days. By far the vast majority of culture lies at the grassroots of society. Hence, by its very definition, culture and tourism contribute actively towards poverty alleviation.

Thailand is primarily popular as a beach and sea destination, primarily due to the fame of resorts like Pattaya, Samui Island, Phuket and Krabi. However, Thailand also has four UNESCO World Heritage sites and a large variety of historical places, palaces and temples with unique architecture, arts and culture.

According to data recently compiled by the Tourism Authority of Thailand, Thailand has 1,364 natural attractions and 1,515 cultural attractions which include not only temples, palaces, buildings and other historically important sites but also handicraft-based communities and festivals. At the moment, cultural tourism in Thailand is primarily focussed on historical places, our royal family, religious traditions and internationally-known festivals like Songkran (the Thai new year) and Loy Krathong festivals. The Loy Krathong is Thailand's most popular festival, marked every November, with candles floated down the river in little banana-leaf boats as a sign of thanks to the Goddess of Water, according to ancient traditions.

The government gives these cultural activities a lot of support to ensure that they remain creative and have adequate infrastructure. It also helps channel private sector support through hotels, shops and other service businesses. The objectives are to distribute income and create jobs for the rural people.

Allow me to cite the example of the Historic Town of Sukhothai, UNESCO World Heritage site, and one of Thailand's most important tourism attractions. When the development began, it was necessary to transfer out some of the people living in the area. However, after the development was completed, and cultural tourism began, it created more jobs and the revival of ancient traditional arts and local products such as ceramics, terracotta, hand woven cloth and gold ornaments. Festivals like Loy Krathong are conducted there annually, along with a light and sound show to illustrate the history of the site.

Although the full Loy Krathong and light and sound show is only held once a year, miniature versions are adapted and held year round to serve groups of tourists who have made reservations. The light and sound show includes a performance, dinner and fireworks, all by the local communities and schools. Also the government plans to develop centres for selling local products which will be located in the communities

---

[12] Mr. Pradech Phayakvichien, Adviser to the Tourism Authority of Thailand

along the route between the historic town of Sukhothai and the province of Kamphaeng Phet.

The government also supports numerous other cultural tourism sites, such as the Historic City of Ayutthaya, also a UNESCO World Heritage Site, the Phranakhonkiri Palace or Khao Wang in Phetchaburi and a Mon (or minorities from Myanmar) community that produces terracotta at Koh Kret, a tiny island in the Chao Phraya River, located in Nonthaburi Province, only 30-45 minutes drive from Bangkok.

In Bangkok itself, the Rattanakosin Island Grand Songkran Festival features cultural parades from every Thai province. The Grand Lanna Civilisation Songkran Festival is held in Chiang Mai to highlight the cultures of the northern Thai provinces and neighbouring countries including Laos, Myanmar and south China. The TAT has also supported the "walking street" project under which sections of main thoroughfares in Chiang Mai are closed to traffic to allow Micro Small and Medium Enterprises (MSMEs) to sell products like handicrafts and paintings along the street. This, too, is aimed at making use of cultural and social activities to attract visitors, and create tourism revenue for lower-income people.

All this clearly indicates that large tourism attractions like World Heritage Sites or small ones like Kho Kret, or large festivals like Songkran or smaller ones like walking street, the government has invested in all these activities in order to help trickle down revenue to the poor.

Grassroot cultural tourism activities conducted by specific communities are emerging as the communities, government departments and the educational sector, as well as private development organisations, begin to notice the potential. Naturally, government policies are instrumental as they are designed to help the local people who are largely living off agriculture and comprise the majority of the country's population.

Allow me to highlight a few specific policies in this direction:
The bureaucratic administrative structure has been decentralised to the provinces by the creation of so-called 'CEO Governors' who become de facto Chief Executive Officers of their respective areas and have to ensure integration of all public and private sector projects and activities. The policy also creates clusters which allow neighboring provinces to take part in the development plan of the area. This allows all involved to better understand the problems and needs of the local communities, and ensure they are addressed rapidly.

The One Tambon One Product Scheme (OTOP) is designed to help small manufacturers develop products and services based on their cultural traditions and local knowledge. This generates additional income and adds value to the agricultural sector.

Just to give you some background, a tambon is a 'subdistrict' which contains many villages. There are about 8,000 tambons in Thailand with populations ranging from a few hundred to a few thousand each. Each of them has unique capabilities for making a huge variety of products ranging from souvenirs to canework, costume jewellery to handbags. The products include not only goods but also tourism attractions and services. Hence, the project reflects "development" in all aspects.

Cultural tourism at the community level could be significantly boosted by helping the local communities with their management and administrative capabilities as well as through better communications, marketing, public relations and promotion. Two case studies include the Plai Pongpang Village and Mae Kham Pong Village, both of which have a unique form of cultural tourism related to the local way of life, which is mainly agricultural. This kind of cultural tourism is thus linked to both village-based tourism and agro-tourism. In addition, it is clear that agricultural activities are inextricably linked with the specific local culture.

Plai Pongpang Village, a community of traditional Thai-Style homes

The Plai Pongpang Village is located about 64km from Bangkok. The community lives within a network of canals that feed into a river. Like in ancient times, the canal is still the main means of internal transport for the local people although most of the area itself is reachable by road. The main occupations of the villagers are fruit farming and coconut-palm sugar production, while the minor occupation is fishery.

The uniqueness of the community is the Thai-style dwellings which are about 50-100 years old. About 160 such homes can be found in the area. Other unique points include the wonderful view and peaceful atmosphere as the area is surrounded by natural habitats and canals. Also, the local life-style has been passed on from generation to generation, including the production of coconut-palm sugar, the floating market and the tradition of offering food to monks on the boats. The community has also preserved its local crafts such as making of equipment for fishing and catching prawns. The local people also take visitors to see fireflies along the canals at night.

The project started in 1999 when the head of the sub-district was contacted by the local government officials about the potential for promoting agro tourism in the community. He then did some additional research and provided more information in a number of areas. Discussions were held with the local community and it was agreed that there was much potential to develop tourism.

He began with members of three homes and has now expanded it to 25. Boatmen help plan the trips, along with the co-operation of the government sector. Tourists stay in their Thai-style homes, tour the community and the surrounding area by boat, see fireflies at night and offer food to monks in the morning with the homeowners.

All the benefits go directly to both the boat-owners and home-owners who are paid for providing accommodation and the boat-rides. They also generate income from selling fruits, souvenirs, and food from fishing, bakery and sugar production. These products are made in the community itself as well as in the nearby villages. Moreover, even though the local people are not benefiting from seeing the fireflies, they are not annoyed by the tourists. They are quite proud to have been visited.

Mae Kham Pong Village, Chiang Mai
The Mae Kham Pong Village is an agro forest community on a hill located about 1,200 metres above sea level, about 40 kilometres from the capital of the northern province of Chiang Mai. The villagers grow tea, and then steam and ferment it for chewing. This is a traditional product in northern Thailand and is very popular.

Jungle tea or 'tea garden' is an ancient agricultural system that combines forestry, agriculture and animal husbandry. The system is designed in a way that focuses on food production, survival needs and environmental balance. Tea is a popularly-grown plant in the mountains from the south of Tibet all through the mountains in Assam State of India to southeastern China, parts of Myanmar and northern Thailand.

The Mae Kham Pong village enjoys cool and cold weather year-round. Surrounded by forest, streams, waterfalls and plants and with its tea and coffee gardens, steaming and fermenting activities as well as hand-made products, the village is unique and very attractive for visitors. Its way of life and natural resources are different from other mountain areas which cultivate land using the slash and burn method which just makes the land barren and then has to be sold off to develop resorts and hotels.

The head of the village, who once was a pack-ox seller, set up a co-operative venture with a local tour operator who graduated with a master's degree in tourism from Chiang Mai University. They brainstormed ways to make the project work. The Thailand Research Fund (TRF) provided support by conducting local research about the tourism potential. In 2000, they began the cultural tourism and home-stay tours with five homes, a number which has risen to 17 at present. It has become increasingly popular with both Thai and international visitors, groups and FITs.

The community has set up a small tourist service centre for the local people, including those from surrounding areas, to sell their products and provide information to visitors. Also, trails have been developed to visit waterfalls, villages and the chewing tea-leaves production areas. However, all activities are developed in such a way that they avoid disturbing those families which are not ready to serve visitors.

Summary of the case studies

Both projects have certain key characteristics:
Good, solid leaders have played an instrumental role in creating an understanding among the villagers and people in the community. They also have the ability to coordinate the support required from external organisations.

The projects took time to be successful. The communities had to be gradually prepared to open up for visitors by doing a lot of research, brainstorming ideas, and mutually agreeing on the plans. In the case of Mae Kham Pong village, the involved parties had prepared one year before opening the village. For the Plai Pongpang Village, they also took time for the preparation and started with three homes. This case study of a bottom-up approach is different from other communities where members only followed the policies of the top-level management without thoroughly considering their readiness and whether there was sufficient demand, and then were forced to close down.

Mae Kham Pong Village project has received some expert advice. Very early on, the village gained valuable support from the TRF and other researchers at educational institutions. It has also created a network with other villages on tourism. On the other hand, Plai Pongpang village was supported by organisations that it itself sought out, such as the Department of Agricultural Extension. This is because the village is located close to the capital. Thus, the educational level and economic status of the local people is slightly better than that of villages located far from Bangkok.

Marketing is also an important factor. In the case of the Mae Kham Pong Village, success resulted from discussions with the tour operators which have experience in ecotourism. Proper discussions took place since the beginning of the project. As for Plai Pongpang Village, success resulted from word of mouth and media promotions that helped to expand the market. Important customer segments are college students and researchers.

Other important factors are the tourism resources and their uniqueness. The Mae Kham Pong Village has focused on it's agro forest culture which is located on the upper levels of hill where the weather is cold year-round, with considerable natural beauty. It is well suited to the method of tea planting and production. The Plai Pongpang village has focused on the preservation of the Thai-style homes with the life-style of people and the river. This is an old lifestyle which has changed little inspite of the many changes in the world around it.

There are, however, some problems which have emerged.

The Plai Pongpang Village has become a victim of conflicting government policies. The Revenue Department is levying a tax on the coordinators of the project by calculating it as part of their total income even though the income is being distributed to community members such as the owners of the boats and accommodations. The coordinators are not able to pay the tax.

In turn, the Mae Kham Pong Village lacks adequate marketing support from the government or related organisations. Both villages need a measurement index to indicate how to sustain it and how tourism is improving the living standards of the community.

Paradoxically, another important problem is the government's projects in the surrounding areas. In the case of Mae Kham Pong Village, as part of its development plans for the entire area, the government is expanding road links among tourist attractions by widening the local existing road which cuts through the centre of the village. Overall, these roads spoil the atmosphere of the village and can even lead to purchasing of land by investors for other commercial developments. This will affect tourism to the community. No efforts are being made to zone the area or establish clear preservation efforts for the village and forest areas. If tourism declines as a result, these villagers will suffer considerably, as they are poor and not well-educated.

Suggestions

There should be both government and local level policies for sustainable tourism promotion in order to alleviate poverty. Support and funding should be given to the potential communities, who should be allowed to share ideas, make decisions and enjoy the real benefit in terms of pro-poor tourism. Projects should focus not just on promoting tourism and big scale development but also other activities that can create direct benefits for the poor in other areas.

A team of local researchers should be set up to provide proper information. They can then consider the real potential, opportunities and the real needs of the village and use the research as a database for making plans and policies, and providing support at the government and local level. In addition, there should be a network of researchers for the entire cluster area to ensure that its development is well managed and integrated.

Support should be given to educational institutions or Non Government organisations NGOs to provide technical training to the villagers to help preserve and develop the local knowledge. These institutions and organisations are more flexible than the government organisations in working with the villages.

The government sector should establish a centre to help the villages with marketing and public relations, as well as with upgrading the quality and standards of their products.

The government should help the community better manage the tourist attractions and related activities by building up their capacities and markets in order to reduce the need to go through middlemen.

Ladies and gentlemen,
In conclusion, I would like to say that tourism can play a major role in both cultural preservation and poverty alleviation. There is no shortage of market potential. But even as we strive to boost visitor arrivals, and raise the standards of living of our people, we also need to ensure that our culture and environment does not suffer from the rush to economic growth and development.

That is why this event is so important because it highlights the fact that all must get equal priority and importance. Doing business is easy but all forms of business must be accompanied by a sense of deeper responsibility to the society, community, culture and environment in which we live. Short-term gain must not result in long-term pain.

Thank you very much and Sawasdee-khrap.

Presentations by Countries and International Organizations

CASE STUDY –DPR KOREA

The Democratic People's Republic of Korea has a long history of over 5000 years, hence its world famous cultural resources with historic relics.

▲ Government Policy

1. In recent years, Korean people have undergone many difficulties in all fields due to the inhospitable elements and repeated natural disasters. However, our Republic has established governmental policies to improve and develop cultural tourism resources in order to improve the standard of living of our people as well as the joint efforts of the National Tourism Administration, Ministry of National Land and Environment Protection, Cultural Preservation Administration.

2. Through the personal initiative and leadership of our Great Leader Comrade Kim Jong Il, a number of historical relics have been developed as follows:

- Mt. Paekdu, the sacred mountain where our Great Leader had his 20 years history of struggle against Japanese colonialism, had been completely converted into an outstanding cultural tourism resort and a great outside museum.
- More than 7 Buddhist temples, Mausoleums and old castles of centuries ago including Ryongtong temple, Simwon temple have been restored.
- The old Kaesong City, which used to be the capital of Koryo Dynasty, the first unified country in Korean history in the 10th century, is abundant in historical relics such as the tomb of HwangJini. She was famous in her appearance and talents as well as poems. Her tomb was restored in recent years and it attracts more than 2000 visitors a year.
  - Other famous places and resorts have also been developed including Mt. Kuwol, Mt.Chilbo, Ulim Waterfalls under the government's care.

3. Eighteen mural wall paintings of Koguryo Dynasty belonging to the nation's cultural heritage will be awarded the status of UNESCO world cultural heritage during their Commission meeting, which will be held in China this year. This includes Jinpa-ri Wall Painting Tomb in Ryokpo District, Pyongyang; 2 Tombs in Sammyo-ry, Nampo City; and Wall Painting Tomb in Dokhoung-ri.

4. Silk Trade Road, which was formed between Asia and Arabia many centuries ago B.C. for trade, has been developed into the Silk Tourism Road for the development of multi-destination.

▲ Concret Result
Under this government policy and its practical desire, numerous cultural assets have been developed and the number of visitors from within and outside the country has increased. This has brought improvement in the living standards of the local population and possibilities of employment either directly or indirectly.

▲ Management Measure
Our Republic maintains and sets out clear strategic policies aimed at developing the country's cultural assets to the utmost so that our people can enjoy and improve their living standards.

There is the need for international technical cooperation and investment for the development and promotion of our specific ecotourism resorts and historical relics. Therefore we need consideration and the active cooperation of international organizations including WTO and the international community for the development of cultural tourism and poverty alleviation of our country.

CULTURAL TOURISM AND POVERTY ALLEVIATION[14]

1. Introduction

So much has been written and discussed among scholars all around the world about tourism. Nevertheless there is still doubt whether there is a common understanding between the scholars and the tourism business or among stakeholders of what tourism is all about. Among the literature, it is estimated that most subject are on the business side of tourism, and on marketing and management in particular. Literature on cultural tourism is not that much, Among the business players cultural tourism is probably just a term to describe a certain kind of product that may be interpreted differently by different people. The seemingly common term of cultural tourism is not a simple understanding, it has different meaning for different stakeholders.

The meaning of cultural tourism has been changing throughout the last two centuries. It was once perceived as the practice of traveling around Europe to study fine arts. The son of English aristocrats would go on a grand tour in the company of tutors and returned home- "cultured". In the subsequent time, cultural tourism was adopted by merchants who traveled in order to develop "class". Cultural tourism may also be interpreted as small, up market, well managed educational tour, some may defined cultural tourism when they go on a tour with cultural performance as part of the agenda.

However, from the very first example it is quite clear that culture and cultural tourism was related to the high class and the rich merchant/traders who was trying to move up their class through tourism. Cultural tourism has become a means for social mobility.

Cultural tourism was once seemed to be for those who belong to the privileged of being noble or rich. When one studied fine arts, they go to an artist or an educational institution. When the young aristocrats traveled, they learned about what they see and experienced along their journey from their tutor as well as what they can absorb individually. The artists who taught fine arts, may also benefit culturally from their selected tourists coming from different part of Europe. Why fine arts ? Because fine arts is perceived as an indication of class. Traveling was also an indication of class perceived by the society. It was so because traveling was expensive and only classy people were able to travel.

With all those as a background how can we relate cultural tourism with poverty alleviation ? Can tourism really be a mean for alleviating poverty ? Poverty has become a social issue and not a t tourism issue . With the new 'movement' of pro poor tourism, it seems that more and more concern are put on poor community in location where tourism exist. The good intention is not always easy to be implemented, and even it is true that tourism create jobs and increase income as well as opportunity for other livelihood benefit, it may not applicable to the poorest. There seems to be a certain level of well being that is needed for the community to be appropriate to get benefit direct or indirectly from tourism.

---

[14] Myra P. Gunawan, Deputy Minister for Tourism Product Development & Tourism Enterprises, Ministry of Culture and Tourism, Indonesia

2. Working definition

One literature referred in this paper underline that cultural tourism is a particular type of tourism, not of anything else (e.g. heritage management).

According to Mc Kercher and du Cros (2002) who are referring to other writers, definition of cultural tourism can be seen from four different angles.

First, is the tourism derived definition, which place **cultural tourism as a special interest tourism**, where culture form the basis of either attracting tourists or motivating people to travel (Mc Intosh and Goeldner 1990, Zeppel 1002, Ap 1999)

Second is the motivational definitions. WTO defines **cultural tourism as movement of persons essentially for cultural motivation** : study tours, performing arts and cultural tours, travel to festivals and other events, visit to sites and monuments, travel to study nature, folklore or art and pilgrimage (WTO, 1985)

Third an experiential definitions, cultural tourism is also **an experiential activity**; Cultural tourism involves experiencing or having contact of differing intensity with unique social fabric, heritage and special character of places (TC 1991, Blackwell 1992)

Fourth is the operational definitions, where cultural tourism is defined by **participation in anyone of an almost limitless array of activities or experiences:** the range of **cultural tourism activity include the use of such cultural heritage assets** as archaeological sites, museum, castles, palaces, historical building, ruins, art, sculpture, crafts, galleries, festivals, events, music and dance, folk arts, theatre, "primitive culture", subcultures, ethnic communities, churches, cathedrals,....and other **things that represents people and their cultures** (Richards 1996a, Goodrich 1997; Miller 1997 and Jamieson 1994)

Cultural tourism in all the above reference are dedicated to tourist while in this paper cultural tourism will also be seen from the host community point of view. Thus **cultural tourism is defined as a process as well as a product**. It is **a process whereby tourist interact with the host community of differing intensity**, whether as the service provider or as the general public in places visited. The process is also experienced by the service provider and the community, tourists may be involved in the community activities and community may also participate in the cultural tourism undertaking. Both the tourists and the host experience a process of interaction for their benefit. The host get jobs, income and pride; beside they may also enrich themselves by knowing and further understanding about different cultures brought by the tourists as the tourist may have experiences by being involved in the community activities.

Cultural tourism as a product is referred **to a combination of tourism and cultural elements: goods and services with cultural ingredients**. Home-stays, local food and cuisine, craft as souvenirs, traditional spa services, agro-tourism are among the examples. Cultural heritage, physical; as well as non physical are also among the ingredients.

Poverty is defined as condition where people are not in a well being condition, not only from economic point of view, but also from social and cultural point of view which is interrelated one to the other. An economically poor people or family may not be able to have proper education and health services for their children and may not be able to perform their cultural need to visit relatives or to undertake their traditional activities. Poverty alleviation in this paper **is understood as giving opportunity to the community to improve their well being in its widest sense.**

When we relate cultural tourism and poverty alleviation, there is a wide policy implications not just as relating two difficult concepts into a more difficult one.

Poverty alleviation in this sense is to be seen as an outcome of **a policy on cultural tourism** (if there is any) and the question is whether there is proof where cultural tourism has really been able to alleviate poverty. What has really been achieved by cultural tourism so far? It is not just making an inventory of what has been done but what has been achieved by doing so. Whether the goals and objectives of alleviating poverty for the community has come into being.

Since there are many dimension of what public policies are, it is necessary to go through all the dimensions to check whether we are going to the right direction.

First is an understanding of policy as a label for a field of activity, in this case of cultural tourism. Do we have a policy that really cater for cultural tourism that may alleviate poverty, say a cultural tourism policy ?

Second, policy as an expression of a desired state of affairs, in this case state of community well being through cultural tourism, Do we have already stated of what is the desired state of affairs ?

Third, policy as a specific proposals, expressing the expectation of a certain group of people. Is there a group of tourism players, NGOs or other stakeholders that propose to the government to do something in relation to poverty alleviations as it relates to cultural tourism ? and whether the government is doing so.

Fourth, policy as decision of government, particularly arising from 'moments of choice'. Is there any decision when I is found that some community surrounding popular resorts are poor ?

Fifth, policy as formal authorization. Is there an Act or statutory instrument which permit or require an activity to take place in relation to poverty alleviation ?

Sixth, Policy as a program. Is there a cultural tourism program that is really geared toward poverty alleviation ?

Seventh, Policy as output. What are the output indicators that can be use to measure poverty alleviation as it relates to cultural tourism ?

Finally, policy as an outcome. When we consider poverty alleviation as an outcome, we are focusing on the impact of decision made, program undertaken, authorization and follow up actions toward the elimination of poverty in cultural tourism places.
This means that it is not only what the government is doing or can do but it is a matter of how we all can commit ourselves to alleviate poverty through cultural tourism, and each play their respective role/s.

3. The Indonesian models for poverty alleviation related to cultural tourism

It is understood that there are 5 different types of cultural tourists, namely:
the purposeful cultural tourists with cultural motivation and deep cultural experience;
the sightseeing cultural tourists with high motivation and shallow experience;
the serendipitous cultural tourist with deep experience and less motivation;
the casual with weak motivation and shallow experience, and
the incidental cultural tourist who "just happen" to participate in some of the cultural activities. (Mc Kercher and du Cros, 2002)

In our case this is understood as the fact that there are culturally rich tourists , and also culturally poor tourists. Those who are cultured and wish to developed their understanding of another culture and those who are only interested to the 'accessories' of culture from the place visited, whereby they can enjoy as part of their recreational purposes.

On the other hand, in terms of the host communities, we can find communities that maybe by a formal quantitative standard are being classified as poor but in fact they are culturally rich with their norms and values that we all have to appreciate.

A matrix of interaction typology can be drawn from above understanding of poor, when we are looking at cultural tourism as it relates to poverty alleviation. There is also a possibility where culturally poor tourists may enriched themselves from poor communities with who are culturally rich.

ILLUSTRATION 1: A CULTURAL TOURIST TYPOLOGY

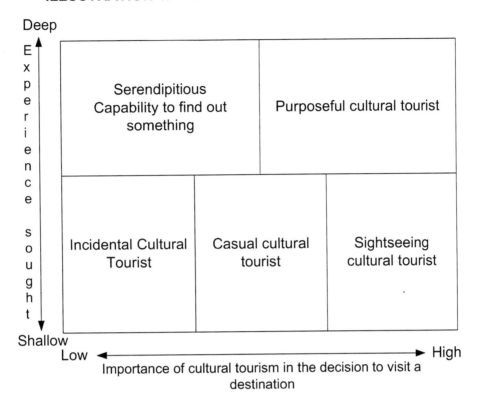

Source: Page 140, Cultural Tourism, Bob Mckercher, Hilary du Cros,
The Haworth Hospitality Press. 2002

Different type of tourists will need a different kind of product and will create a different way of cultural interaction with the host community. The purposeful cultural tourists will need a well planned product ready to serve the purpose of the tourists, the serendipitous tourists need an original traditional daily life, both in selected communities. The sightseeing cultural tourists need famous or popular product. Physical establishment of cultural heritage will play an important role for the casual tourists who may have a broad range of different interest, and in the meantime the incidental cultural tourists will need an interpreter who can interpret whatever cultural elements available in the place visited.

In this latest case the community can be indifferent of the tourist existence, or the may also be proud of being visited and becoming point of interest. Experience gain by the community will vary from low to high and the need for promotion will also differ in catering different market segments.

ILLUSTRATION 2: A CULTURAL TOURISM FROM THE HOST POINT OF VIEW

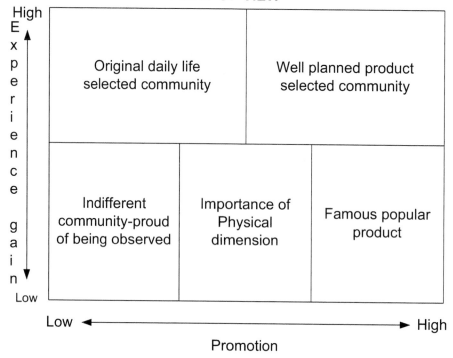

While cultural tourism can take place in many different form, how it contribute to the enhancement of human development for the local community may appear in many different ways. Some has direct impact through the direct interaction and others may have indirect impact that enable people to gain something from tourism undertaking. The possibility where tourists, particularly culturally poor tourists may gain from visiting a culturally rich community is still beyond our observation. Different cases in Indonesia can be categorized as follows :

Cultural tourism as seen from the community side.

The cultural need of the community to be fulfilled , where the tourists or tourism industries can benefit from The program is undertaken for the community need, and not specifically for the tourists who may enjoy as well. (incidental group of cultural tourists)

Facilitation for the community to be able to implement a certain traditional activities which can be enjoyed by the tourists/tourism industries. The poor community with their very limited resources to fulfill their physical need , will not be able to fulfill their need for traditional cultural need. In this respect either the government or the NGOs can facilitate by organizing the needed ceremony. For instance in the tradition for circumcision in West Java which is attributed with a traditional dances and festivals. The well off people will have this traditional need, organized by themselves for their son when the son has reached a certain age. The facilitator, in this can organize such an event for a group of boys from the under privileged families supported/subsidized by the other group of community or by the local government and businesses. When there is a fixed agenda it can be informed to tourism industries to be included in their itinerary.

Indirect cultural benefit from tourism undertaking, the case of Bunaken where each diver is charged for a certain amount of money which is used for the conservation of the environment. In addition the business also set aside a certain amount to be donated to the nearby villages , dedicated for educational purposes.

Tour operator can also play a role as voluntary mediator to contribute to the villages they visited , since the village that the tourists are enjoying the local life, some of the villager maybe in poverty are not charging an entrance fee.

Cultural tourism for the tourist with indirect benefit for the poor community

A cultural tourism product using local product produced by poor community. In the case of spa industries in Indonesia, they get their medicinal plant supply from the farmers who may not produce it without the demand or may not be able to sell their product. This is a case whereby the tourism industry, catering for purposeful cultural tourists, is playing a role to make the market ready for the community product.

There is also a case where the community get economic opportunity by being close to a main cultural attraction such as Borobudur which cater the purposeful as well as the sight seeing cultural tourists

Cultural tourism as seen from both the tourists and the community (casual tourists, sightseeing tourists, as well as serendipitous tourists)

direct contact and interaction between the tourists and the community

The community is directly involved in the provision of services, for example as food vendors, as massager, as guides and others for the fulfillment of the tourist's need. The host community can also be empowered to provide accommodation services : home stay.

In his respect the community can get a direct benefit from the tourists expenditure.
Both parties get their benefit in different forms.
In the case of serendipitous tourist, it is not the economic benefit which is most important, but the built up friendship and understanding of different cultures.

Cultural tourism business play a role in the cultural preservation and development of local culture for serendipitous and purposeful cultural tourists. Visit to a culturally rich village such as in Baduy in western part of Java may enrich the serendipitous tourist while the community may not like being intensively visited. There is also another case where children from the surrounding villages are getting place and tutors for dance training, music or any other cultural related activities and when they are ready, they perform for the tourists. The business, the community as well as the tourists are getting benefit in different form.

4. Concluding remarks

There are many different ways whereby tourism in general and cultural tourism in particular can contribute positively to poverty alleviation.

Even that the tourism Act or other legal document do not explicitly mention poverty alleviation, but the spirit is there. Tourism is not seen as an end, but a mean to achieve welfare for the community at large, especially those at the closest location. There are many undertaking going to the direction, but inventory has not systematically been done.

Poverty alleviation is seen as a social issue and not as a tourism issue, therefore programs for poverty alleviation is under the umbrella of the Coordinating Ministry of Social Welfare, which covers among others : education and health. They also have a division on tourism related matters. There is also an Act to protect the cultural heritage. Cultural heritage conservation in Indonesia include not only protection, but also usage for tourism and development of culture : tangibles and the intangibles.

Government program related to the issue is among others the development of a community based tourism development model and the empowerment of the mini and small scale tourism related enterprises such as home-stays. The Community based tourism model is seeking for instrument whereby the community can be empowered and directly or indirectly benefit from the tourism undertaking. The government should take the lead and work hand in hand with NGOs and other stakeholders in making tourism as an alternative source of income for the community and also providing the community the opportunity to benefit from tourism infrastructure.

The Indonesian government is also very keen in encouraging people to travel to fulfill their cultural need and gradually become "cultured". Tourism, especially domestic tourism is seen as a means for mutual understanding among the diverse culture and to stimulate economic activity both in sending and in receiving regions, and therefore also contribute to local economy.

Even that there is a common understanding that the success of tourism has to be measured from the improvement of community well being and not only from the number of tourists and expenditure, it has to be acknowledged that measurement of such an improvement is still limited to academic exercises and to particular places and has not been widely used.

It is therefore necessary to have a more explicit tourism policy dedicated for poverty alleviation and apply the relevant measures in promoting tourism as an alternative source of income for the community as well as an alternative economic base for a poor region. Pro poor tourism need to be promoted more to arouse stakeholder's concern. One way or another the community need to be involve in planning for tourism undertaking, as an acknowledgement of their existence. It is best if the community can be positioned as shareholders rather than only as stakeholders in cultural tourism undertaking.

Bibliography

Mc Kercher, Bob and Cros, Hilary du, 2002, Cultural Tourism, The Partnership between Tourism and Cultural Heritage Management, The Haworth Hospitality Press, New York

Hogwood, brian W and Gunn, Lewis A, 1984, Policy Analyses For The Real World, Oxford University Press, Oxford

Ashley, C, Boyd C and Goodwin H, ?? , Pro-Poor Tourism : Putting Poverty at the Heart of the Tourism Agenda

CULTURAL TOURISM, POVERTY ALLEVIATION AND THE LAO NATIONAL ECOTOURISM STRATEGY AND ACTION PLAN[15]

Introduction

The government of the Lao People's Democratic Republic (Lao PDR) acknowledges the significance of its environmental resources and, to help protect and ensure their sustainable use, has become a signatory to the International Convention on Biological Diversity (CBD). As party to the CBD, Laos has developed and recently approved a National Biodiversity Strategy and Action Plan (NBSAP). Given strong national and regional interest to develop tourism as key development sector, the ecotourism component of the NBSAP acknowledged the value and potential of this activity to help strengthen and fund the management of the Lao protected area network. This interest served as the starting point for the development of a National Ecotourism Strategy and Action Plan. The ecotourism strategy, being a detailed extension of both the NBSAP and the National Tourism Master Plan, provides a useful example of integrated government planning. This paper focuses upon the cultural component of the National Ecotourism Strategy and describes practical steps underway at the local level to ensure that new pro-poor tourism products and services reflect the richness of Lao PDR's cultural heritage.

Before examining these issues, it is helpful to clarify the role of SNV Lao PDR in supporting the Lao tourism sector. SNV (the Netherlands Development Organisation) – operating in 26 countries in Africa, Asia, Latin America and Europe – provides advice on demand to local organisations, with the aim of fighting poverty through capacity building and institutional development. In the Lao PDR this work is conducted in the ecotourism, non-timber forest products and governance sectors. In relation to ecotourism, SNV has centre-level service agreements with the National Tourism Authority, the Science Technology and Environment Agency and the Division of Forest Resources and Conservation. At this level, assistance is focused upon advising on the design and implementation of the ecotourism strategy, together with wider capacity and institution building, including advice on policy issues, training and assistance with networking and identifying funding partners. At the provincial level, SNV has service agreements with three Provincial Tourism Offices (PTOs) where advice is delivered through the placement of both Lao national and international advisors within the PTOs. Support is provided, for example, on management and administration systems, the supply of visitor information, programme development, proposal writing and seeking donor funding. As this paper also makes clear, product development is a further important function at the provincial level – with advice and support provided in relation to site and visitor surveys and a range of community-based tourism planning & management activities – examples of which are summarised below.

Cultural Tourism & the National Ecotourism Strategy

International tourism to the Lao PDR is relatively new with activity confined largely to the cities of Vientiane and Luang Prabang. A key aim for the future is to diversify the tourism product and develop new resources and attractions around the country. Central to this aim is the development and promotion of ecotourism – and hence the design of

---

the country's first National Ecotourism Strategy and Action Plan. Cultural heritage is firmly embraced in the strategy's vision statement, guiding principles, ten-year goals and the five key objectives.

A vision statement for the strategy was developed in full consultation with tour operators, accommodation providers, national and local government stakeholders and development agencies active in the sector. Through this process, the following long but inclusive statement was developed to help raise awareness of the concept and approach of Lao ecotourism.

> *"Laos will become a world renowned destination specialising in forms of sustainable tourism that, through partnership and cooperation, benefit natural and cultural heritage conservation, local socio-economic development and spread knowledge of Lao's unique cultural heritage around the world."*

At the same time, through the same consultations and workshops, guiding principles for Lao ecotourism were developed to inform, guide and direct the sector. These principles are based heavily on those identified by the International Ecotourism Society, but have been adapted by local stakeholders to suit the Lao context. The principles that relate to, or focus upon, cultural issues are underlined.

Guiding Principles for Lao Ecotourism

Minimise negative impacts on Lao nature and culture
> *Increase awareness among all stakeholders as to <u>the importance of ethnic diversity</u> and biodiversity conservation in the Lao PDR*
> *Promote responsible business practices, which work cooperatively with local authorities and people to support poverty alleviation and deliver conservation benefits*
> <u>*Provide a source of income to sustain, conserve and manage the Lao protected area network and cultural heritage sites*</u>
> *Emphasise the need for tourism zoning and visitor management plans for sites that will be developed as eco-destinations*
> *Use environmental and <u>social base-line data</u>, as well as long-term monitoring programmes, to both assess and minimize negative impacts*
> *and illustrate the measurable benefits of Lao ecotourism*
> *Maximize the economic benefit for the Lao national economy especially local businesses and people living in and around the protected area network*
> <u>*Ensure that tourism development does not exceed the social and environmental limits of acceptable change as determined by researchers in cooperation with local residents*</u>
> <u>*Promote local styles of architecture and infrastructure that are developed in harmony with the Lao culture and environment, that use local materials, minimise energy consumption and conserve local plants and wildlife*</u>

With these statements setting out the vision and grounding principles for Lao ecotourism, three clear policy statements in the form of *ten year goals* were also developed, these are to:

- strengthen national and provincial capacity and expertise in the ecotourism sector;
- coordinate and, where necessary, guide and regulate the development of ecotourism to ensure it adheres to the guiding principles; and,
- support local communities, the public and private sectors and ensure they are given sufficient freedom and assistance to develop and promote the sector

It can be seen that two of the goals relate directly to cultural issues – in the second emphasis is given to the guiding principles that cover cultural heritage, while the third emphasises the need to work closely with local communities who (certainly from a tourist perspective) can be described as the gatekeepers of Lao culture. A practical example of an action to support this goal is the production of a manual for small businesses and entrepreneurs. The manual contains a wealth advice on a range of issues relating to the construction and management of restaurants, small lodges and guest-houses.

To achieve the three broad ten year goals, five key objectives that serve as the working areas of the strategy (under which the strategy's actions are grouped) have been developed. The wording of the fourth objective in particular provides a strong emphasis on culture. The *five key objectives* are to:

- strengthen institutional arrangements for planning and managing ecotourism growth;
- support training, capacity building and the promotion of good practice;
- support environmental protection and nature conservation;
- provide socio-economic development and cultural heritage protection for host communities; and,
- develop ecotourism research and information.

Developing the Cultural Components of Community-based Tourism and Ecotourism

Turning to practical issues concerning the implementation of the ecotourism strategy, community-based projects function as important spotlights to help ensure strong take-up of the strategy at the local level. Community-based tourism projects serve to:

- raise awareness of (eco)tourism planning and management processes;
- provide working models to promote good practice & encourage replication;
- identify management concerns & help to formulate policies and regulatory mechanisms; and,
- identify incentives to encourage entrepreneurship & public and private sector investment.

Focusing upon one province, SNV has been working with the Savannakhet PTO and other stakeholders to develop the Dong Phu Vieng National Biodiversity Conservation

Area as an ecotourism destination. This particular example involves a trek, home-stay and boating experience. From a cultural perspective, the product includes an introduction to, and interpretation of :

- folk stories about features of the landscape (Plate 1);
- a home-stay with an explanation of traditions and taboos associated with local houses (Plate 2);
- a Lao Thueng baci ceremony (Plate 3);
- folk music (Plate 4);
- a local sacred forest (Plate 5);
- a nearby *coffin cave* (Plate 6); and,
- local ancestral poles (Plate 7).

To develop the product SNV is working with local stakeholders in a number of different ways. Part of this process involves forming service-groups and undertaking a series of participatory planning exercises. In the Dong Phu Vieng example, the following service groups were formed:

- cooking group (mainly young women – Plate 8);
- cultural group (for ceremonies and folk music – Plate 9);
- village guides (for trekking, and wildlife watching – Plate 10);
- home-stay group (to develop and oversee a home-stay roster – Plate 11);
- handicrafts group (Plate 12); and,
- boating group (Plate 13).

After several months of planning and preparatory activities, the first trial products were made available to tourists in January 2004. In the opening three months a total of six treks, each with 10 tourists, were sold. Figure 1 illustrates the cost breakdown of providing the product. The headings indicate that some 32% of the total product price goes to the target communities, while some 16% benefits provincial guides who are typically young Lao starting out in the tourism sector (40% of the guides trained through the project are women). The wildlife viewing bonus also goes to local village guides (rather than provincial guides) and serves as an important tool in helping to protect and conserve local wildlife. It is also worth stressing that another 21% of the product price is spent on transport – some of which is provided by local villagers and therefore makes a meaningful contribution towards poverty alleviation objectives. Finally is noted that funds are also allocated to NBCA management and the provincial government through the inclusion of local taxes.

Figure 1   Dong Phu Vieng Cost Breakdown

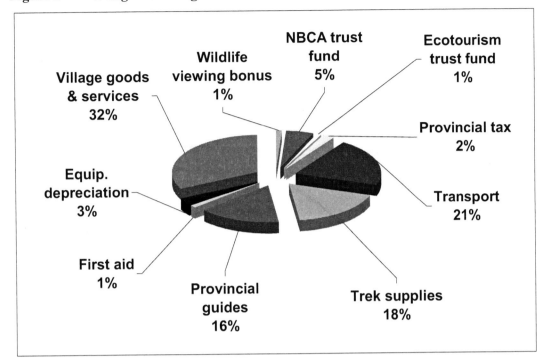

Focusing further on the impact of this activity on local incomes, Figure 2 illustrates the income gained by the target villages and in local taxes from one trek of 10 people. Similarly, Figure 3 illustrates the total income received by these parties from the six treks organised in the opening 3 months. While it can be seen these sums are modest in terms of national incomes, it is stressed the target communities are among the poorest in Laos, which implies they currently exist on less than US$1 per day and have few if any opportunities to earn cash incomes. At the local level, the US$300 earned by Vong Sikaeo makes an enormous difference to local incomes. The greater earnings of this village are accounted for by the sales of local crafts to the tourists, which in itself illustrates the potential value of tourist-related handicraft production to local communities. It is also of note to stress that these figures represent the initial launch phase of the product, in other words it is very early days for this product and incomes can be expected to increase further as the product is consolidated during the first twelve months of operation.

Figure 2 Income Received by Target Villages and Through Taxation from one Trek (10 people)

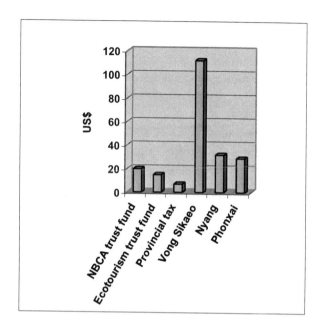

Figure 3   Income Received by Target Villages and Through Taxation from Six Treks

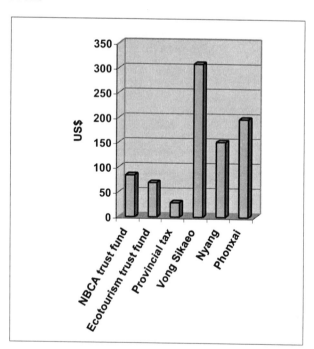

Problems and Ways Forward

A variety of challenges have been faced in developing tourism opportunities in and around Dong Phu Vieng NBCA. Five main challenges include: the lack of tourism awareness on the part of local communities; the role of local women in tourism planning and management; the use of trust funds; language barriers; and, marketing and investment. This concluding section summarises the context of these problems and, where possible, sets out mechanisms for addressing such issues.

Working with local communities with little or no experience of international tourism is a complex, difficult and time-consuming process: the poorer the target community, the longer the development process. Work with the communities around Dong Phu Vieng NBCA has however illustrated the value and potential of ecotourism activity to villages that are endowed with rich landscapes and cultural resources. A tour operator from the UK who participated in one of the treks, for example, noted the cultural experience of the product was extremely rewarding and of strong interest to European markets. As programme is consolidated, it will be used as a model to raise awareness among other target villages and, by introducing them to the planning and management processes, will provide greater access to the tourist dollar.

Among the target villages, problems were encountered in trying to involve local women – it is not considered appropriate, for example, for married women to engage with tourists. To help overcome gender issues in developing tourism a series of planning exercises focused on specific target groups were convened. This helped to reveal an interest in the value and role of non-timber forest products (NTFPs) to the local communities. NTFPs are harvested by local women and used in food preparation and processed for sale in local markets. It was discovered that some tourists are particularly interested in different types of NTFPs that are used by local communities to the extent they are motivated to accompany women to help harvest and observe the processing of the products. This interest has served as an important means to engage local women in tourism planning and management.

The development of trust funds or income streams that re-cycle tourist income for both NBCA management and local community development are important components of many tourism models. While the value and purpose of these funds is widely recognised among development and donor agencies, their implementation is often beset with a series of practical difficulties at the field level. In this case as elsewhere, for example, different stakeholders have conflicting views on how and where the funds should be used. To overcome such issues participatory planning steps are underway to set out guidelines that stipulate how these funds can be used and targeted towards conservation and development activities.

Overcoming language and interpretation barriers is one of the most essential obstacles to overcome in developing a high quality cultural tourism experience. Considerable time and effort is required to train provincial and local guides, and provide them with a range of skills to facilitate an easy exchange of stories and information with tourists. Further focus is required in the months ahead to strengthen guiding skills, particularly in relation to language training.

Also related to guiding are issues associated with the marketing and promotion of the product. At the provincial-level Lao PDR has very few tour operators with sufficient funds and expertise to develop and market pro-poor community-based tourism and ecotourism. A series of supportive planning steps are therefore being developed that will: a) ensure experienced guides become integral and essential components of the final product; b) promote the sale of products through local tour operators; and c) encourage private sector investment in small scale infrastructure to improve the quality and standing of the product.

In conclusion, it is noted that cultural tourism is an important component of the Lao National Ecotourism Strategy, as expressed in the vision statement, guiding principles and key objectives on the document. Carrying this expression forward through definitive actions to ensure cultural tourism is linked to poverty alleviation requires clear planning and action. Developing and promoting community-based tourism products, through carefully planned projects and programmes, helps raise stakeholder awareness of the interest in, and value of, cultural diversity. While the process of working with poor families to develop new tourism products and services is lengthy and complex, the economic and social contribution to the livelihoods of target communities is highly significant. A continued investment of time and effort is expected to result in greater benefits to: target communities; biodiversity conservation and protected area management; and, wider provincial and national development objectives. The Dong Phu Vieng example illustrates that cultural integrity is an extremely valuable component of pro-poor tourism.

HOMESTAY PROGRAMME IN MALAYSIA[16]

I. OVERVIEW OF TOURISM DEVELOPMENT AND THE ECONOMIC IMPACT OF TOURISM

Tourism was virtually unknown in Malaysia until the late-1960s. Since then it has developed into a major sector of the economy - the second largest foreign exchange earner after manufacturing. In addition to the more traditional goals of generating foreign exchange, increasing employment, fostering regional/rural development and diversifying the country's economic base, tourism is seen by the Malaysian Government as one of the keys to promote greater understanding of Malaysia's multi-ethnic diversity. It also gives Malaysia an opportunity to contribute to international peace by showcasing Malaysia as a modern and progressive Islamic country when people of different races lived harmoniously together and are free to practice their own religions.

The performance of the tourism industry in terms of tourist arrivals to Malaysia since 1999 had been encouraging despite the world's economy slowing down, international conflicts and the threats of safety issues to tourists. Tourist arrivals to Malaysia recorded a double-digit growth from 1999 with a growth of 42.9% in 1999 followed by 28.9% in 2000 and 25.0% in 2001. This positive trend continued until 2002 with a total of 13,292,010 arrivals representing an increase of 4% over that of 2001. However, it experienced a severe drop 20.4% bringing down tourist arrivals to only 10,576,915. This was largely due to the severe impact of Severe Acute Respiratory Syndrome (SARS). Figure A below shows tourist arrival figures for Malaysia from 2000 - 2003.

Figure A: Foreign tourist arrivals 2000 – 2003

Year	Number of foreign tourists	Change over the previous year (per cent)	Tourism Receipts (US$ billion)
2000	10,221,582	28.9	4.6
2001	12,775,073	25.0	6.4
2002	13,292,010	4.0	6.8
2003	10,576,915	- 20.4	5.6

Source: Tourism Malaysia

---

[16] Mrs. Junaida Lee Abdullah, Principal Assistant Secretary, Ministry of Tourism, Malaysia

II.   TOURISM DEVELOPMENT AND POVERTY ALLEVIATION

Poverty in Malaysia is conceptualised in both absolute and relative terms. Absolute poverty is measured in terms of the Poverty Line Income (PLI) which is USD 139 (RM 529) whilst relative poverty is defined in terms of inequality between ethnic urban and rural. Households whose gross monthly incomes were below half the PLI were classified as hardcore poor.

Poverty eradication is certainly one of the key concerns in Malaysia's five-year plans. Under the present Eight Malaysia Plan (2001 - 2005), the Government has managed to reduce the incident of poverty from 7.5% in 1999 to 5.1% in 2002 and the number of poor household by 25.6% to 267,900. The general poverty rate for the country as a whole is around 4.5% in 2002. The incident of rural poverty declined from 12.4% in 1999 to 11.4% in 2002 with the number of poor household reduced by 26.8% to 198,300 in 2002. The incident of urban poor also declined to 2% in 2002 with the number of poor household reduced to 69,600 compared to 89,100 in 1999.

The Government of Malaysia will continue to play the leading role in poverty eradication efforts by promoting income-generating projects, providing amenities to improve the quality of life and implementing programmes to inculcate positive values among the poor. In addition, the private sector and NGOs (Non Governmental Organisations) are expected to complement the government efforts.

The reduction in the incidence of poverty was due to the implementation of specific programmes towards increasing the productivity and improving the living standards of the poor. This includes efforts of the Government to address the issue of income imbalance, particularly between ethnic groups, urban-rural population and regions. Efforts are also taken to intensify the creation of a bigger and more prosperous middle-income group as well as to improve the income of the lower-income group. To meet the objectives of balanced development between different regions and states, the Government undertook measures to increase the growth rates of less developed states through the promotion of the manufacturing, tourism and modern agriculture sectors.

The following are some of the measures undertaken by the Malaysian government at federal, state and district levels for poverty eradication:
- providing housing assistance
- financial and material assistance to conduct economic activities such as micro-credit, better clones crops, life stocks and fisheries rearing such as cattle, goats, ducks, chicken, pigeons, prawn, fresh water fish, cultivation of seaweed, etc.
- other programs which are related to rural tourism such as the homestay programme and training for the poor and hardcore poor.

Some of the programmes implemented under the Eight Malaysia Plan (2001 - 2005) for poverty eradication include the following:
- Attitude Rehabilitation Programme
- Food Supplement Programme

- Pre-School Nursery Programme
- Program for the Urban Poor
- Housing Rehabilitation Programme
- Income Generating Programme
- Income Generating Programme - Agriculture
- Resettlement and In-Situ Community Development Programme

In terms of participation in tourism activities as one of the measures to generate additional income for the rural poor, the Ministry of Tourism Malaysia (MOTOUR) works closely with the Ministry of Rural and Regional Development, Ministry of Agriculture and Agro-Based Industry, and Ministry of Entrepreneurship and Cooperative Development as well as with the various State Governments through the participation of their respective State Tourism Action Council. Among some of the measures undertaken to eradicate poverty which provides opportunities for tourism activities are as follows:

- the promotion of "One District One Product" which have tremendous potential to attract tourists arrivals;
- the promotion of heritage and cultural villages;
- the provision of the basic tourism infrastructure and amenities to villages with tourism potential to promote day visits and implementation of the homestay programmes;
- the promotion of local handicrafts to produce more souvenir items;
- the provision of training programmes to educate the poor on the importance of customer care, cleanliness and hygiene, standards and quality of products and services, packaging of products, marketing, budgeting and accounting;
- training of localised guides; and
- training of activists to run homestay programmes in their own village.

The successful implementation of the Homestay Programme depends largely on the following factors:

- the attractiveness of the village itself in terms of its cultural heritage, natural assets as well as the willingness of the villagers themselves to accept foreign guests;
- the accessibility of the village;
- whether the village is located within a tourist path and or situated in a nearby natural, cultural, historical/heritage setting;
- the existence of local activists to lead the villagers to run this programme more effectively;
- the commitment of the homestay operators to change their mind-sets:

  - adopt more businesslike approach in the management of foreign visitors
  - give attention to the importance of cleanliness and hygiene, customer care and safety
  - improve English and other foreign languages to facilitate communication

- work with local travel agents, hoteliers and MOTOUR to promote their villages as homestay products

> obtain support of everyone in the village especially those who are not participating in the homestay programme to avoid and minimize community disputes, discord as well as envy.

All homestay operators are required to register with MOTOUR first. Upon receipt of such application, MOTOUR will send its officials down to evaluate the viability of the villages in terms of its attractiveness, location as well as the existing infrastructure and amenities. The implementation of the homestay programme is only meant to help supplement the villagers' income while they continue with their daily economic activities. Operators are required to attend homestay courses so that they are aware of the importance of customer care and safety, cleanliness and hygiene, conducting of interesting activities for their guests, managing their expenses, production of local handicraft and local produce such as cakes, traditional herbs, vegetables, flowers, fruits and others that could be sold to their guests. In addition, they would also visit other successful homestay programme in other villages to learn and experience themselves as to how a homestay programmes should be run.

At the moment there are about 70 villages and 1,000 homestay operators that have been registered with MOTOUR. A Homestay Directory has been produced to promote these homestay villages. Successful homestay operators usually receive a lot of visitors from the promotion of youth tourism, students' tourism, education tourism as well as domestic tourism'. MOTOUR and other government departments and agencies also which arranges for such villages to receive and act as host/foster villages for foreign guests and local students who are interested to experience a traditional rural lifestyle.

III. RECOMMENDATIONS

The government will continue to play a major role in the development of tourism activities to help alleviate poverty among the poor by providing the necessary support in terms of financial support, know-how and training as well as guidance and promotional support for their products and services.
Amongst some of the tourism activities that help improve the livelihood of the poor in the rural areas are as follows:

> produce local handicraft as souvenir items that are not too bulky, expensive, using local materials and design for tourists;
> conduct farm stay and homestay programmes for tourists who are interested to experience rural Malaysia lifestyle where the majority of the homestay operators are involved in the agriculture and fishing sector;
> provide transportation services to homestay villagers;
> develop local guides to provide guiding services for tourists staying in hotels/resorts or homestay programme;
> work in nearby hotels/resorts;

> sell traditional herbs or produce to visitors visiting their village/ areas;

> become an activist to motivate their own villagers to participate in tourism activities such as setting-up food stalls, handicraft shops, homestay, marketing of local produce and services (including traditional healthcare/massage); and

> work with the various government departments and agencies to promote youth tourism, students' tourism and domestic tourism.

IV. A CASE STUDY - CULTURAL TOURISM AND POVERTY ALLEVIATION THROUGH HOMESTAY PROGRAMME

Profile of Village: **Kampung Wang Tok Redung, Kuah, Langkawi**

Date of Settlement: Phase I (1986), Phase II (1987)

Project Cost: RM3.48 million or USD 916,842.10

Land Origin: Government Land

Size of house lot: 4,000 sq. ft

Size of Village: 113 acres

Land Use:
a) housing - 45 acres
b) Industry - 11 acres
c) State land - 16 acres
d) Future plan for Phase III - 41 acres

Status of Village: Resettlement

Population: 995 people (males = 513; females - 482)

Age groups	Males	Females	Total
45 & above	91	63	154
17 - 44	195	205	400
12 - 16	90	75	165
11 & below	137	139	276
Total	513	482	995

Education: Low educational qualification. Only 6% with Form Five/Form Six and Vocational/Technical qualifications; 15% with Form Three, 19% with no education and the rest mostly primary school levels.

Occupation: Fisherman, traders, carpenters, small scale entrepreneurs, factory workers, working in the hotel industry, operating tourist boats and ferries, mechanics, general labour, government servants

Estimated income of main breadwinner: USD 79 - USD 658

Estimated household income: USD 118 – USD 921

Village Assets:

Camps: 3 bays (USD 789)

Chairs :   100 chairs and 30 tables (USD 658)

P.A. System:	1 unit (USD 395)
Equipment Store:	1 building (USD 789)

Infrastructure

Road:	1,047 km (vicinity of village)
Pipe water:	100%
Electricity:	100%
Amenities:	Mosque - 1; Public Hall - 1, Kindergarten - 1; Public phones - 3; Children's Playground - 1; Football field - 1; Education Centre - 1; Orphanage - 1; Cemetery - 1

Associations and Organisations

Types	Total Membership
Parents Teacher Association	330
Youth Association – 4B Branch	60
Farmers Association	20
UMNO Political Association	350
Women Grouping	80
Voluntary Security Group	30
Silat Martial Arts Group	60
Nasyid Choir Group	30
Development Cooperation	155

Economic Activities/Employment

Types	Details
Commercial agriculture	30 acres of maize
Integrated project of cattle rearing and maize cultivation	6 participants
Grocery shops	5 participants
Tailoring	3 participants
Food stalls	4 participants
Craft workshop	1 participants
Satay processing	3 participants
Prawns and crabs breeding	2 participants
Boat builders	2 participants
Food processing	1 participants
Traditional medicine	16 workers
Small noodles factory	4 workers
Boat and canoe industry	6 workers
Packaging of cooking oil factory	7 workers
Laundry service	6 workers
Wood chips and compost factory	6 workers
Furniture and door frames factory	4 workers
Homestay Programme	30 participants

Participating in Government Programmes

- International Youth Exchange Programme - selected as the village to foster 30 participants from Saudi Arabia, Singapore, India, Pakistan, Japan, Taiwan, Philippines, Indonesia and Thailand
- One Village One Product Programme - as a tourism product based on agro-tourism and homestay
- National Landscape Programme - planting of trees
- Women Entrepreneurship Programme - 120 women participants undergo a course in business training, which resulted in 30 participants now active in small business
- Computer Literate Programme - 45 school children given training in basis computer
- IT programme - setting up of a Computer Centre for the youths
- Recycle Programme - recycle of tree trunks and leaves as decorative materials and fertilisers
- Homestay courses - participation in homestay courses conducted by the Ministry of Tourism

Organisation Chart of the Village Development and Security Committee

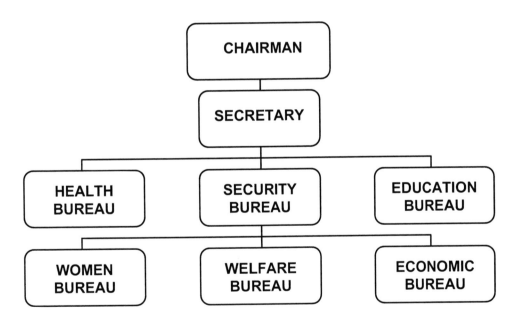

HOMESTAY PROGRAMME - A CULTURAL EXPERIENCE FOR VISITORS

There are presently 30 homestay operators registered with the Ministry of Tourism (MOTOUR) who are participating in the Homestay Programme in this village. This village is suitable for homestay as it has the necessary basic tourism infrastructure and amenities provided by the various government agencies and authorities in charge of poverty alleviation as well as being located on the beautiful island of Langkawi which is already a popular international tourist destination. As a result, this village receives a lot of daily visitors as it lies in the path of the day visitors/tourists which could total to more than 400 a day during peak season. Day visitors will get to see how the villagers go about in their daily lives as well as to visit the small-scale factory producing a special kind of medicinal oil made from sea-cucumber and such produce are sold to the interested tourists especially the local tourists who are aware of the efficacy of this oil for certain ailments. In addition, day visitors buy food and drinks from the various stalls run by the villagers themselves. It is estimated that each day visitor can spend about USD 3 - USD 10 in this village.

For homestay tourists, the operators charged USD 50 for a 3-day/2-nights full-board stay. Most of the 30 participants have only one extra room for guests staying with them under this programme. Among some of the activities organised by the operators for their guests include taking them to all the interesting places in the islands, fishing, organising a Kampung night for them with the traditional cultural performances and serving them local popular dishes, showing them how to wear traditional clothing such as the sarong, and helping them to get married according to the traditional Malay customs, if they wish with no extra charges. At the end of the departure, most of them will feel sad as the guests who have stayed with them are now no longer treated as paying guests but regarded as part of the family. In this regard, they become foster families or foster parents for the younger guests.

Participating in the homestay programme has indeed enhanced the income and improves the livelihood and standard of living of the homestay operators in this village. It is estimated that they are able to earn extra income of about USD 52 - USD 132 a month. The 30 operators felt that they have benefited from the homestay programme and have become more aware of the economic potential of tourism activities by allowing visitors to come into their village and share their daily cultural lifestyle. As a result, they have also become more committed to keeping their village clean and carried out own landscaping activities to beautify the surroundings so that their village appears more attractive and welcoming to their guests. To overcome the feeling of envy from other villagers who are not participating in this programme as well as to maintain general good-will, all villagers are invited to the 'Kampung night' organised by the homestay operators where free food are given to their fellow villagers. In this respect, the homestay operators reported no profit in the provision of this event but felt that it is a good event where everyone enjoys and get to know one another better especially with their guests. During the Kampung Night, the guests and the villagers will karaoke to their hearts content singing songs from the 60sl.

The homestay operators also often received support from various government agencies such as being asked to host Motivational courses for youth in their camp sites which could take up to a maximum of 200 people. Such courses usually last for 5-day / 4-nights and are meant to get the younger people especially those from the cities to have a better understanding and appreciation of traditional rural lifestyles.

When hosting a big event/group, the homestay operators also get help from other villagers where they formed groups to carry out a specific task. For example, a few women groups are formed to bid for the hosting of the food and drinks. All bids tendered are considered and decided by the Village Committee. Successful bidder will be given the task to do the job at the price quoted. Young adults are normally involved in the setting-up of the place, acting as security guides and helping the instructor to handle the groups. Sometimes they can earn as much as USD 4 for each course conducted in the village.

The implementation of the homestay programme in Kampung Wang Tok Redung is expected to continue with more villagers participating in the homestay programme given the increased interest generated as a direct result of the success of the existing 30 participants and the government will continue to support them in this venture by providing the appropriate form of loan financing, training, infrastructure and promotional support.

Problem Encountered in Other Less Successful Homestay Programmes

- ➢ Visitors less than 20 people becomes less economical and viable
- ➢ Not enough promotional efforts
- ➢ Village not easily accessible
- ➢ Lack of leadership - too dependent on governmental efforts
- ➢ Need to enhance cleanliness and hygiene standards
- ➢ Language problems
- ➢ Require more training to enhance better understanding of customer care and safety requirements
- ➢ Local travel agents not interested to promote homestay
- ➢ Not enough interesting things for tourists to see and do in the village

CASE STUDY ON SRI LANKA[17]

Introduction

Sri Lanka is an island that centrally located in the world map enable international tourist to access easily from both east and west particularly from the Europe and Asia Pacific. This country is also known as the **Pearl of the Indian Ocean** because of its rich heritage, culture, nature and location in addition to high literary people and their social norms etc.

There are about 189 world heritage sites declared by the UNESCO in the world. Out of them 7 exist in Sri Lanka which is one of the height sites available in the single country. Those sites are Anuradhapura, Polonnaruwa,Dambulla, Sigiriya, Kandy, Galle and Sinharaja. Among these seven sites, five are located within cultural tranquil of Sri Lanka. i.e. Anuradhapura, Polonnaruwa , Dambulla, Sigiriya, and Kandy. The Case Study selected for our subject is Sigiriya which also considered as the tourism symbol of Sri Lanka.

Culture open to tourism in Sigiriya

The culture and heritage in Sigiriya goes back to third century B.C. which means 2,300 years old. There the ancient culture heritage, art, literature developed by ancient kings and their people exist even today,. Culture and heritage in Sigiriya belongs to three periods as listed below;

1   As a Buddhist monastery complex before 3rd century B.C.(before 2300 years)
2   King Kashyapa's period in 3rd century B.C..
3   Later as a Buddhist monastery complex and a place of worship.

Sigiriya has about 600 acres of area including inner & outer kingdom. So far only 1/4 of inner kingdom has been excavated (the west entrance) and the whole Sigiriya kingdom is surrounded by a outer wall and a mode. Between west entrance and the rock from outer wall, the water garden, pleasure garden are unique attractions. Frescoers, mirror wall and its graffiti upto the main entrance has the most important cultural expressions of the past. On top the rock ruins of the King kashyapa place exists. In all this components reflects the hidden rich culture that present visitors admire today as probably the eight-world wonder of the world.

This site and its sounding are famous among both international and domestic with 500 to 3000 visitors daily. By providing transportation and other facilities to visitor has generated many employment opportunities both direct and indirect in the area.

Employment of the poor in tourism enterprises

There are medium and small size hotels and guesthouses available in Dambulla, Sigiriya, Habarana focusing the main attractions in Dambulla, Sigiriya, and peripheral attractions around Sigiriya. About 40-45% people employed in these tourism enterprises are from the area. Before tourism develop in these areas most of their means of

---

[17] Mr. P.U Ratnayake, Assistant Director/Planning & Development, Sri Lanka Tourist Board

employees was agriculture and their level of income was very low due to climatic changes droughts, less price for crops etc. Today most of the farmers produced their vegetables, fruits fishing for tourism service establishments. This backward link has stimulated the economy in the region by generating employment opportunities direct and indirect and income to the area.

Supply of goods and services to tourism enterprises and employing the poor

Most of the people who involved in guiding, sale of souvenir and handicrafts are mainly from the area. In addition they have equal opportunities to study in satellite hotel schools established in Anuradhapura and Kandy to possess professional skills to work in hotels. This shows that there are many opportunities available human resource requirement in the area.

Establishment and management tourism enterprise by the poor

Tourism enterprises by the public are in the area still to be developed in Sri Lanka. Government involvement in empowering people for tourism enterprises is limited therefore, there are no much enterprises managed by the poor in the area. But with the initiatives by Eco-tourism Foundation (NGO) and some of small investors more people getting involved in tourism enterprises presently.

Tax/levy on tourism income - benefiting the poor

Local government collect one per cent on turn over from all tourist service establishment which is spent back in the area development mainly on infrastructure and garbage disposal etc.

Voluntary given /support by tourism enterprises and tourist

In Kandalama area particularly the Kandalama hotel has scholarship scheme for year five students and O/L qualified students encouraging village students for further studies and tourism. They also have foster parents programme to help the poorest but intelligent children selected from the area.

Infrastructure development stimulated by tourism benefiting the poor

Ribbon infrastructure development has took place in the past but today more people are getting mainly access roads, electricity, and water. In the area like Kandalama the poor people who are living both sites of the access roads to Kandalama Hotel got electricity because of the project. Local Authority is also taking initiate to develop more and more infrastructure to internal areas with the time.

LINKING TOURISM WITH ONE TAMBON ONE PRODUCT(OTOP) FOR SUSTAINABLE DEVELOPMENT: A CASE STUDY IN CHIANG MAI AND CHIANG RAI[18]

Rationale

According to the Sustainable Tourism – Eliminating Poverty (ST-EP) Framework of the World Tourism Organization, sustainable tourism has been linked with poverty elimination.

OTOP Tourism Villages are villages with community strength and produce quality products of 3 – 5 stars, one kind of product per one district. The community members voluntarily need to develop their villages linking their products with tourism sites in order to increase number of tourists, length of stay and more money spent.

OTOP Tourism Villages are located on or near high potential tourism routes, with attractive atmosphere and interesting legends. The producing processes of products are unique and appropriate to demonstrate to target group of tourists.

Objectives of Establishing OTOP Tourism Villages:

To generate incomes for those communities producing OTOP products,

To link the ways of life of local people with tourism sites nearby in order to increase competitiveness potentials, incomes and added values,

To give importance on understanding in producing process, appreciation in skills of Thai local people, local wisdom, value of local techniques,

To elevate standards of products and services for tourists with hospitality, understanding, confidence in communication, honesty, cleanliness for nutrition products, facilitation and modernization for transports and communication as well as punctual, accurate and reliable delivery services.

Concept

The development of tourism sites linking with OTOP tourism villages aims to increase competitiveness potentials in tourism. The tourism sites will be developed and linked with those tourism villages which are product champions. The interesting process of production avails an opportunity for tourists to participate in demonstrating the production, as well as keeping the local ways of life with the identity of Thainess and diversity of each area. This is a means of marketing promotion of experiential tourism.The experiential tourism development gives importance on the participation of tourists in the ways of life of the local people living in the tourism sites.

Tourism sites and tourism villages with quality products are the target to be linked. The 6 Ps are to be developed as follows:

---

[18] Dr. Sasithara Picharchannarong, Director General, Office of Tourism Development, Thailand

1. Place   Infrastructure and landscape are to be improved such as building more toilets and rest areas, information centers with telephone/internet services, money auto telling machines, post offices, roads/footpaths, direction signs as well as boards telling history of the communities or products, parking areas with shuttle vehicles (may be carts or bicycles) from the parking areas to tourism sites,

2. Products   Products and services are to be diversified and elevated standards such as demonstrating producing process, folk cultural performance, delivery services, massage, etc.,

3. People   Human resources are to be developed such as increasing skills in working, language, product design, work safety, providing services, administration in finance, marketing, environment,

4. Planning and Management Systematic planning, clear targets and indicators, integrated implementation among governmental, non-governmental and local authorities should be developed.

5. Presentation Legends of villages and products are to be presented, displaying product designs and packaging, in an atmosphere of traditional ways of life.

6. Promotion   Marketing and promotion such as public relations on tourism sites, promotion to attract tourists to purchase more through travel agents or tourists themselves or advertisement.

Implementation Plan

Pilot OTOP Tourism Villages will be implemented over the country as follows:

January – April 2004
Wood craving at Baan Tawai, Hangdong District, Chiang Mai
Oolong Tea at Baan Mae Salong, Fa Laung District, Chiang Rai
Wiang Kum Kam Ancient City, Sarapee District, Chiang Mai
May – July 2004
Bamboo wicker work at Baan Wat Yang Tong, Potong District, Angthong
Earthern wares at Baan Chiang, Nong Han District, Udornthani
Batik at Baan Aownang, Muang District, Krabi
August – December 2004
Beach cloth at Baan Lumpoo, Muang District, Narathiwas
Traditional coffee at Betong, Betong District, Yala
Kapiyoh hats at Baan Takae, Yaring District, Pattani
Earthern wares at Baan Tung Luang, Kirimas District, Sukhothai
Earthern wares at Baan Daan Kwian, Chokchai District, Nakhon Ratchasima
Natural colour dyed cloth at Baan Kiriwong, Muang District, Nakhon Sithammarat
Hundred colour Pha Khao Mah (loin cloth) / broom at Baan Nong Khao, Tamuang District, Kanjanaburi

The Ministry of Tourism and Sports has planned to link tourism with OTOP in 2 pilot provinces of northern part of Thailand:

Baan Tawai in Chiang Mai   There are 2 groups in the community. The first one is developed with shops selling things to foreigners. Another one is along the canal, where people still have traditional ways of life, low potential and unskilled. It is necessary to link these 2 groups for sustainability of the community by using the 6 Ps.

During 5 – 9 March 2004, there will be Northern Craft Design Festival at Art Museum, Chiang Mai University. Another Handicraft Festival will be organized in April 2004 to celebrate the Thai Traditional New Year's Day (Water Festival).

Procedure

An integration approach has been applied in working among governmental, non-governmental, private sectors and state enterprise (Tourism Authority of Thailand). For infrastructure development, we have been working with Ministry of Interior, for skill development, we have been working with Community Development Department and Export Promotion Department. For marketing and promotion, Tourism Authority of Thailand has been working with Association of Thai Travel Agents (ATTA) and Thai Hotels Association (THA). Familiarization trips have been organized for tour operators in order to enhance marketing. The Governor of Chiang Mai and local authorities have encouraged this project to be a pilot example showing the difference of the village where one side consists of quality products to world market but lacks Thainess, another side is a traditional community with expertise in wood craving but lacks administration skill in marketing. At present, there are a lot of tourists coming to Baan Tawai, spending 2 hours on buying products, then going back. The improvement of services to tourists of Baan Tawai increases the number of tourists, spending longer time and more money on quality products, and learning more Thainess, while the local people earn more from the tourists.

Baan Mae Salong in Chiang Rai   where Chinese immigrated from Yunnan 30 years ago. The land used to grow poppy and there were a lot of political controversies. Now this village is being considered an OTOP Tourism Village for health and relaxation to taste the best Oolong Tea in the world. Baan Mae Salong is not far from the well known Golden Triangle and the Historical City of Chiang Saen where is 700 years old. Chiang Saen was an important port town on Mekong River Bank in the past. Thailand is going to develop Chiang Saen and Luang Phra Bang, to facilitate the land, air and boat transportation, to increase the number of tourists coming to visit the two cities.

In 2004, Ministry of Tourism and Sports will develop at least 10 OTOP Tourism Villages such as Krabi where located PP Islands and batik village, bamboo wicker work in Angthong which is near Ayutthaya – a World Heritage, earthern wares at Baan Chiang – a World Heritage.

Technical Seminar on Cultural Tourism & Poverty Alleviation

Mr Duncan PESCOD
Deputy Commissioner for Tourism
8 June 2004

Asia's world city

**Technical Seminar on Cultural Tourism
& Poverty Alleviation**

Mr Duncan PESCOD
Deputy Commissioner for Tourism
8 June 2004

HONG KONG

Tourism Commission

- Established in May 1999 in the former Economic Services Bureau
- Headed by the **Commissioner for Tourism**
- Formulating and coordinating the **implementation** of policies, plans and strategies for tourism development
- **Regulating** travel agents

Poverty and Relative Poverty

- **No universal** and **objective definition** of poverty
- **UN poverty line - US$2** a day

Tourism in Hong Kong

- Recognised as one of the four **pillar industries** supporting **economic development**
- **Major foreign exchange earner**
- **Job creation**
- Major source of **new skilled and unskilled jobs**
- Helping to drive **service quality and hospitality**

Cultural Tourism Resources

Modern vs ancient

East vs West

Modern vs traditional artistic performances

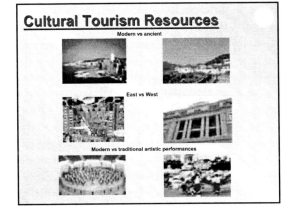

Northern New Territories

- Emphasis on **cultural** tourism and **nature-based** tourism

Appropriate planning

- **Consultancy** study
- Determine the **tourism theme** and products
- Ensure **adequate accommodation** and **supporting infrastructure** (water, sewage, electricity)
- Comprehensive **consultation** with locals and stakeholders
- **Action plan** and **environmental conservation plan**

Local participation

- **Complementary tourism products** engaged by locals
  - bed-and breakfast operations
  - catering and food vendoring services
  - oral stories/histories about local traditions, culture and heritage
- Enhance **awareness** of tourism benefits

Impact assessments

- Ensure **sustainability**
- Perform **impact assessments** for -
  - **technical feasibility**
  - **financial cost and benefit**
  - **accessibility**; and
  - **heritage and environmental** conservation

Partnership

```
   Government          Local community

          Interdepartmental
             Committee

          Private stakeholders
```

Objectives & Benefits

Objectives

- **Investment** in and by **local communities**
- **Creating jobs**
- **Lower skills** required

Benefits

- Enable visitors to see and understand **cultural and social history**
- Enhance **interaction** between visitors and local residence
- Encourage **private sector investment**
- Regenerate degraded areas

Pilot projects

- Tung Ping Chau

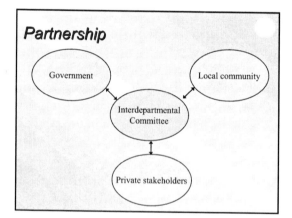

Pilot projects

- Plover Cove Reservoir and Tolo Harbour

Essential factors

- Appropriate policy framework
- Adequate planning mechanism
  - existing culture and heritage is protected
  - necessary infrastructure improvements
  - adequate accommodation
  - projects properly assessed for their impacts on the local community & environment
- Government commitment
- Encourage local community and private sector participation
- Effective collaboration between parties
- At all times working to ensure sustainable development

Asia's world city   HONG KONG

DEVELOPING LOCAL CAPACITIES FOR CONSERVING HERITAGE RESOURCE AND MANAGING TOURISM AT HERITAGE SITES[20]

1. Tourism Development and Local Heritage

As the fastest growing and one of the most profitable industries in the world, tourism offers unparalleled opportunities for the economic development of local communities living in or near heritage sites in Asia and the Pacific. Properly managed tourism development can help to stem the out-migration of youth and other marginally-employed members of the community, alleviate poverty by providing new employment opportunities, revitalise traditional building and craft industries, enhance both the physical and the intangible heritage and offer a positive, peaceful way for communities to express pride in their cultural identity.

Painful experience in many areas of the world however, has shown that unplanned tourism development, although it may be profitable in the short term, can do irreversible damage to humankind's most precious heritage sites. Tourism can undermine the heritage value of these sites, despoiling them for future generations of inhabitants, students and visitors. The tourism juggernaut has the power to destroy the landscape with inappropriate infrastructure, force the out-migration of indigenous populations and cause over-exploitation and deterioration of the fragile cultural and natural resources. This vicious downward spiral also undermines heritage tourism by degrading and devaluing the very resources on which the tourism is based.

Local communities, heritage conservationists and tourism industry professionals operating in this region are acutely aware of the problems confronting them, and in particular that the development of tourism as an economic sector is being threatened by the lack of articulation of interests and cooperation between the parties involved. These groups sought assistance from UNESCO as well as other bodies, to provide workable solutions to find common ground between stakeholders and to help develop models for mechanisms that will create a sustainable cultural tourism industry that is beneficial to all and preserves the heritage resources of the community.

2. UNESCO Project on "Culture Heritage Management and Tourism: Models For Co-operation Among Stakeholders"

The UNESCO Project on **"Culture Heritage Management And Tourism: Models For Co-operation Among Stakeholders"** (1998-2003) addressed these concerns directly and brought into play action plans for the sustainable management of heritage and tourism which have been built up from the community level. The project provided all stakeholders -- and in particular women and youth - the opportunity to represent their own interests and play an important role in the development of sustainable tourism industries. Coming from a variety of circumstances and areas of expertise, partners - especially those in weaker positions, with less power - had the opportunity to learn from each other and develop ideas and opportunities.

2.1 Objective

---

[20] Mr. Ricardo Favis, UNESCO, Bangkok Office, Thailand

The project aimed to open and structure avenues of communication between the tourism industry and those responsible for the conservation and maintenance of cultural heritage properties. By developing and testing models for the preservation of heritage and development of tourism as a local resource, the aim is to form mutually-beneficial alliances that will be both economically profitable and socially acceptable to local inhabitants and other stakeholders.

2.2 Implementation strategy

The project fostered the creation of key networks within heritage and tourism sectors, utilising in particular UNESCO's LEAP ('Integrated Community Development and Cultural Heritage Site Preservation in Asia and the Pacific Through Local Effort') network of heritage site managers, and heritage experts from the private and public sectors. The project developed closer networking ties with the tourism industry through industry bodies and national tourism organisations.

The project was implemented in five phases:
- **Phase I**:   Case studies to evaluate tourism potential
- **Phase II**:   Workshop to formulate action plans
- **Phase III**:   Action plan implementation period
- **Phase IV**:   Workshop to construct and test models
- **Phase V**:   Evaluation and mainstreaming workshop

2.2.1. Phase I: Preparation of case studies

Eight historic heritage towns were selected for pilot project implementation. They are: Bhaktapur (Nepal), Melaka (Malaysia), Lijiang (China), Levuka (Fiji), Luang Prabang (Lao PDR), Hoi An (Viet Nam), Vigan (Philippines) and Kandy (Sri Lanka) - sites located in developing countries where cultural tourism development is a development priority by policy and by practice.

In each of these pilot sites, a team of local experts and/or stakeholders prepared an in-depth case study on the impact of tourism on heritage preservation, analyzing the following components:

> heritage resources
> tourism infrastructure
> econometric statistical analysis
> management, staffing and employment
> revenue capture and reinvestment

2.2.2. Phase II: Workshop to formulate action plans

Following the elaboration of the case studies, a regional workshop was organised in Bhaktapur, Nepal in April 2000 where teams from pilot sites presented their case studies to an audience of stakeholders from a wide selection of communities throughout the region. The workshop was facilitated by experts in heritage conservation, tourism economics and community development.

During the workshop, the expert resource persons provided guidance to pilot site team members in formulating site-specific action plans to address the problematic issues of communication and coordination between the tourism and heritage sectors identified during the Phase I studies. Components of the action plan were as follows:

re-direct investment from infrastructure development into meeting the increased maintenance costs of cultural sites, in order that they are not degraded by expanding tourist flows

put into place mechanisms and indicators which would give warning in advance when a cultural resource is approaching its carrying capacity, so that preventive action can be taken

establish and enforce professional standards of renovation and interpretation, in order to preserve the authenticity of cultural sites

measure the economic success of actions not on the basis of capital accumulation or international capital flow, but on the basis of local employment and job creation

2.2.3. Phase III: Action plan implementation period

The pilot sites implemented their action plans for a period of eighteen months from April 2000 to October 2001. Towards the end of this period, the pilot sites were requested to prepare their report on the implementation of their action plans, highlighting stakeholders involvement, sourcing and nature of funding; and evaluation of outcomes.

2.2.4. Phase IV: Workshop to construct and test models for co-operation among stakeholders

A workshop was organized in Lijiang, China in October 2001 to evaluate and reformulate site action plans and to construct replicable models for co-operation among stakeholders, based on the outcome and analysis of the test applications of these models in the pilot sites over the course of the previous 18 months. The resultant models were intended to: secure conservation and management of the cultural heritage in a sustainable way; respect the living traditional ways of life; include the local population and promote competence building, employment and other benefits especially among the poor part of the population; and induce tourism industry to compensate the heritage by increased revenues.

2.2.5. Phase V: Evaluation and mainstreaming workshop

A final project evaluation and mainstreaming workshop was organized in Penang, Malaysia from 15-18 January 2003 to: (1) evaluate the impact in the eight pilot sites of their participation in the project, in order to understand and make explicit the benefits of the process; (2) refine the Lijiang Models of Cooperation; and (3) to mainstream the lessons learnt from the pilot site activities into government policy at local, provincial and national level, thus transforming the Lijiang Models into action across the board.

The pilot site self-evaluations included the mapping of inputs which have resulted in the most significant and sustained results, the identification of indicators which most reliably measure their successes, and documentation of their 'wise practice' case studies for other sites to emulate.

2.3 The Lijiang Models of Cooperation Among Stakeholders

The outputs of the UNESCO project on "Culture Heritage Management And Tourism: Models For Co-operation Among Stakeholders" are currently being compiled into a user-friendly "Manual for Tourism Management in Heritage Cities and Towns in Asia and the Pacific", which will be distributed in the region. They are currently available online at http://www.unescobkk.org/culture/norad-tourism/index.html

The key outputs are the models for cooperation among heritage tourism stakeholders in the region, which were developed on the basis of the locally developed plans by the participating sites. The models provide an operational strategy for sustainably developing tourism, especially with long-term local involvement and benefits. The models are as follows:

2.3.1 Models for fiscal management of heritage conservation, maintenance and development at the municipal level achieved through: review of the impact of income generating mechanisms; and identification and implementation of new income generating mechanisms.

(Refer to Annex I: Flowchart of the Model for Fiscal Management)

Mainstreaming into government policy would entail the following:
- comprehensive financial planning based on an agreed conservation management plan, considering environmental and social carrying capacity, risk management, preparedness and assessment, public-private partnerships, conservation incentives and financial support systems for private conservation efforts, and restructuring of tourism revenue collection for conservation and maintenance
- support heritage management programme with legal, administrative and institutional framework
- financial support for core programme from internal and external sources, external debt and revenue capture from special events and innovative activities

2.3.2 Model for investment by the tourism industry in the sustainability of the cultural resource base and supporting infrastructure achieved through: education of tourism operators on the value and conservation needs of the heritage; and formulating mechanisms by which the tourism industry can contribute financially and in other ways to preservation activities.

(Refer to Annex II: Flowchart of the Model for Investment by the Tourism Industry)

Mainstreaming into government policy would entail the following:
- identify and implement tourism revenue-capture schemes to finance 'material goods' and services, such as: heritage capital to restore built heritage and improve site presentation; tourism capital to enable community provide more convenient parking spaces, public toilets, food and accommodation facilities; 'carrying capacity' capital for tourism support services like electricity, water and waste management.
- Increase cultural awareness level and understanding among policy makers and community stakeholders on culture resource base and its economic potentials
- Establishment of interpretation and tourist information centers to educate tourists and tourism operators on the value and conservation needs of the heritage

2.3.3 Model for community education and skills training leading to employment in the heritage conservation and culture tourism sectors, with emphasis on opportunities for women and youth, achieved through: identifying new businesses and employment opportunities which can be made available locally; and designing programmes of skills training plus financial incentives to turn these potential opportunities into reality at the local level.

(Refer to Annex III: Flowchart of the Model for Community Education and Skills Training)

Mainstreaming into government policy would entail the following:

strong political will and commitment among policy makers
formulate human resource development plan based on the demand of the tourism industry
preparation and implementation of educational and training programmes
local government to facilitate the establishment of partnerships in education and training with prival tourism industry
allocate public funds for tourism promotion and skills training programmes

2.3.4 Models for conflict resolution and consensus building among tourism promoters, property developers, local residents and heritage conservationists achieved by: providing a structured venue where all stakeholders can raise and discuss situations and concerns, as well as receive education and information about heritage conservation needs and tourism development activities; and empowerment of local stakeholders through joint participation and implementation of both heritage conservation projects and culture tourism activities

(Refer to Annex IV: Flowchart of the Model for Community Education and Skills Training)

Mainstreaming into government policy would entail the following:
community empowerment through education and awareness
early stakeholders' involvement in planning and strategizing
consensus building through equal access to information and respect for every stakeholder idea
form community committees to monitor activities and to report back findings to the community

3. Regional Application of the UNESCO Tourism Project: Linking Tourism Development To Preserving Cultural Heritage In The Buddhist Circuit

The Buddhist temples and the associated knowledge and traditions found in Southeast and South Asia represent a unique and representative heritage, not only to Asia and the six percent of the world's population who are Buddhist, but to mankind at large. A large number of these sites are found in what is becoming one of the world's most successful tourism growth areas. However, the traditional heritage at the Buddhist sites faces great pressures from international tourism which too often promotes superficial, non-authentic cultural products, and the rise in global construction materials and techniques. These factors have led to the degradation of traditional practices which define Buddhist communities, including unique building crafts and decorative arts.

3.1 Developing the Buddhist Circuit

As a precursor to further developing the Buddhist Circuit as part of the Asian Development Bank (ADB) South Asia Sub-regional Economic Cooperation (SASEC) Tourism Working Group (TWG) project, attention must be paid to strengthening the conservation of Buddhist heritage in these sites - both in terms of the built monuments as well as the living traditions. The tourism strategy which will be implemented in Bhutan, Bangladesh, India and Nepal for promoting these sites should take into account the need to build capacity among care takers of the heritage, so as to promote long-term sustainable development of the sites, while maintaining their cultural authenticity intact.

During the ADB SASEC Fourth Tourism Working Group (TWG) Meeting in Thimphu, Bhutan from 26-28 May 2004, UNESCO has been designated as the lead agency in the formulation of the conceptual framework for the development of Buddhist circuits under the following themes:
> Living Buddhism in the Himalayas
> Buddhist Art and Archaeology in South Asia

A third sub-theme on Footsteps of the Lord Buddha is currently the subject of on-going cooperation with JBIC and the Government of India.

3.2 UNESCO Project on "Cultural Survival and Revival in the Buddhist Sangha"

In this context, UNESCO seeks to strengthen the on-going Buddhist traditions within the framework of the Buddhist community itself through the on-going 3-year project **"Cultural Survival and Revival in the Buddhist Sangha".** The project is implemented in co-operation with the Nordic World Heritage Foundation with funding from the Government of Norway. The sub-regional implementation of the project is a continuation of a successful pilot project in Luang Prabang, Lao PDR. The following countries are included in the co-operation: Cambodia, China (Yunnan Province and Tibet), Lao PDR, Myanmar, Sri Lanka and Thailand. Additional implementation sites are situated in Bhutan, India, Nepal and Mongolia. The total budget for the three-year project period (2004-6) is approximately US $1,800,000.

3.2.1 Objectives

The project aims to build traditional local capacity in heritage conservation in Buddhist sites by reviving traditional decorative arts and building crafts, and developing preventative conservation skills among local caretakers of heritage, in particular amongst religious communities, such as the Buddhist *sangha*.

The project was developed in response to requests from monks and communities that see their heritage threatened by the disappearance of traditional skills and knowledge, and the tear and wear of tourists. Only if local traditions are preserved in a way that strengthens local people's identity, will local communities be prepared for handling increased tourism in a responsible manner.

Most of the selected sites are situated in poor areas with great development needs. Without mobilisation of necessary resources needed to preserve the authenticity and integrity of this unique heritage, these sites and communities run the risk of gradually being destroyed as a tourist attraction.

At the same time, many sites are inscribed on the UNESCO World Heritage List or are on the countries' Tentative List. The national responsibility and the priority accorded to the conservation of the tangible as well as the intangible heritage of these sites by both national authorities will facilitate the successful implementation of the project.

Partnerships and networks will be built by engaging actors form multiple sectors in the project in order to put into place innovative mechanisms which will guarantee the project's long-term sustainability with support from local communities and authorities at all levels. Moreover, the project will strengthen the social cohesion of local communities by reaffirming values implicit in their heritage and identity, while supporting sustainable production and consumption systems.

The recent Information and Strategy Development workshop for launching the expansion of this project, held in Luang Prabang, Lao PDR from 10-14 May 2004, provided a forum for representatives from Buddhist sites throughout the Mekong sub-region as well as the South Asia region to identify their needs and resources in conserving their living Buddhist traditions.

The situational reports presented by the site teams indicated that the living traditions of Buddhism in the region are a vibrant, integral part of the local identity and cultural resources. At the same time, they are under threat from development pressures; shifting socio-cultural tastes which privilege modern ways; and discontinuities in transmission of traditions and skills to the younger generation, brought about by political changes or lack of qualified trainers and interested trainees.

3.2.2 Implementation strategy

In response to these issues, site representatives identified modalities of project implementation as follows: awareness-raising amongst Buddhist *sangha*, community members and key decision makers about the conservation of Buddhist heritage; documentation and practical training in reviving dying or lost crafts associated with Buddhist practices; development of curricula concerning heritage conservation and management targeting the secondary and tertiary educational institutions for monks; training of monks and decision makers in preventative conservation, especially of key Buddhist landmarks. The overall output as a result of these project streams is to revive the living Buddhist practices in these sites.

In addition to local-level implementation, a sub-regional strategy for sharing resources and addressing linked concerns was developed. Sub-regional caucuses will provide the forum for sub-regional strategies for creating a network for training and technical mentoring, as well as monitoring and creating key partnerships with other initiatives, such as the ADB SASEC TWG. In the case of the South Asian sites, a sub-regional caucus to be spearheaded by the Indian National Trust for Art and Cultural Heritage (INTACH), will be convened in the third quarter of 2004.

In the context of the future influx of tourism along the Buddhist Circuit, the proposed site projects must be explicitly linked to the development of the cultural infrastructure which is needed to maintain, manage, and in some cases, revive the authentic practices of these communities. From the demand side of the equation, the visitors to the Buddhism sites will be drawn by reasons of religious pilgrimage or educational interest in Buddhist traditions. This demand will be translated into a desire to interact with genuine Buddhist heritage at these sites. The challenge is then to preserve the heritage while also facilitating increased tourism flow.

As such, the projects will be undertaken in a framework which offers three benefits:

Reinvigoration of traditional Buddhist practices, including ritualistic or devotional crafts central to the on-going practice and transmission of Buddhist heritage, such as production and caretaking of "thanka" paintings, palm-leaf manuscripts, among others.

Development of knowledge resources within existing Buddhist institutions, which will serve as a repository for local cultural resources, as teaching resources for future transmission among the local community, as well as educational tools for outside visitors. For instance, the establishment of monastery-based museums will develop a much-needed inventory of Buddhist artifacts, while serving as best-practice teaching models for undertaking such crafts in the present-day. At the same time, the museums will serve an important function in educating visitors about the broader historical and social context of the living traditions which they will experience on-site.

The strengthening of socio-economic opportunities for Buddhist communities, including linking the crafts revival to poverty alleviation as well as education, particularly within the traditional modes of Buddhist temple-based community capacity building.

Given this, an approach which heavily emphasizes the development of visitor amenities over the maintenance of authentic local heritage will likely deliver the pitfalls of mass-market tourism, leading to the dilution of the local heritage in the service of the lowest common denominator.

However, if the planned tourism strategy respects this framework, the visitors will serve as a catalyst for raising the awareness of the significance of these sites, even amongst local or national stakeholders. This will allow for a respectful approach to socio-economic development which will enhance the sites both in the short-term as well as the long-term.

3.3 Future steps

The ADB initiatives to strengthen tourism development in the Greater Mekong Sub-region and in the South Asian "Buddhist Circuit" provide a timely opportunity to cooperate with UNESCO in jointly developing a strategy for conserving and developing the cultural heritage resources of the region. A holistic approach to managing these local resources should bring together concerned stakeholders from the tourism as well as culture sectors. In particular, the application of the tourism development models developed through the UNESCO Project on "Culture Heritage Management and Tourism: Models For Co-operation Among Stakeholders" will provide the modalities to ensure the sustainable development of the Buddhist sites.

CONFERENCE PROGRAMME

Tuesday, 8 June 2004

09:00 – 09:40 hrs.   *Opening Ceremony*

- Welcome address by H.E. the Minister of Tourism of the Royal Kingdom of Cambodia, Mr. Veng Sereyvuth

- Remarks by H.E. the Secretary-General of the World Tourism Organization, Mr. Francesco Frangialli

- Opening speech by H. E. the Prime Minister of the Royal Government of Cambodia, Samdech Hun Sen

09:40 – 10:00 hrs.   **Coffee/tea break**

                                  Technical Session

10:00 – 10:05 hrs.   Introduction by Mr. Xu Jing, Regional Representative for Asia   and the Pacific, WTO

10:05 – 11:00 hrs.   Keynote Presentations by WTO

"Poverty alleviation through sustainable tourism development" by Mr. Eugenio Yunis, Chief, Sustainable Development of Tourism, WTO

"The socio-economic benefits of community involvement in cultural tourism" by Mr. Ruud Klep, WTO Consultant

11:00 – 11:20 hrs.   *Presentations on ST-EP Programme*

- by Dr. Dawid de Villiers, WTO Deputy Secretary-General

- by Mr. Yoo Beong-heok, Director of International Tourism Division, Ministry of Culture and Tourism, Republic of Korea

11:20 – 11:35 hrs.   Country Presentation by Cambodia

11:35 – 12:30 hrs.   *Special WTO case study presentations*

Presentation by Mr. S. K. Misra, Chairman of the Indian National Trust for Art & Cultural Heritage (INTACH)

Presentation by Ms. Wiendu Nuryanti, Secretary-General of International Centre for Culture and Tourism, Indonesia

Presentation by Mr. Pradech Phayakvichien, Adviser to the Tourism Authority of Thailand

Questions and answers

12:30 – 13:30 hrs.	**Lunch break**

13:30 – 15:00 hrs.   *Presentations by Countries and International Organizations*

- DPR Korea
- Indonesia
- Laos and SNV
- Malaysia

15:00 – 15:15 hrs.   **Coffee/tea break**

15:15 – 16:45 hrs.   *Presentations by Countries and International Organizations*

- Sri Lanka
- Thailand
- Hong Kong
- UNESCO

16:45 – 17:00 hrs.   Questions and answers

17:00 – 17:15 hrs.   Conclusions and recommendations

17:15 – 17:30 hrs.   Closing statements by the Minister of Tourism of the Royal Kingdom of Cambodia, Mr. Veng Sereyvuth and H.E. the WTO Secretary-General, Mr. Francesco Frangialli.

List of Participants

AUSTRALIA

Mr. Rowan MACTAGGART
Director – South East Asia and
Sustainable Tourism
GRM International Pty. Ltd.
Lennons Commercial Tower
Level 29, 76 Queen Street
BRISBANE, Queensland 4000
Tel. 61 7 3025 8500
Fax. 61 7 3025 8555
Email: rowanm@grm.com.au

BHUTAN

Mr. Lhatu WANGCHUK
Director-General
Department of Tourism
DOT, Ministry of Trade & Industry
THIMPHU
Tel. 975 2 325 225
Fax. 975 2 323 543
Email: lwangchuk@tourism.gov.bt

CAMBODIA

H.E. Mr. Veng Sereyvuth
Senior Minister and Minister of
Tourism
Ministry of Tourism
3 Preah Monivong Boulevard
PHNOM PENH
Tel: (855-23) 427 107
Fax: (855-23) 213 741
Email: veng@mot.gov.kh

H.E. Mr. Thong Khon
Secretary of State
Ministry of Tourism
3 Preah Monivong Boulevard
PHNOM PENH
Tel: (855-23) 427 107
Fax: (855-23) 213 741
Email: asean@mot.gov.kh

H.E. Mr. Nuth Nin Doeurn
Secretary of State
Ministry of Tourism
3 Preah Monivong Boulevard
PHNOM PENH
Tel: (855-23) 427 107
Fax: (855-23) 213 741
Tel/Fax: (855-23) 213 912
Mobile: 012 811 062
Email: doeurn@mot.gov.kh

Mr. Kousoum Saroeuth
Director General
Ministry of Tourism
3 Preah Monivong Boulevard
PHNOM PENH
Tel: (855-23) 427 107
Fax: (855-23) 213 741
Email: kousoum@mot.gov.kh

Mr. Tith Chantha
Deputy Director General
Ministry of Tourism
3 Preah Monivong Boulevard
PHNOM PENH
Tel: (855-23) 427 107
Fax: (855-23) 213 741
Email: chantha@mot.gov.kh

Mr. In Thoeun
Director - Intl. Coop. & ASEAN Dept.
Ministry of Tourism
Tel: (855-23) 213 911
Mobile: (855) 12 821 114
Fax: (855-23) 426 107/364/877
Email: asean@mot.gov.kh

H.E. Mr. Chuch Phoeurn
Under Secretary of State
Ministry of Culture and Fine Arts
PHNOM PENH

H.E Mr. Tep Hen
Deputy Director General
ASPARA Authority
PHNOM PENH

Mrs. Chao Sunkeriya
ASPARA Authority
PHNOM PENH
Mr. Net Barom
Vice Rector
Royal University of Phnom Penh

Mr. Sun Bunna
ASEAN University
PHNOM PENH

Mr. Om Pharin
Cambodian Association of Travel
Agents
PHNOM PENH

CHINA

Mr. Ya Ping XUE
Director
China National Tourist Office (SEOUL)
#1501, Daeyungak Bldg.
25-5, 1 –ka, Chungmu-ro, Chung-ku,
SEOUL
Tel. 82 2 773 0393
Fax 82 2 757 3210
Email xueyp@cnta.gov.cn

DPR KOREA

Mr. Hak Song RYO
Director General
National Tourism Administration
Haeoun 2 – Dong
Pyongchon District
PYONGYANG CITY
Tel. 850 2 18111
Fax 850 2 381 4547
Email: nta@silibank.com

Mr. Song Jo KIM
Director – International Affairs
Department
National Tourism Administration
Haeoun 2 – Dong
Pyongchon District
PYONGYANG CITY
Tel. 850 2 18111
Fax 850 2 381 4547
Email: nta@silibank.com

Mr. Kon Ho RI
Director – Tourism Promotion &
Development Department
National Tourism Administration
Haeoun 2 – Dong
Pyongchon District
PYONGYANG CITY
Tel. 850 2 18111
Fax 850 2 381 4547
Email: nta@silibank.com

HONG KONG

Mr. Duncan PESCOD
Deputy Commissioner for Tourism
Tourism Comisión, Economic
Development & Labour Bureau
2/F., East Wing, Central Government
Offices
Lower Albert Road, Central
HONG KONG
Tel. 852 2810 3249
Fax 852 2801 5792
Email duncanpescod@edlb.gov.hk

INDIA

Mr. S.K. MISRA
Chairman
Indian National Trust for Art & Cultural
Heritage (INTACH)
71, Lodhi Estate
NEW DELHI
Tel. 91 11 2465 4090
Fax 91 11 2461 1290
Email intach@del3@vsnl.net.in

Mr. Sheldon Albert Daniel SANTWAN
Editor – Hospitalityç
Indian Express Newspapers Ltd.
Express Towers, 1st Floor
Nariman Point
MUMBAI-21
Tel. 91 22 2204 0109
Fax 91 22 5630 1007
Email ehc@vsnl.com

Mr. Mark MENDES
Editorial Consultant
Indian Express Newspapers Ltd.
Express Towers, 1st Floor
Nariman Point
MUMBAI-21
Tel. 91 22 2204 0109
Fax 91 22 5630 1007
Email ehc@vsnl.com

INDONESIA

Ms. Myra P. GUNAWAN
Ministry of Culture and Tourism
Deputy Minister for Product
Development and Tourism Enterprises
Jalan Medan Merdeka Barat 17
YAKARTA, 10110
Tel. 62 21 383 8803
Fax 62 21 306 2522
Email myra@budpar.go.id

Mrs. Ni Wayan Giri
ADNYANI
Deputy Director for Multilateral
Cooperation
Ministry of Culture and Tourism
Jalan Medan Merdeka Barat 17
YAKARTA, 10110
Tel. 62 21 383 8413
Fax 62 21 348 33601
Email nwgia@budpar.go.id

Dr. Ir Agung Suryawan WIRANATHA
Executive Secretary of Research Centre
for Culture and Tourism
Ministry of Culture and Tourism
Jalan P.B. Sudirman
DENTAR, Bali
Tel. 62 361 22 9508
Fax 62 361 23 6180
Email baligreen@indo.net.id

DR. Wiendu NURYANTI
Secretary-General
International Centre for Culture and
Tourism
Jalan Lingkar Utara, 234
YOGYAKARTA 55281

Tel. 62 274 520 907
Fax 62 274 583 783
Email stuppa@yoyga.wasantara.net.id

JAPAN

Mr. Satoru KANAZAWA
Director General, Tourism Department,
Policy Bureau
Ministry of Land, Infrastructure and
Transport
2-1-3 Kasumigaseki
Chiyoda-ku
TOKIO 100-8918
Tel. 81 3 5253 8325
Fax. 81 3 5253 1563
Email: kanazawa-s57if@mlit.go.jp

Mr. Satoshi SHIBATA
Senior Officer for Convention
Promotion, Tourism Department
Ministry of Land, Infrastructure and
Transpor
2-1-3 Kasumigaseki
Chiyoda-ku
TOKIO 100-8918
Tel. 81 3 5253 8325
Fax. 81 3 5253 1563

Mr. Yuichiro HONDA
CEO & President
JR West Japan Communications
Company
2-5-2 Umeda Kita-ku
OSAKA
Tel. 81 6 6344 5138
Fax 81 6 6344 7517
Email: ----

LAOS

Mr. Vang RATTANAVONG
Vice Chairman
Lao National Tourism Authority
Lane Xang Avenue
PO Box 3556
VIENTIANE
Tel. 856 21 21 2251
Fax. 856 21 21 2769
Email: ----

Mr. Sounh MANIVONG
Director of Planning and Cooperation
Division
Lao National Tourism Authority
Lane Xang Avenue
PO Box 3556
VIENTIANE
Tel. 856 21 21 2251
Fax. 856 21 21 2769

Mr. Paul ROGERS
Senior Ecotourism Advisor
SNV Lao PDR
PO Box 9781
VIENTIANE
Tel. 856 20 55 26 166
Fax. 856 21 414 068
Email: progers@snv.org.la

MACAU

Mr. Manuel PIRES
Deputy Director
Macau Government Tourist Office
Alameda Dr. Carlos d' Assumpçao, n
335-341
Edificio "Hot Line", 12 andar
MACAU
Tel. 853 397 1533
Fax. 853 374 321
Email: pires@macautourism.gov.mo

Ms. Silvia SI TOU
Head of Research & Planning
Department
Macau Government Tourist Office
Alameda Dr. Carlos d' Assumpçao, n
335-341
Edificio "Hot Line", 12 andar
MACAU
Tel. 853 397 1533
Fax. 853 374 321
Email: silviat@macautourism.gov.mo

MALAYSIA

Mrs. Junaida Lee
ABDULLAH
Principal Assistant Secretary

Ministry of Tourism – Tourism
Division
Level 33, Menara Dato' Onn
PWTC, Jln. Tun Ismail
50694 KUALA LUMPUR
Tel. 60 3 2696 3140
Fax 60 3 2693 2399
Email: junaidalee@mocat.gov.my

MALDIVES

Mr. Ismail FIRAG Deputy Director
Planning and Development
Ministry of Tourism
Ghazee Building – 1st Floor
MALE
Tel. 960 32 3224
Fax 960 322 512
Email:
planning@maldivestourism.gov.mv

PHILIPPINES

Mr. Roberto M. PAGDANGANAN
Secretary
Department of Tourism
T.M. Kalaw Street, Rizal Park
PO Box 3451
MANILA
Tel. 63 2 524 1751
Fax 63 2 521 7374
Email: otdp@tourism.gov.ph

Mr. Phineas ALBURO
Action Officer, International Coop.
Dept.
Department of Tourism
T.M. Kalaw Street, Rizal Park
PO Box 3451
MANILA
Tel. 63 2 524 1751
Fax 63 2 521 7374
Email: otdp@tourism.gov.ph

Ms. Josefina Leona O. RIEL
Officer
Department of Tourism
T.M. Kalaw Street, Rizal Park
PO Box 3451

MANILA
Tel. 63 2 524 1751
Fax 63 2 521 7374
Email: otdp@tourism.gov.ph

REPUBLIC OF KOREA

Mr. Beong Heok YOO
Director
Ministry of Culture and Tourism
82-1 Sejong-no, Jongno-Gu
SEOUL 110703
Tel. 822 3704 9771
Fax 822 3704 9789
Email: bhyoo@mct.go.kr

Mr. Moo Jin CHUN
CEO & President
CNK Bridge Company
752-2 Gong-dul Dong
Mapo-ku
SEOUL
Tel. 822 757 2572
Fax 822 318 8834
Email: ceo@cnkcon.com

SRI LANKA

Mr.Parapelage Upali
RATNAYAKE
Assistant Director
Sri Lanka Tourist Board
80, Galls Road
COLOMBO 3
Tel. 94 11 238 2622
Fax 94 11 243 7062
Email: ratna923@yahoo.com

THAILAND

Dr. Sasithara PICHAICHANNARONG
Director-General
Office of Tourism Development
Ministry of Tourism and Sports
National Stadium, Rama I Road
Pathumwan
BANGKOK, 10330
Tel. 662 215 3788
Fax. 662 214 1491

Ms. Pantipa SRIKONG
Policy & Plan Analyst
Office of Tourism Development
Ministry of Tourism and Sports
National Stadium, Rama I Road
Pathumwan
BANGKOK, 10330
Tel. 662 612 4024
Fax. 662 216 6658
Email: talumpuk@yahoo.co.uk

Ms. Prapa TANTASUPARUK
Tourism Development Officer
Office of Tourism Development
Ministry of Tourism and Sports
National Stadium, Rama I Road
Pathumwan
BANGKOK, 10330
Tel. 662 612 4024
Fax. 662 216 6658
Email: prapatanta@yahoo.com

Mr. Wiroj PANJAKHAJORNSAK
Tourism Development Officer
Office of Tourism Development
Ministry of Tourism and Sports
National Stadium, Rama I Road
Pathumwan
BANGKOK, 10330
Tel. 662 612 4024
Fax. 662 216 6658
Email: baoxen@yahoo.co.uk

Mr. Pradech PHAYAKVICHIEN
Advisor
Tourism Authority of Thailand
1600 New Pechaburi Road
Makkasan
BANGKOK, 10400
Tel. 662 652 8203
Fax. 662 685 8204
Email: Pradech@tat.or.th

Ms. Ubolwan PRADABSOOK
Official
Tourism Authority of Thailand
1600 New Pechaburi Road
Makkasan
BANGKOK, 10400
Tel. 662 652 8203
Fax. 662 685 8204
Email: Ubolwan.pradabsook@tat.or.th

USA

Mr. Christopher EDMONDS
Research Department
THE ECONOMIST
1001 East-West Center
HONOLULU, HI 96848-1601
Tel. 1 808 944 7362
Fax. 1 808 944 7399
Email: Edmondsc@eastwestcenter.org

VIETNAM

Ms. Pham Ngoc DIEP
Official, International Cooperation
Department
Vietnam National Administration of
Tourism
80 Quan Su Street
HANOI
Tel. 84 4 942 1061
Fax. 84 4 942 4115
Email: pndiep@yahoo.com

UNESCO

Mr. Ricardo FAVIS
Consultant for Culture
UNESCO Bangkok Office
5th Floor M.L. Pin Malakul Centennial
Building
920 Sukhumvit Road
BANGKOK 10110
Tel. 66 2 391 0577
Fax. 66 2 391 0866
Email: r.favis@unescobkk.org

WTO Delegation

Mr. Francesco Frangialli
Secretary-General
World Tourism Organization
Capitán Haya, 42
28020, MADRID
Tel. 34 91 567 8100
Fax. 34 91 571 3733
Email: omt@world-tourism.org

Dr. Dawid de Villiers
Deputy Secretary-General
World Tourism Organization
Capitán Haya, 42
28020, MADRID
Tel. 34 91 567 8100
Fax. 34 91 571 3733
Email: omt@world-tourism.org

Dr. Harsh Varma
Chief – Technical Cooperation
World Tourism Organization
Capitán Haya, 42
28020, MADRID
Tel. 34 91 567 8100
Fax. 34 91 571 3733
Email: omt@world-tourism.org

Mr. Eugenio Yunis
Chief – Sustainable Development of
Tourism
World Tourism Organization
Capitán Haya, 42
28020, MADRID
Tel. 34 91 567 8100
Fax. 34 91 571 3733
Email: omt@world-tourism.org

Mr. Xu Jing
Regional Representative for Asia and
the Pacific
World Tourism Organization
Capitán Haya, 42
28020, MADRID
Tel. 34 91 567 8100
Fax. 34 91 571 3733
Email: omt@world-tourism.org

Mr. Harunori YUKI
Chief, WTO Regional Support Office
for Asia and the Pacific
24 F Gate Tower Bldg. 1 Rinku-Orai
Kita, Izumisano
OSAKA
Tel. 81 724 60 1200
Fax. 81 724 60 1204
Email: yuki@aptec.or.jp

Mr. Yukio SHIMA
Director, International Affairs
WTO Regional Support Office for
Asia and the Pacific
24 F Gate Tower Bldg. 1 Rinku-Orai
Kita, Izumisano
OSAKA
Tel. 81 724 60 1200
Fax. 81 724 60 1204
Email: shima@aptec.or.jp

OTHER DELEGATES

Mr. Ruud Klep
Consultant
World Tourism Organization
Capitán Haya, 42
28020, MADRID
Tel. 34 91 567 8100
Fax. 34 91 571 3733
Email: omt@world-tourism.org

Ms. Vanessa Satur
Assistant – Technical Cooperation
World Tourism Organization
Capitán Haya, 42
28020, MADRID
Tel. 34 91 567 8100
Fax. 34 91 571 3733
Email: omt@world-tourism.org

Ms. Christine Brew
Assistant - Regional Representation
for Asia and the Pacific
World Tourism Organization
Capitán Haya, 42
28020, MADRID
Tel. 34 91 567 8100
Fax. 34 91 571 3733
Email: omt@world-tourism.org

Ms. Victoria J. Baker, Ph.D
Professor of Anthropology
Eckerd College
4200 54th Avenue South
St. Peterburge, Florida 33711
USA
Tel: 1-727 866 65 44
Fax: 1-727 864 7995
Email: bakervj@eckerd.edu

Mr. Chrysostom Graves
Eckerd College
4200 54th Avenue South
St. Peterburge, Florida 33711
USA
Tel: 1-727 866 65 44
Fax: 1-727 864 7995
Email: bakervj@eckerd.edu

MINISTERIAL CONFERENCE ON CULTURAL TOURISM AND POVERTY ALLEVIATION

Hue, Vietnam
11-12 June 2004

1. Introduction

This report contains an overview of the presentations and debates held during the Ministerial Conference on cultural tourism and poverty alleviation.

The conference was held in the city of Hue, Viet Nam from 11-12 June 2004. The conference was a joint initiative of the Government of the Socialist Republic of Viet Nam and the World Tourism Organization.

2. Background

Poverty alleviation is a subject many least developed countries and developing countries have been grappling with for a long time. It is now the top priority on the international agenda for the 21st Century set out in the United Nations' eight Millennium Development Goals that were endorsed by the Heads of State and representatives of Governments of 191 countries in September 2002. The UN spurred on to make the eradication of abject poverty its priority owing to the fact that approximately 4 billion people live on less than two dollars a day, half of whom subsist on less than one dollar.

Tourism is a powerful instrument for the socio-economic development of especially developing countries because of its job and income potential. This was given a universal recognition in December last year when the UN, at the 58^{Th} Session of its General Assembly, conferred on WTO the status of a full-fledged specialised agency of the UN in the field of tourism.

WTO's *Tourism 2020 Vision* forecasts that international tourist arrivals are expected to reach over 1.56 billion by the year 2020. With the projected increase, cultural tourism stands out as it outperforms other tourist segments in terms of growth. The Asia-Pacific region, from the Indus Valley civilization in South Asia to the Chinese kingdoms and dynasties of East and Southeast Asia, is endowed with a vast and ancient cultural heritage that is more than 2000 years old. And it is precisely in Asia where about two-thirds of the world's poorest live. Many of these reside in the vicinity of World Heritage monuments and sites of renown such as Angkor Wat, Taj Mahal, the Great Wall and Borobodur. These treasures of humanity as well as the traditional culture of the poor people including their lifestyles, festivals, folklore and handicrafts are cultural resources that are potential generators of income and jobs for the host destinations.

3. Objectives

The Conference had the following main objectives:

- To rally political support of policy makers for the effective application of tourism programmes oriented towards poverty reduction.

- To examine ways in which cultural tourism can be channelled effectively to achieve poverty alleviation in Asia.

- To identify policies that governments could adopt to increase their share of the cultural tourism market and increase its contribution to poverty alleviation.

- To identify the roles that local authorities can play in cultural tourism management to ensure that socio-economic benefits are fairly distributed among the local poor.

4. Organization and structure of the Conference

The Ministerial Conference on cultural tourism and poverty alleviation was inaugurated by H.E. the Deputy Prime Minster of the Socialist Republic of Viet Nam, Mr. Vu Khoan, the chairperson of the Viet Nam National Administration of Tourism Mdm. Vo Thi Thang and the Secretary General of the World Tourism Organization Mr. Francesco Frangialli.

The conference started with a brief introduction on the aim and structure of the conference. A keynote presentation by WTO gave an in depth analysis of the principles, challenges and opportunities that cultural tourism provides in relation to poverty alleviation. In addition, the conclusions and recommendations from the technical seminar held at Siem Reap, Cambodia, on 8 June 2004 were presented.

Representatives of the Government of the Socialist Republic of Viet Nam gave an introduction to the current status of tourism development in Viet Nam after which the Ministers or heads of the delegations were invited to make a 15-minute statement on the issue of cultural tourism and poverty alleviation in their countries.

The second day of the conference was mainly devoted to further shape and adopt the Hue Ministerial Declaration on cultural tourism and poverty alleviation. During the first part of the morning a panel discussion was held among three senior experts and the Head of the WTO Sustainable Development of Tourism Department that, combined with the active input from all delegates, generated further input and ideas for the ministerial declaration. During the second part of the session the ministerial declaration was discussed and edited according to the remarks and observations made by delegates. During the last part of the morning session the Ministers of Tourism officially adopted the Hue Ministerial Declaration on cultural tourism and poverty alleviation.

The conference was concluded by the Deputy Prime Minister of the Socialist Republic of Vietnam, H.E. Mr. Vu Khoan, Dr. Dawid de Villiers, WTO Deputy Secretary-General and H.E. Mr. Veng Sereyvuth, Minister of Tourism of the Royal Kingdom of Cambodia.

5. Presentations and discussions

Key issues raised during the panel discussion:

- Putting together and implementing tourism policies are essential conditions for a successful (cultural) tourism development. A sound policy should contain elements that:

1. Conserve and protect the (living) culture
2. Enhance and facilitate interpretation, that is not being used optimally at this moment, and save guard the local authenticity
3. Ensure that income is distributed fairly among all communities involved in cultural tourism

- The public sector should play a mediating and facilitating role for the private sector and the local communities, which are the two most important key players in tourism development.

- The issue of poverty alleviation should be tackled at the micro level of the village.

- It is important to determine the local carrying capacity and slowly expose villagers to the tourism industry by bringing in domestic tourists in the first place and international tourists in the second place.

- For successful tourism projects it is essential to identify villages below the poverty line, which are rich in cultural traditions and also meet other basic tourism conditions such as close proximity to existing tourism destinations and good accessibility.

- Tourism development at the village level can only be successful if the development is for the interest of the villagers and if the villagers perceive this as such.

- It is important to give local villagers time to adjust local structures to deal with tourists and to be able to control the process of tourism development.

- Indicators for development defined by the local villagers can also guide the tourism development process as cases from Thailand have shown. Based on these indicators the villagers asses the local development after two years, and determine what has changed and are offered different scenarios to deal with these changes in line with the desires of the local community.

- The input of different stakeholders is required to provide different facilities and requisites for a successful tourism development, such as an appropriate infrastructure (by regional government) and training (by international donor). The central role in the tourism development is played by the Indian NGO National Trust for Art & Cultural Heritage (INTACH).

- Once a pilot project is successful there is a need to duplicate it to other villages.

- Successful tourism development at the village level requires no forced participation and no large budgets to make villagers participate.

- It is essential that a bottom up approach is used in which local villagers, supported by academic researchers, built up their own knowledge in terms of local resources, tourism potential and social status.

- There is the contradiction of areas that are rich in culture but receive less tourists compared to areas that are less rich in culture but receive more tourists. To ensure that the benefits of tourism development trickle down to all levels there is a need for clear-cut policies at government level including elements for private sector and community involvement.

Finally, the delegation of Iran stressed the need to raise awareness on the demand side for cultural tourism. They proposed the idea to designate 2006 the Year of Cultural Tourism, and to have a conference on this subject at the city of Bam, Iran.

Opening Speeches

INAUGURATION DECLARATION BY THE DEPUTY PRIME MINISTER OF THE SOCIALIST REPUBLIC OF VIETNAM[1]

His Excellency Mr. Francesco Frangialli, Secretary-General of the World Tourism Organization,
Distinguished Heads of Delegations,
Ladies and Gentlemen,

I have the great honor, on behalf of the Government of the Socialist Republic of Viet Nam, to extend my warmest welcome to all distinguished delegates to the Asia-Pacific Tourism Ministerial Conference under the Theme "Tourism, Culture and Poverty Alleviation".

I would also like to take this opportunity thank the World Tourism Organization (WTO) for its decision to choose the Imperial City of Hue, one of Vietnam's famous tourist sites recognized by the UNESCO as the World Cultural Heritage, as the venue for this important conference. It should be noted that the conference takes place at the threshold of the Hue Festival, a Vietnam's major cultural event. This clearly demonstrates your strong confidence and valuable support to our country and to our tourism industry, in particular. We strongly believe that this Conference will mark an important milestone in the close cooperation between Vietnam and the World Tourism Organization as well as with other countries in the regional and world tourism family.

From the bottom of my heart, I wish the Conference a fine success, creating a new momentum for tourism development in our region.

The Conference's theme "Tourism, Culture and Poverty Alleviation" has a very profound meaning. Tourism is not purely a socio-economic activity but also deeply imbued with cultural characteristics. Apart from magnificent and appealing natural landscapes, the uniqueness of culture and history as well as tranquility and hospitality are the factors of vital importance to attract tourists. In return, tourism will help promote cultural exchange, consolidate solidarity, friendship and enhance mutual understanding among peoples, thus making great contributions to safeguarding peace and opening up cooperation opportunities for treasuring, restoring and preserving cultural values, tangible and intangible heritages of each country as well as of mankind. On the other hand, tourism is an effective way to improve the people's life, reduce poverty, step by step narrow the gap between the rich and the poor and between regions. The Conference's theme is relevant to the Asia-Pacific region, which is characterized with age-old and diverse cultures, dynamic development and strong tourism growth. In the meantime, poverty alleviation remains an urgent task for the region as a large of population is living in poverty and backwardness.

The combination of tourism, culture and poverty alleviation will contribute to the promotion of development for each of our nations as well as for the region as a whole. Only through close cooperation, mutual assistance among regional countries and tourism industries, could we succeed in developing tourism, treasuring cultural values, reducing poverty, and fulfilling the UN Millennium Development Goals. We look

---

[1] H.E. Mr. Vu Khoan

forward to interesting ideas and important agreements at this conference for the benefit of the noble goals as indicated in the theme.

Distinguished Delegates,

For the last 20 years, thanks to the *Doi Moi* (reform) and open-door policy, our country has traveled a long way in the national development. In this regard, tourism has an increasingly important role to play and recorded proud achievements. In the early 1990s, only about 300,000 foreign tourists visited Vietnam annually. In 2003 alone, the year was fraught with difficulties and challenges caused by SARS, Vietnam was still able to welcome nearly 2.5 millions of foreign visitors. In first years of the 21st century, foreign tourists increased from 15 to 17% per year. Efforts have been doubled to turn tourism into a spearhead economic sector in the process of the country's industrialization and modernization.

We are confident that Vietnam will be able to achieve the set goals. First, the country is endowed with exciting scenic spots, long and beautiful coastline and primitive tropical forests. Second, Vietnam has an age-old and unique culture with numerous valuable relics, among those Hue is an example. Third, we have a history with glorious victories. Fourth, Vietnam is situated a convenient geographic location in Southeast Asia and Asia-Pacific that can be connected as a destination in famous package tours. Fifth, the country's stability is firmly maintained and her people are hospitable and friendly to visitors from all over the world. Sixth, Vietnam pursues an open-door policy and is willing to be a friend of all peoples near and far. With these conditions, Vietnam has become one of the most attractive destinations for eco tourism, cultural tourism and historical tourism.

In order to better tap the existing potentials, our policy for tourism development is in line with the Conference's theme. Tourism is an important factor not only for economic growth but also for job creation and poverty alleviation. Along that line, all economic sectors are encouraged and given favourable conditions to participate in the tourism development. Tourism is not only a primary product of culture. Tourism is also a thread by which the heart and soul of the Vietnamese people and international friends can be woven.

For socio-economic development in general and tourism promotion in particular, international cooperation is given high priority by the Vietnamese Government. On behalf of the Vietnamese Government, I take this opportunity to express our deep gratitude to the World Tourism Organization and international organizations, to the tourism industries of countries in the Asia-Pacific region and other nations in the world for their strong support and close cooperation with Vietnam Tourism.

I really hope that distinguished delegates will spend some time to visit well-known tourist sites in this area, which are recognized by the UNESCO as world cultural and natural heritages such as Imperial City of Hue, Hoi An Ancient Town, My Son Sanctuary, Phong Nha-Ke Bang Cave to explore the potential of tourism development in Vietnam.

With that in mind, I wish all distinguished delegates health, happiness, success and an enjoyable stay in Vietnam!

ADDRESS BY THE CHAIRPERSON OF VIETNAM NATIONAL ADMINISTRATION OF TOURISM[2]

Honorable Deputy Prime Minister Vu Khoan, Chairman of the State Steering Committee for Tourism,

H.E Mr. Francesco Frangialli, Secretary-General of the World Tourism Organization,

Excellency Ministers,

Distinguished Guests and Delegates,

Ladies and Gentlemen,

First of all, on behalf of the leaders of Vietnam Tourism, I would like to express sincere thanks to Honorable Deputy Prime Minister Vu Khoan, Chairman of the State Steering Committee For Tourism, for taking time out of his precious schedules to participate in the opening session of the Asia-Pacific Ministerial Tourism Conference, held in Hue City of Vietnam.

I would also like to warmly welcome esteemed Mr. Francesco Frangialli and other senior officials of the World Tourism Organization, Excellency Ministers and Heads of delegations representing national tourism organizations of countries in Asia-Pacific region, international and national delegates, media agencies to ancient capital of Hue, our tourism city, to attend and take coverage on the Asia-Pacific Ministerial Tourism Conference, which is collaboratively organized by the Vietnam National Administration of Tourism and the World Tourism Organization.

This is the first time ever Vietnam hosts a regional ministerial tourism conference under the umbrella of the World Tourism Organization. We are really proud of that and would take this opportunity to thank H.E Mr. Francesco Frangialli, Secretary-General of the World Tourism Organization for this sound decision as well as for World Tourism Organization's assistance and support given to Vietnam Tourism so far.

In recent years now, Vietnam Tourism has gradually been affirming its role and position as a spearhead economic sector in the national economy. The Strategy for Tourism Development in Vietnam for the period of 2001-2010 has been approved in line with a sustainable-oriented approach, which is built up on the basis of the country's potentials and advantages in terms of eco and cultural tourism, aimed at enhancing the people's quality of life.

Vietnam is home to plentiful natural landscapes and unique natural tourism resources with her long-standing historical prides and profound cultural identities of 54 fraternal ethnic groups. These traditional legacies have left to both present and future

---

[2] Mdm. Vo Thi Thang

generations a huge treasure comprising of thousands of national cultural and historical relics and of which 7 are recognized as world heritages.

With its rapid growth rate that Vietnam Tourism has witnessed for the past few years, it has step by step re-ensured its role as a spearhead economic sector of the country, by increasing its share to the national GDP from 1.76% in 1994 to 3.5% in 2003. Tourist activities have been burgeoning from cities to rural areas, from the coastlines and islands to mountainous areas and highlands. The development of tourism has made significant contribution to changing the appearance of urban and rural areas, creating more jobs for different people from all walks of life. Wherever tourism develops, the quality of life for people there is improved. It is obvious that the development of tourism has played an important and active part in the cause of hunger alleviation and poverty reduction in Vietnam.

We have been mindful that in order to ensure sustainable tourism development, the issue of conservation and management to be addressed against commercialization tendency of cultural heritages, together with natural scenery preservation, and safeguarding of social safety would be of great significance to the future development of Vietnam Tourism industry. The continuous growth rate of annual 11.1% in number of international arrivals and 16.3% of domestic visitors in the last 10 years is an obvious evidence for that. For the first 5 months of 2004, although Vietnam was severely suffering from avian influenza but the number of international arrivals to Vietnam was still on the 19% increase comparing to that of the previous year and therefore, with the Asia-Pacific Ministerial Tourism Conference held in Vietnam this time is indeed a big source of encouragement for us.

Ladies and Gentlemen,

World Tourism continues growing even in the most recent circumstances that it has been under innumerable pressures and negative impacts caused by natural calamities, epidemic diseases, terrorism and wars. The development of tourism will be an important contribution to conserving traditional cultural values and helping improve quality of life for people living in poverty. However in reality, currently 49 least developed countries have been able to receive about only 1% share of the total tourist arrivals and earn 0.5% tourism revenue of world tourism. It is clearly seen that these figures are so diminutive comparing to what tourism can bring to developing countries and poor community all over the world. Therefore, in order to successfully achieve the Millennium Development Goals set forth by the United Nations that by the year 2015, the number of 1.2 billion poor people who are living with an income less than $US 1 per day will be cut down by half, we - who are directly working in tourism industry – must make all efforts to further promote tourism activities so as to bring more benefits for countries, localities and regions where life is still under much hardships. On the other hand, by getting involved in tourism businesses, various communities particularly the poor will have greater opportunities to generate incomes and improve living conditions, and at the same time making an important contribution to the conservation and preservation of traditional cultural values.

Therefore, I do believe this Asia-Pacific Ministerial Tourism Conference will have significant contribution to the development cause of regional and world tourism, strengthening closer and stronger development cooperation in conserving and bringing into full play the human cultural values as well as successfully realizing the UN Millennium Development Goals in hunger alleviation and poverty reduction.

Finally, I would like to wish the conference productive and fruitful. May I wish Honourable Vice Prime Minister Vu Khoan, Secretary-General of the World Tourism Organization and all distinguished delegates good health.

Thank you.

SPEECH BY THE SECRETARY-GENERAL OF THE WORLD TOURISM ORGANIZATION[3]

Your Excellency, the Deputy Prime Minister of the Socialist Republic of Vietnam, Mr. Vu Khoan,

Your Excellency, the Chairperson of the Vietnam National Administration of Tourism, Madam Vo Thi Thang,

Your Excellency, the Chairman of the Hue People's Committee, Mr. Nguyen Xuan Ly,

Hon. Ministers of Tourism from the Asia-Pacific Region,

Distinguished Delegates,

Ladies and Gentlemen,

It is a pleasure and an honour for me to welcome you today at this auspicious occasion - the celebration of the first Ministerial Conference ever held by the World Tourism Organization (WTO) in the Asia-Pacific region on the issue of poverty alleviation through cultural tourism. As a specialised agency of the United Nations system, WTO attaches great importance to poverty alleviation through tourism in line with UN Millennium Development Goals.

I would like to take this opportunity to express my sincere thanks and appreciation to the Government of the Socialist Republic of Vietnam for its warm and generous hospitality in organizing this Ministerial Conference. I would also like to thank His Excellency, the Deputy Prime Minister of Vietnam for taking the time out of his extremely busy schedule to join us this morning. Your presence here is a great source of encouragement for all of us as it shows the importance which you attach to the tourism industry as an engine for socio-economic growth of Vietnam.

As you may be aware, the organization of this Conference was programmed intentionally to coincide with the inauguration of the prestigious Hue Festival whose theme this year of "Cultural Heritage with Integration and Development" provides a unique background to our deliberations.

WTO and the Government of the Socialist Republic of Vietnam enjoy a very warm and mutually beneficial relationship. I have witnessed with great pleasure the rapid growth in Vietnam's tourism industry and would like to take this opportunity to express my respect and admiration for the Hon. Chairperson of the Vietnam National Administration of Tourism, Madam Vo Thi Thang, who, through her dynamic leadership, has been the driving force behind the success of Vietnam's tourism industry.

WTO has provided its technical assistance to the Government of Vietnam on numerous occasions. In the recent past, we have formulated a Revised Master Plan for Sustainable Tourism Development, a Tourism Master Plan for Cua Lo, a Sustainable Tourism Development Plan for Phu Quoc, and, we are currently assisting the Government of

---

[3] Mr. Francesco Frangialli

Vietnam in drafting the terms of reference for Vietnam's first Tourism Law. We are also assisting the city of Ho Chi Minh in developing MICE tourism.

The Asia-Pacific region is the region that has experienced a constant and steady growth in international tourism. The diversity of its tourism attractions and its strong economic growth have made it the second-most visited region of the world after Europe. WTO has focused its attention on tourism development in Asia and we aim to assist the region in developing a sustainable tourism industry which could contribute towards social development, economic growth and environmental preservation.

One of the greatest challenges that the Asia-Pacific region faces is that of poverty. It is also a challenge that has been taken on by the international community whose commitment, through the Millennium Development Goals and the recommendations of the World Summit held in 2002 in Johannesburg regarding sustainable development and poverty alleviation, illustrate this. The MDGs and the WSSD recommendations now serve as a guide for WTO's actions, since we are full partners of the United Nations.

It is evident that cultural tourism has the characteristics to make it a most suitable economic activity for Asia: the richness and diversity of Asian cultures, both in terms of monumental sites and living cultural heritage, provide your countries with a unique opportunity to base tourism development on these resources. But this wealth should be correctly conserved and managed, in order for it to contribute significantly to the long-term sustainable development of the continent and to the reduction of poverty. Cultural tourism, including community-based initiatives through which the tourists like to experience the daily life and living cultures of local communities, lends itself to small and medium sized entrepreneurial developments, offering thus opportunities to incorporate important poor segments of population.

Innovative research has been undertaken by WTO since 2002 in order to identify the different ways in which tourism has effectively been contributing to reduce poverty in many parts of the world, and on the most practical approaches to further develop this potential. Two publications have been issued, the first of which was launched at the Johannesburg Summit, while the second one, with specific recommendations for action, was presented at ITB Berlin last March. We will provide you with an electronic copy of the latter and we shall also present during this Conference, its main conclusions and recommendations, as they apply to cultural tourism in Asia.

Furthermore, and for the purpose of multiplying the contribution of tourism to poverty reduction efforts, our Organization has undertaken to establish a foundation called the ST-EP Foundation. Its aim will be to help developing countries to design and implement sustainable tourism projects that can contribute to the creation of jobs in disadvantaged areas and to the improvement of the living standards of local populations. We foresee that Asia and Africa will be the first two regions to benefit from actions by the ST-EP Foundation.

ST-EP intends to make tourism work for the people – work with communities and work in rural areas – where most of the poverty is often found. It is an ambitious programme that will require substantial funding. At the ST-EP Forum at ITB in March this year, the Republic of Korea announced a contribution of 5 million US$ to kick-start the project -

and more sponsors are showing interest, either to provide a cash contribution or to put their capacities at the service of ST-EP objectives.

But overcoming poverty is a shared task, in which different institutions and actors have to take their share of responsibility. This is why we are undertaking a number of other activities, such as this Conference, in parallel with the creation of ST-EP. We are convinced that governments, and more particularly the national tourism administrations, can already make better use of their own human and financial resources in order to guide the benefits of tourism in favour of the poor segments of their populations.

I am pleased to see such a large number of participants at this Conference and am especially encouraged at the presence of so many Ministers of Tourism as this convinces me of the importance which your Governments attach to tourism as an engine for poverty alleviation. As you may be aware, we have just arrived from Siem Reap, Cambodia where we organized a Technical Seminar on the Cultural Tourism and Poverty Alleviation. We shall present to you today the main conclusions and recommendations of the seminar and we shall benefit from the Ministerial Statements which will inform us on the policies and strategies adopted by Asia-Pacific nations to develop cultural tourism as a means to eliminating poverty.

I am convinced that this Conference, which shall culminate in the adoption of Hue Declaration on Cultural Tourism and Poverty Alleviation, will provide all of us with practical, efficient guidelines and policies for poverty alleviation through tourism development while preserving the rich cultural heritage of the Asia-Pacific region.

I thank you for your kind attention and wish you good luck in your deliberations.

INTRODUCTION BY WTO[4]

Poverty alleviation is a subject which has been a constant source of concern to many developing countries. It is now the top priority on the international agenda for the 21st Century set out in the United Nations' Millennium Development Goals which were endorsed by the Heads of State and representatives of Governments in September 2000. This decision was influenced by the fact that approximately 4 billion people live on less than two dollars a day, half of whom subsist on less than a dollar.

There is no denying the fact that tourism is a powerful instrument for the socio-economic development because of its capacity to generate jobs and income. This was acknowledged in December last year when the UN, at the 58th Session of its General Assembly, designated the WTO as its specialised agency.

WTO's *Tourism 2020 Vision* forecasts that international tourist arrivals are expected to touch 1.5 billion by the year 2020. Of these arrivals, an overwhelming majority would be for cultural tourism purposes. The Asia-Pacific region, from the Indus Valley civilization in South Asia to the Chinese kingdoms and dynasties of East and Southeast Asia, is endowed with a vast and ancient cultural heritage that is more than 2000 years old. And it is precisely in Asia where about two-thirds of the world's poorest live. Many of these reside in the vicinity of World Heritage monuments such as the Angkor Wat, the Taj Majal, the Great Wall and the Borobodur temples. These cultural treasures on one hand, as well as local festivals, folklore, and arts and crafts on the other, are resources that have the potential to generate employment and income for the local host communities.

With this background, the *Ministerial Conference on Cultural Tourism and Poverty Alleviation* is being organised with the objectives which are central to the alleviation of poverty through cultural tourism:

- to rally support of policy makers for the formulation and application of effective tourism programmes which are oriented towards poverty alleviation;

- to examine ways in which cultural tourism can be efficiently channelled to achieve poverty alleviation;

- to identify policies and strategies that governments could adopt to increase their share of the cultural tourism market and its resultant socio-economic benefits; and

- to identify the roles that local authorities can play in cultural tourism management to ensure that socio-economic benefits are fairly distributed at all levels of society.

The conclusions and recommendations that will emerge from the deliberations shall constitute the basis for the Hue Declaration on Cultural Tourism and Poverty Alleviation that will clearly reflect the commitment of governments to adopt and implement measures leading to poverty alleviation through cultural tourism.

---

[4] Dr. Harsh Varma, Chief, Technical Cooperation, WTO

After a keynote presentation on "Contribution of Cultural Tourism to Poverty Alleviation" by my colleague, Mr. Eugenio Yunis, Chief of Sustainable Development for Tourism of WTO, there will be two case study presentations from Vietnam - first, from the Vietnam National Administration of Tourism on the national scenario followed by a Hue-specific case study presented by the Chairman of the People's Committee.

The Conference will then proceed with Ministerial and Heads of delegation statements. The day's deliberations would conclude with a presentation by UNESCO.

The session on 12 June will open with a panel discussion featuring three distinguished panellists from India, Indonesia and Thailand.

Based on various presentations and discussions, a draft Hue Declaration on Cultural Tourism and Poverty Alleviation will be read out to the participants for their review and comments. Once the text is finalised, the Declaration would be formally adopted by the Conference.

CONTRIBUTION OF CULTURAL TOURISM TO POVERTY ALLEVIATION[5]

Asia is host to 65 per cent of the world's poor, as defined by the World Bank. This means 712 million people living with less than one dollar per day. There is, therefore, an ethical obligation for the tourism sector in the region to find practical ways in which this activity, particularly when it is motivated by cultural attractions, could more effectively contribute to alleviate the poverty situation. In addition to fulfilling an ethical imperative of our times, helping to reduce poverty is a key element for the long term sustainability of tourism development in Asia, since tourism cannot eventually survive under extreme poverty conditions, since it becomes unsafe, risky and somehow anachronistic in the eyes of many visitors.

Can tourism contribute to reduce poverty?

Looking at the location of poverty in the world, and then at tourism flows, two key points emerge. Firstly, tourism is increasingly playing a major part in the economy of poor countries. In 2001, international tourism receipts accruing to developing countries amounted to US$ 142,306 million worldwide, of which 31 per cent correspond to Asian developing nations (i.e. US$ 44,380 million). Tourism is the principal export in a third of all developing countries and, amongst the 49 Least Developed Countries (LDCs), it is the primary source of foreign exchange earnings. In some countries it plays a major part in their sustainable development strategy. In Africa for example, it was tourism that enabled Botswana to cease to be an LDC back in 1994.

International tourism receipts in Asian countries, $millions

	1990	2002	% change 1990-2002
Low income countries	3,165	10,413	229
Lower middle income countries	7,965	18,002	366.3
Upper middle income countries	1,674	1,606	332.3
High income countries	19,552	20,464	112.3
Asia Total	**32,356**	**140,762**	**335**
World Total	*265,316*	*457,890*	*72.6*

World Tourism Organization; World Development Report 2003 (World Bank)

Secondly, tourism is growing much faster in developing countries than in developed countries. The graph below shows the relative growth of international tourist arrivals in low+middle- and high-income countries of Asia in recent years.

---

[5] Mr. Eugenio Yunis, Chief, Sustainable Development of Tourism, WTO

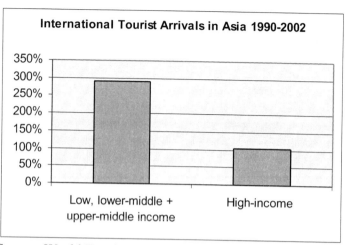

International Tourist Arrivals in Asia 1990-2002

Source: World Tourism Organization

In line with this, a predicted growth rate of around 5.9% per annum between 2000 and 2020 for South Asia, which is home to most of the world's poorest people, is considerably greater than for the world as a whole; and much of such growth will be motivated by the continuous incorporation of more and more cultural attractions into the tourism offer of these countries.

Many reasons, in addition to market growth, serve to explain why cultural tourism development can serve as tool for poverty alleviation:

- Tourism is one of the few industries in which many developing countries actually have a comparative advantage over developed countries in terms of cultural heritage, particularly considering cultural assets and traditions that are very different and less known to the main generating markets of Europe and North America.

- The attractiveness of some interesting cultural heritage sites located in remote rural areas, accompanied by the living cultural traditions of the corresponding rural communities. This point is particularly important, since three quarters of people in extreme poverty live in rural areas.

- The opportunity to support, through cultural tourism, traditional activities such as ancient rice cultivations, tea growing, collecting and roasting, and a wide range of handicrafts. Tourism can also offer opportunities to maintain traditional building methods for the construction of tourist lodges or for the restoration of monuments.

- Tourism, as a labour intensive and diversified industry, can provide jobs for women and young people within and around cultural heritage sites, ranging from basic tourist services in hotels and restaurants that require little training, to jobs in artistic performances, festival and other cultural events.

- It is also an industry where entry barriers to establishing new small businesses can be quite low, or can be easily lowered to allow poor people to establish new activities or to formalise existing micro-ventures.

- And leaving aside economics, it can bring non-material benefits such as pride in local culture and a valorisation of the surrounding natural environment and cultural landscapes in the eyes of local communities. Besides, since cultural tourism can positively contribute to the fame and renown of a place, it can help to attract new companies and investors, which would like to associate their name with its image.

Having revisited the advantages of cultural tourism and having looked at the international policy context, WTO has identified a series of overarching principles that should be borne in mind when seeking to address poverty through tourism. These are:

- **Mainstreaming**: Ensuring that sustainable development of all segments of tourism, including the cultural one, is included in the national poverty reduction strategy and relevant programmes. And, conversely, including poverty reduction measures within overall strategies for the sustainable development of all segments of tourism. In parallel, programmes linking culture and poverty have to be established, like the Dutch-supported initiative "Learning and Research on Culture and Poverty" which at improving poverty reduction efforts by mobilizing cultural strengths and assets.

- **Partnership**: Developing partnerships between public bodies and private sector companies and trade associations, with a common aim of poverty alleviation. In addition, since culture and tourism cannot be considered like competitors but rather as collaborators, partnerships have to be established between tourism administrations and tourism companies on the one hand, and cultural authorities and cultural site managers on the other, with a view to examine ways in which the local poor could be trained and employed at sites to help serve the tourists' requirements.

- **Integration**: Adopting an integrated approach with other sectors and avoiding over-dependence on tourism. And within the tourism sector, linking the cultural tourism offer with other tourism segments (e.g. nature, beach, and also business tourism, etc).

- **Equitable distribution**: Ensuring that development strategies of cultural tourism focus on achieving a more equitable distribution of wealth and services, since growth alone is not enough. This contributes also to raise the awareness among local populations about the fact that cultural assets have to be protected, since they provide them with additional income and job opportunities.

- **Acting locally**: Focusing action at a local destination level (a village, a site or a city), within the context of supportive national policies. And establishing partnerships between tourism and cultural authorities at the local level too.

- **Retention**: Reducing leakages from the local economy and building linkages within it, focussing on the very long tourism supply chain, especially that referring to hotels. Collaboration initiatives with local manufacturing industries and with farmers can bring important progress in this respect.

- **Viability**: Maintaining sound financial discipline in tourism enterprises and assessing the commercial viability of all actions taken.

- **Empowerment**: Creating conditions to enable the poor to have access to information and to influence and take decisions, and provide them suitable training to continue and strengthen their involvement in cultural tourism activities.

- **Human rights**: Removing all forms of discrimination against people working, or seeking to work, in tourism and eliminating any exploitation, particularly against women and children. Indeed, in many communities women are the guarantors for traditional continuity and must be included in the decision-making process regarding cultural tourism activities. Reciprocally, tourism development must consider the right to self-determination and cultural sovereignty of indigenous communities, including their protected, sensitive and sacred sites as well as their traditional knowledge.

- **Commitment**: Planning action and the application of resources for the long term.
- **Monitoring**: Developing simple indicators and systems to measure the impact of cultural tourism on poverty, as well as the impacts of tourism on the cultural assets and values. It regards, among others, increases in revenues, employment statistics, possible physical deterioration of assets (caused by tourists or not), the dependence of communities living close to the sites on the tourism resources, their loss of control over cultural properties, leakages, etc.

The best strategy for a country or region to conserve its comparative advantage in the tourism market is to maintain and develop its combination of cultural assets, traditions and arts that make up its uniqueness. Yet, for this to occur in a sustainable manner, it is necessary to achieve a mutually beneficial relationship between tourism and cultural heritage. This requires:

- Collaboration and understanding between the tourism sector and the cultural heritage specialists and conservation professionals.
- Preparing a tourism master plan for the heritage site and its surrounding areas.
- Applying modern planning and monitoring techniques and methodologies (e.g. environmental impact assessment, carrying capacity, the definition of sustainability indicators).
- Responding differently to the needs and preferences of cultural travellers and of other categories of visitors.
- Interpreting the heritage sites for the visitors, including the living cultural elements around them.
- Setting up a marketing strategy and a pricing policy for tourism at heritage sites, and establishing appropriate mechanisms for ensuring that a significant proportion of tourism earnings revert to conservation purposes.

The 7 WTO approaches for poverty reduction through cultural tourism

- The above evidence and principles regarding tourism and poverty have pushed WTO to initiate specific research about the various forms and conditions in which tourism does contribute to reduce poverty in different countries and in different segments of the tourism industry. In a recent publication *Tourism and Poverty Alleviation: Recommendations for action*, WTO has presented the results of such research, identifying seven different ways of addressing poverty through tourism. These can be applied in almost every country, provided a number of issues are suitably addressed. I will attempt today to adapt these 7 approaches to cultural tourism and to Asia in particular.
-
- The first way is simply through **the employment of the poor in tourism companies, but also in cultural enterprises,** within or outside cultural sites or monuments. This can occur in small as well as large enterprises and in rural and urban areas. In Asia there are many large hotel establishments catering for cultural tourists, and they could be encouraged to replace foreign staff with local people, strengthening at the same time the local cultural image of the destinations; policies and laws that encourage the employment of local people, such as those recently approved in the Maldives for example, clearly open up opportunities for the poor.

The advantage of addressing poverty through existing tourism enterprises is that it enables the poor to benefit from the entrepreneurial skills and market access of others, and can potentially reach quite large numbers of people. Many issues need to be addressed in Asian companies in order to secure potential advantages for the poor through tourism employment, such as:

- Establish proper contracts and offer fair pay conditions.
- Offer part time work, enabling poor people also to attend to other commitments, and also helping in this way to reach more people.
- Disseminate the flows of tourists towards less visited cultural assets close to famous sites, in order to create job opportunities for even more people and in a wider radius.
- Promote and advertise job opportunities in such a way that the poor are suitably and timely informed and are able to apply.
- Look at seasonality issues, if any, and the need to provide more year round opportunities, which in the case of cultural tourism should be easier, since tourists are not motivated by, or dependent on climate conditions.
- The choice of location of new developments, giving greater importance to sites or monuments surrounded by poor populations, and to living cultural expressions of poor communities.
-
- The second way is through **the supply of goods and services to tourism enterprises by the poor**. This can happen at various points in the tourism supply chain, including the choice of products featured by tour operators as well as goods and services provided to hotels, such as food and textile furnishings, especially if these are is produced with traditional techniques, thus doubly enhancing the cultural experience of visitors, handicrafts and decorations, building services at the construction stage (including heritage restoration works), and so on. The advantage in the supply-chain approach is that this can make use of existing skills in poor communities and of the existing hotel and other tourism infrastructure, encouraging it to examine its supply chain and to strive to use locally supplied goods and services instead of imports. The two main issues to address are:
- How to encourage and help enterprises to identify new sources of supply.
- Working with poor communities to enable them to provide an assurance of quality and reliability.
-
- A practical approach is to take small steps, making a few carefully selected linkages, where success seems most likely, and then building on this. NTAs can help in establishing the linkages between the hotel and catering sector and the local manufacturers of different goods.
-
- The third way is through **direct sales of goods and services to visitors by the poor.** This is about the informal economy, and includes stalls selling food and handicrafts, portering, some forms of transport, and informal accommodation. The informal sector is very important in many developing countries and this can be one of the most direct ways of getting visitor spending into the hands of the poor. However it is characterised by chaotic trading conditions, congestion in the site access and over-supply. Issues here include:

- providing some order and quality control, which may include licensing or training (for example, in the framework of a cultural visit, it requires a good knowledge from the guides to provide tourists with a high-quality experience),
- giving some reassurance to visitors as potential purchasers. However, it is important still to maintain the ease of access to such trading by poor people, which is the main advantage of the informal economy.
-

Fourthly, there is the process of supporting the **establishment of tourism enterprises by the poor.** These may be micro, small and medium sized enterprises (MSMEs), or community based enterprises. Compared with working in the informal economy, this is about helping poor communities develop something for the longer term, and about placing power and control in their hands. In the case of cultural tourism, the corresponding authorities can grant technical, financial or simply marketing support poor communities to produce traditional shows, performances, and even improve their traditional handicrafts in order to complement and diversify the cultural tourism offer. The challenges are many, including:

- access to capital, and the forthcoming International Year of Microcredit might be a suitable opportunity to address this issue,
- acquisition of skills, confidence and motivation,
- property rights and legal recognition, and especially
- securing access to tourism markets.

The fifth way in which tourism can address poverty is through a **tax or levy on tourism income or profits with proceeds benefiting poverty reduction programmes.** This has the advantage of enabling resources to be channelled to the most needy people and communities without requiring their involvement in tourism activity either directly or indirectly. The approach can be at a national level, or at a local level. There are a number of examples showing how this can work quite well at a local level – such as negotiating concessions with tourism enterprises involving a proportion of income per bed night being given to the local community. Fiscal income can also be perceived on monuments or sites as entry fees, one part being affected to conservation purposes, the other part to poverty alleviation programmes. However, approaches involving taxes and charges have to be treated with caution in order not to deter investment and income flows in the long term.

The sixth way is about **voluntary giving by tourism enterprises and tourists.** This may include payments into general charities and programmes, such as HIV/AIDS programmes, by tourists and tour operators, or more specific support for projects in destinations visited. Many tourism enterprises are engaged in supporting social programmes in their neighbouring communities. Funds from tourists may be collected in the country of origin or in the destination, through voluntary supplements or invitations to donate. During the visit of a cultural asset, the guide could be the "spokesperson" of the surrounding poor communities and raise awareness among visitors about the role they could voluntarily play in helping them financially to undertake specific improvements in the village, etc.

Finally, poor communities can benefit from **investment in infrastructure stimulated by tourism.** This is about the provision of roads, energy supplies, sanitation, clean water and telecommunications, on the back of tourism investment. Careful planning in such situations is clearly very important and local communities should be involved from an early stage.

WTO has also identified a certain number of common themes that keep recurring across all these methods. These include:

- Understanding the nature of poverty and its link with the cultural assets in an area and how engagement in tourism will complement and support other livelihood options.
- The key issue of capacity building and training.
- Trying to introduce simple processes of quality control, if necessary in cooperation with cultural site managers or with cultural authorities that supervise art performances, etc.
- Raising consumer awareness: providing visitors with better information to direct their purchasing.
- Creative, realistic and viable cultural product development and marketing, and
- Adopting an integrated approach to planning and management at a local destination level.

It is also important to provide a framework for action by the different stakeholders:

National governments should pay more attention to cultural tourism in their poverty reduction strategies and in trade negotiations, where they should ensure that sustainability and poverty issues are considered alongside export promotion. Governments are often in a position to influence the location and nature of new tourism development and should seek to benefit poor communities in so doing. Other relevant instruments include legislation affecting employment and credit. Governments can also support capacity building, appropriate marketing and undertake monitoring of the impact of tourism on poverty. They are also very important in contributing to heritage conservation and supporting appropriate cultural product development and marketing. Finally, they can stimulate cooperation among cultural and tourism authorities in a common effort to fight poverty.

Intra-regional bodies can play an important role in supporting the development and marketing of appropriate tourism, including tourism based on cultural assets and traditions and cultural routes through developing countries, which may lack the scale or resources to make an impact on their own. They could encourage a joint approach to poverty issues across the region, including the sharing of good practice.

NGOs have a particularly valuable role to play in networking and forging relevant linkages, in representing and championing the poor, in capacity building and in identifying social programmes that can be supported through cultural tourism income.

Destination management organisations, which may be local authorities, private public partnerships or possibly protected area bodies, have a critical role to play in issues such as developing local supply chains and improving the relationship between the informal economy and sites visitors.

Tourism enterprises, including international tour operators, incoming operators and tourism service providers, especially hotels, must be central to any strategy to tackle poverty through cultural tourism. They should include concern for poverty as part of their commitment to corporate social responsibility. This should be reflected in employment policies, supply chain management and support for local communities. They also have a critical role to play in providing relevant information to their guests, especially in respect of local cultures and styles of life.

Looking back over these various stakeholders, it is very important that they do not take action in isolation. Joint action is needed. One suggestion is the establishment of joint committees for tourism and poverty at a destination level, which seek to engage all stakeholders, as has already been done by the government of Cambodia.

So, and to conclude, this is a considerable challenge. It requires purposeful, well-directed action. Tourism in general, and cultural tourism in particular, will not address poverty automatically. It also requires commitment and political will, making poverty alleviation a primary objective of tourism policies and development plans.

Fighting poverty on the one hand, and facilitating inter-cultural understanding through cultural tourism on the other, are the main pillars to establish more stability, more security and more peace in our world at a time of international tensions.

Thank you.

CULTURE TOURISM DEVELOPMENT FOR POVERTY ALLEVIATION IN VIETNAM[6]

H.E. Mr.Vu Khoan, Deputy Prime Minister
H.E. Mr. Francesco Frangialli, Secretary General of WTO
H.E. Tourism Ministers
Distinguished Guest
Ladies and Gentlemen

Vietnam, a country with a thousand-year history in the cause of national construction and defence, has abundant potentials of culture tourism including 2,269 national cultural and historical sites, hundreds of traditional festivals, handicraft villages etc., which were all generated from creative labour, simple life style, especially from Vietnam people's struggles against foreign invaders & natural disasters. The Vietnamese people itself today are creams of Vietnamese struggles with brave & steady characters but they are very simple, industrious, attractive to international travellers. Moreover, the resources of culture tourism in Vietnam are very diversified and abundant with 54 ethnic groups of which most of the Northern mountainous region; Cham, Gia Rai, Eda, Banar living in the Central culture values. Among 5 World Heritage Sites in Vietnam recognised by UNESCO, Hoi An Ancient Town and My Son Sanctuary. Therefore, culture tourism is the unique character and comparative advantage of Vietnam Tourism Besides natural tourism resources.

Based on exploitation of tourism resources, especially culture tourism resources and along with open-door policy and supports from the Government of Vietnam, with supports from countries around the world and international organisations, particularly the World Tourism Organisation (WTO), Vietnam Tourism has kept pace with regional countries in terms of tourism development. In 1990, Vietnam only received 250,000 international visitors and over 1 million domestic travellers. In 2002, Vietnam did received over 2.6 million foreign travellers and 13 million domestic tourists with tourism receipt of 1.5 billion USD. Over the past years, Vietnam Tourism Industry has been recognised as a spear-head economic sector creating over 250,000 direct employees and over 450,000 indirect employees accountable to 6% of total working population. It is estimated that the tourism employment will take 12% of total working population in 2010.

The Government of Vietnam reaffirms that the development of tourism. Particularly of culture tourism, must be closely connected to the objective creating more jobs, increasing employee's income with contribution to poverty alleviation. This idea is concretely stipulated in the Tourism Ordinance issued by the National Assembly in 1999 as "The State of Vietnam defines that tourism is multisectoral economic sector with profound culture content of intersectional , interregional and socialised characteristics;...Develop tourism to increase intellectual standards, create jobs and develop national social-economy" as well as"...secure the development of tourism in the way of culture tourism, eco-tourism so as to protect and bring into full play the cultural identity and fine customs traditions of Vietnamese people."

---

[6] Asst. Prof. Dr. Pham Trung Luong, Deputy head of Advisory unit of Industry Development, Vietnam National Administration of Tourism (VNAT)

With priority to develop culture tourism and eco-tourism in the Mster plan for tourism development in Vietnam with in the period of 2001-2010 and with supports from the Government of Vietnam in the National Plan of Action for Tourism and tourism infrastructure upgrade, tourism in general and culture tourism in particular has been developed in remote areas where there are unique tourism potentials but local people, especially ethnic minorities still live a hard life. The development of culture tourism in those areas has initially made a certain contribution to the national efforts on poverty alleviation. The effectiveness of operation models on community-based culture tourism in Sapa (Lao Cai province), Mai Chau (Hoa Binh province), Hoi An Ancient Town (Quang Nam province), Thoi Son (Tien Giang province) etc…are typical examples of what the Vietnam Tourism Industry in conjunction with central and local relevant authorities carrying out the National Poverty Alleviation Plan by promoting culture tourism.

In its development plans, the VNAT will focus on developing new culture tourism products enriched with Vietnamese culture characters based on village culture values of Vietnam which can be more competitive and attractive to international travellers so as to fulfil its strategic targets. But it is more important that developing community based tourism will protect and bring into full play the local culture values and give more chance to local community in the rural area which is now accountable to 80 per cent of Vietnamese population to take an active part in the tourism industry to create more jobs, more income for bettering their lives.

Along with in-time supports from State and Government of Vietnam, especially with assistance and cooperation from international organisation and countries around the world, Vietnam Tourism Industry has tried its best to develop in the sustainable way, particularly promote culture tourism in accordance with poverty alleviation and "Step by step makes Vietnam become a popular tourist centre in the region so that in 2010 Vietnam would be ranked among countries of high developed tourism industry in the region".

Thank you for your attention.

PRESENTATION BY THE LEADER OF THE PEOPLE`S COMMITTEE OF HUE PROVINCE[7]

First of all, on behalf of the leadership of Thua Thien Hue, I would like to warmly welcome the Honourable Mr. Vu Khoan, Deputy Prime Minister of the Socialist Republic of Vietnam, the Honourable Mr. Francesco Frangialli, the Excellency Ms. Vo Thi Thang, Head of the Vietnam National Administration of Tourism, and distinguished guests coming to Hue Ancient Capital City for Ministerial Conference on Culture Tourism and Poverty Alleviation of Pacific Asian countries. I am thankful to the warm sentiments and deep interest that the Central Government of Vietnam, the Vietnam National Administration of Tourism, the World Tourism Organization, and distinguished guests have saved for Hue. We are honoured to host this important and significant conference.

Ladies and Gentlemen,

Thua Thien Hue is a province located in the key economic hub of the midland of Vietnam, with a natural surface of 5,054 sqr. Kilimeters, a population of 1.1 million. It is geographically situated in the middle of the country, 660 kilometers away from Hanoi and 1,080 kilometers from Ho Chi Minh City. The Province stretched in the North-South traffic route. It is the convergence of natural, socio-economic condition of the North and the South. The Province is also located near the National highway No. 9. the East-West corridor linking Laos, Thailand to the East sea. Therefore, Thua Thien Hue can be recognized as an important leverage accelerating the socio-economic development of the midland of Vietnam. Thanks to its diversified reserve amount of non-metallic materials and minerals, aquaproducts at high economic value, and a forest cover rate of more than 73%, Thua Thien Hue has convenient conditions for developing processing industry and construction material production. Thua Thien Hue is also an important centre for scientific research, higher education, university training, which provides scientific, management staff and skilled workers for midland and highland provinces. At present, it is an intensive medical centre of the midland of Vietnam. Additionally, with its convenient location in the world heritage region of Vietnam, Thua Thien Hue has been commonly known as a famous cultural and touristic centre of Vietnam with diversified cultural and touristic resources. Especially, Hue was once the centre of the South, the capital city of Vietnam under Nguyen Dynasty, and probably the only ancient capital city which remains intact as the capital city of the last Dynasty in Vietnam with distinctive historical monuments recognized as world culture heritage, one component of priceless properties of the mankind. Besides, Hue is also famous for particular garden houses, ancient pagoda, gastronomic culture, traditional festivities, traditional musical varieties, especially Hue royal music and dance-the masterpiece of world intangible cultural entities-lately recognized by the General president of the UNESCO in Paris on November 7,2003. Hue is also noted for its heroic revolutionary tradition. It is the place where many revolutionary relics closely related to the political life of President Ho Chi Minh and other former revolutionaries are maintained. A great

---

[7] H.E. Mr. Nguyen Xuan Ly, Chairman of the People's Committee of Hue

many locations have entered into the 2 patriotic wars such as Duong Hoa, HoaMy, A Luoi, the legendary "Ho ChiMinh trail". etc.

With a 127-kilometer-long coastal line, Thua Thien Hue possesses many beautiful beached with soft sand and blue water such as Thuan Anm Canh Duong, Lang Co. Also, the province is located beside marvellous natural landscapes such as: Bach Ma National Park with a surface of 22,000 hectares and a mountain peak of 1,440 meters, where exist various valuable flora and fauna, and pure climate, the Tam Giang-Cau Hai lagoon system, the largest in South-East Asia with a total surface of 22,000 hectares, which is one of the 4 national integrated tourism centers. With the abovementioned touristic resources, Thua Thien Hue is able to develop diversified tourism strategies: cultural tourism, beach tourism, mountainous convalescence, ecological tourism, adventurous tourism etc.

In recent years, Vietnam has made important changes in the process of regional and global development and integration. During the process, the midland of Vietnam in general and Thua Thien Hue in specific, given difficulties in infrastructure planning and development is highlighted, the face of the urban areas is enhanced, the power, freshwater supply, and communication systems are gradually upgraded, the inter-provincial traffic systems have been considerably improved; the trade transaction between Hue and mountainous, coastal districts, and neighboring provinces has been developed. Phu Bai airport has been extended to receive big-sized airplanes such as Airbus A320, A321, and even Boeing 747; the first berth of Chan May deep seaport has been operated and compatible to ships of 30,000 DWT, and recently received the Superstar Leo with 2,800 passengers; foreign investment has achieved positive changes.

At present, there are 20 foreign-invested projects with a total registered capital of 151 million USD in the fields of cement manufacturing, food industry, touristic services etc; and many ODA and NGO projects are being implemented with a total funding of tens of millions of USD. Various investors are seeking for investment opportunities in the national integrated touristic zone Lang Co-Bach Ma-Hai Van; touristic activities over the past ten years has made use of their potentials, and are continuously developed in bith quantity and quality, reaching initial important achievements. This greatly contributes to the socio-economic development of the province as well as tourism development of Vietnam, showing in high and stable development rate (17%) over a long period. Thua Thien Hue is considered among the largest tourist centers in the Central Vietnam but has low rate of development compared with Hanoi and Ho Chi Minh City and has not developed as it is expected with its potentials due to a number of internal and external reasons. However, a face of a tourism city, in the true sense of tourism, is shaping in reasons. However, a face of a tourism city, in the true sense of tourism, is shaping in reality, especially in 1998, the city was supported to be a typical Festival City of Vietnam by the Government, ministries and branched of Vietnam. Then Hue Festival 2000 and 2002 were organized, and tomorrow, June 12, 2004, the opening ceremony is going to actually a festival of culture and tourism for the whole nation with international standards. It significantly strengthens external affairs of culture by introducing typical features of Vietnam in general and Thua Thien Hue in particular in exchange with cultures of attending nations. Conducted every two years, Hue Festival functions not only as a chance for culture exchange for building Hue "A typical Festival City" of Vietnam but also a great event which helps to take advantage of traditional culture values of Hue, making Hue Festival "a typical commercial name of Vietnam" to

186

further attract domestic and international tourists, extend the staying period, and drive tourist products of Thua Thien Hue more attractive, especially by organizing festivals, culture activities which have attracted the participation of many economic sectors and communities, raising remarkably social income from tourism. Therefore, tourism contribution rate of tourism to GDP increases significantly.

In the time to come, the task of socio-economic development of Thua Thien Hue Province is to be connected with the development of the focused economic area of the Central Vietnam, and the East-West Corridor. It also aims at gradually restructuring the economy in the orientation of Industry-Tourism-Services and raising the GDP contribution percentage of the services sector up to 47% by 2010. Tourism is planned to develop as a spearhead sector to tap the competitive strengths and create a motive force for economic development and generate accumulation and positive impacts on both coastal and western areas of the province.

In future, in parallel with expansion and upgrading of National Route No. 1, the trans-Vietnam railway, Phu Bai Airport, Chan May Deep Sea Port, National Road No. 49 and No. 9 linking Laos and northern areas of Thailand, Myanmar are going to favor Thua Thien Hue's integration with countries in Mekong Sub-region, ASEAN and other regions of the world. In addition, investment incentives policies by Vietnam Government and Thua Thuen Hue Province such as favorable conditions for land rental, tax, and land preparation, etc. Among them, the public administration reform appears as the most important for investment procedure which have created an open and attractive ground for investors to Thua Thien Hue. As a result, a stable position and strengths are to be generated for socio-economic development of the province in general and the provincial tourism sector in particular to qualify it one of the most important tourist centers of Vietnam.

Ladies and Gentlemen,
For our Hue City, tourism plays a dominant role with two culture heritages of mankind(tangible and intangible). Therefore, in order to maintain sustainable tourism development in Thua Thien Hue, we have to strengthen all the three internal components. Firstly the Government shall focus more on conservation and rehabilitation of historical monuments, to protect humankind's heritages by policies, guidelines and specific countermeasures. Besides, local people, especially inhabitants of Hue City shall be aware of their important tasks as an owner to well protect the heritages and their pure environment. The local people, in turn, benefit satisfactorily from activities of community-based tourism and heritages conservation as an economic motivation. All three factors will create good conditions for the awareness and particular actions of people, of community for tourism development in Hue. On the other hand, tourism proves highly interdisciplinary, inter-regional and socialized. In this sector, the cooperation among regions, areas, and nations plays a crucial role in diversifying products, improving quality and creating original products, which are attractive and of truly national culture. Currently, in the context of international economic integration, many countries share the initiatives of linkage for a tourism product such as "ASEAN-A shared destination" or the proposal "Three nations-One destination" by three Indo-China nations. Those initiatives are clear proof for the cooperation tendency. We do hope that at this conference, leaders of tourism sectors from different nations will make orienting proposals for cooperation in tourism to link this sector with culture and to balance the proposals for cooperation in tourism to link this sector with culture and to

balance the tasks of economic, cultural, political and social development. This helps to create more jobs for working people, improving spiritual and material life for people as well as fight against poverty and hunger. It also aims at preserving environment, securing national defense and enabling high growth rate as a chance for Vietnam tourism in general and Thua Thien Hue tourism in particular to have more favorable conditions. Accordingly, more attractions are given to visitors from around the world to explore and experience special culture features of Culture Heritage Central Vietnam and of Vietnam.

Once again, on behalf of leaders and people of Thua Thien Hue Province, I would like to express our sincere thanks to Vietnam Government, General Administration of Tourism of Vietnam and the General Secretary of World Tourism Organization for giving Hue City a great honor to be the host for this important conference. We do hope that Thua Thien Hue leaves you all, ladies and gentlemen, good impressions. Taking this opportunity, I would like to extend to the Deputy Prime Minister, Mr. Vu Khoan, and the General Secretary of WTO and you all, distinguished delegates, the best wished. I wish the Asia-Pacific Minister Conference a great success.

Thank you very much.

Ministerial Statements

MINISTERIAL STATEMENT OF INDIA[8]

Namaste from Incredible India

Excellencies, distinguished delegates and friends, I am honoured to be with you today.

After the recent turbulences, the Asian-Pacific region with over 130 million arrivals in 2002, overtook the Americas to become the world's second-most visited region after Europe. In this context, South and South East Asia have had an important emerging role.

Our tourism assets have many similarities with that of ASEAN region. To name a few, your great Mekong artery shares a timelessness aspect with our Ganga and its many tributaries that rise in the Himalaya Renowned sites such as the ham monuments in your "My Son Sanctuary" in Central Vietnam and our historic city of Agra with the Taj Mahal, also universally treasured – providing high value visitor satisfaction compatible with stakeholder communities livelihood through tourism revenues.

Critical impacts such as 9/11, Bali, Mombassa, economic slowdown, the Iraq war and SARS have adversely affected tourism in our region in the recent past. At the same time, it has been demonstrated that domestic and international tourism carry inbuilt resilience which, if sustainably managed, will enable swift recovery.

The tourism sector's capability as a development driver, especially for rural livelihoods, can be viewed in the context of India's current 10th Five Year Plan, our National Tourism Policy 2002 and our global "Incredible India" campaign.

We view tourism as a multiple-interest, all-season catalyst for development and employment – as the operational partner in an enabled environment, blending with our overall social and economic objectives.

For India, the success of the Tourism sector lies in its potential to change the lives of the rural poor, its strengths in generating employment, particularly in the rural regions, and its commitment towards harnessing the economic muscle for the betterment of the disadvantaged. In our thrust for pro-poor, community-based tourism we have initiated several schemes.

We are targeting ten million employment opportunities per year over the Tenth five year plan period till 2007. We have earmarked tourism as a priority sector since it can maximise the productivity of India's natural, human, cultural and technical resources. This attribute goes in tandem with tourism's capacity to create large-scale employment opportunities especially in remote and backward areas, with the potential of being sustainable and non-polluting. Further, it is labour intensive and is thus able to provide extensive forward and backward economic linkages to build income and employment especially for women, youth, and the disadvantaged and structured on the country's cultural heritage and indigenous traditions and can utilise local resources and skills.

---

[8] H.E. Mrs. Renuka Choudhury, Minister of Tourism

By 2007, direct and indirect employment from tourism in India is slated to rise to 66 million from 41 million at present. The tourism multiplier per Indian Rupee 1 million invested creates 47 jobs or virtually four times the 12 jobs for equivalent investment in other sectors, exemplified in the Indian Provinces such as Kerala and Rajasthan through visitor services.

This income route holds special possibilities for the most disadvantaged segments of society including unemployed youth, women and the physically challenged while also bridging the shoulder period to the lean season with regular income from a variety of tourism products.

With the global emphasis on sustainability, we see a major marketing opportunity to position the Indian rural tourism product as a unique visitor experience in a low-impact setting. The primary target is low-volume but high-yield visitors, compatible with local community acceptance, the carrying capacity of the natural environment and visitor satisfaction.

To achieve our overall vision, among the five strategies in India's National Tourism Policy 2002 is the positioning and maintaining tourism development as a national priority activity.

The Policy aims to undertake poverty eradication in an environmentally sustainable manner by enhancing "employment potential within the tourism sector as well as to foster economic integration through developing linkages with other sectors".

The employment generation potential of tourism in India can be further gauged from the volume of domestic tourism, estimated at 230 million annually, which uses a range of services and accommodation especially that provided by the small sector. However, strategic safeguards are required to harness the sector's economic capabilities without irreversible negative impact on bio-diversity.

Our approach is to facilitate both the "hardware" and "software" components of village tourism. We recognise the rationale for sustainable tourism resource management as based on the reality of finite bio-mass whereby nothing on earth is limitless. Against this backdrop, our Rural Tourism Scheme encourages our Provinces to formulate proposals for our support to the alternative tourism "hardware" activities in potential village location.

Locally active NGOs are being enlisted for mass communication and extension support of the Rural Tourism "hardware" Scheme, we now have a first-time agreement with UNDP for the Endogenous Tourism "software" Project with the rural poor as target beneficiaries. The project will offer tourism products based on rural culture, craft and eco-tourism for sustainable livelihoods and integrated rural development, in proximity with existing tourism circuits. Within this ambit and available resources, eighteen Project pilot at rural community level sites have been identified in different places through a lengthy consultative process yielding a representative all-India skill network.

The pilot project's income generating potential will especially focus on women, unemployed youth and disadvantaged groups. "Software" work plans to complement the "hardware" proposals, consensually evolved through extensive field visits and discussions with principal host community stakeholders, district administration representatives and the State Tourism Departments. Project implementation will encompass enhancing the host community's awareness of the tourism process, gender sensitisation, art and craft skill development, capacity building and training in visitor handling and tourism services marketing to both the domestic and international visitor. The community's pride in traditional skills and process direction are among the principal intended outcomes of the Project. Here again, for Project implementation, capable local NGOs have been identified to support the district focal point.

Through endogenous tourism we aim at both domestic and international visitors not for pleasure alone but also for broadening the visitor's experience platform- where the source of attraction lies "within" the host community or environment. It attempts to transform attitudes and mindsets, imparting local pride and visitor appreciation of the diverse cultural heritage.

A few of our site examples of this innovative Project which complements conventional tourism models will illustrate how we would reach the rural poor as target beneficiaries, through the dynamics of brand leadership.

The Pochampalli village, in Nalgonda district of our southern state of Andhra Pradesh, is its renowned traditional Ikat weaving skill in silk and cotton. Pochampali saris are known the world over. Two hours by road from the state capital Hyderabad, the village has an attractive setting in the environment of the Deccan plateau. The Project will strengthen community livelihoods through extended visitor stay in Pochampalli via the experiential aspect of Ikat, combining the possibility of home stays, local heritage attractions and the scenic plateau backdrop.

Hodka village of Kachchh district in the western state of Gujarathas some of the most vibrant skills in traditional embroidery extending to circuit attractions of the fabulous Rann of Kutch, Dholavira in the "Indus Valley" matrix and Mandvi on the edge of the Arabian Sea. Award winning crafts-persons, working here in a hard environment, are the repositories of cross-cultural heritage that will fascinate any visitor. Hodka with its keen village panchayat, is a two-hour drive away from the state capital, Bhuj, which has dailu air connections with Mumbai.

Naggar village of Kullu district of our Himalayan state of Himachal Pradesh is an adventure tour hub for trekking and Lahul-Ladakh safaris, complementing the famous Roerich Art Gallery, Naggar Castle and shawl & cap weaving. It thus has diverse all-year visitor interest, craft skills, the scenic Himalayan Beas valley and, potential market access. Its articulate women's group has shown leadership interest in home-stays, facilitating the scope for convergence with other national initiatives and community-government partnership.

Raghurajpur village in Puri district of the eastern state of Orissa has witnessed the classical revival of the rural Patachitra painting skill. It links up with Orissa's Golden Triangle of Puri-Bhuvaneshwar-Konark, thereby enabling the host community draw livelihood support from ongoing development action through convergent initiatives.

This Project will enable rural host communities to acquire ownership of the innovative tourism products based on their traditional art & craft skills, and their natural environment, for sustainable livelihoods through visitor interest.

All of this links up with our other programmes such as the Destination Development and Circuit Development Schemes.

I hope that the deliberations of this Conference will pave the way for a sustained and concerted effort to harness tourism for bringing benefits to the poor and disadvantaged. I compliment WTO on this timely initiative, as well as the Government of Vietnam for hosting this great meeting.

I thank you for your attention and look forward to our enduring partnership.

Thank you.

MINISTERIAL STATEMENT OF
REPUBLIC OF THE PHILIPPINES[9]

Your Excellencies, Deputy Prime Minister Vu Khoan of the Socialist Republic of Vietnam, Secretary General Francesco Frangialli of the World Tourism Organization (WTO), Madame Minister Vo Thi Thang of the Vietnam National Administration of Tourism, fellow tourism ministers, distinguished delegates, ladies and gentlemen, good morning.

I am deeply honored and privileged to be able to address this Ministerial Conference on Cultural Tourism and Poverty Alleviation under the auspices of the WTO and the Government of the Socialist Republic of Vietnam. Having been on this job for just over three months, I consider this conference as a great opportunity for me not just to meet and share my thoughts with you my dear colleagues in the industry, but also to listen and learn as well.

The tourism industry continues to be one of the largest industries in the world. In the year 2002, it accounted for seven hundred three million international arrivals worldwide with receipts of about $700 billion. The industry showed great resiliency in 2003 despite the economic downturn, the SARS epidemic and threats to peace and order. On 7 November 2003, the United Nations Assembly in New York gave the WTO a status within the system equal to that of the UNIDO, FAO and other UN agencies. To quote Secretary General Frangialli, "the tourism industry is in the midst of a great turning point. Tourism is now considered by international society with other major activities of humanity: industry, agriculture, education and culture, health and labor."

The role of the tourism industry in poverty alleviation especially in developing countries cannot be over-emphasized. It is an effective catalyst and a powerful tool for winning the war against poverty. The challenge to all of us is to maximize its benefits to improve the quality of life of our peoples.

Poverty which has been defined by the Asian Development Bank (ADB) as the "lack of access to essential assets and opportunities" has always been a major concern in the region. ADB had reported that more than one billion people in the Asia Pacific region survived on less than US$1 a day in the year 2000.

Before President Gloria Macapagal Arroyo assumed office in January 2001, more than one-third of Filipinos were living below the poverty line according to the UNDP Human Development Report. Our President therefore immediately launched priority programs to create job opportunities and provide basic services like education, access to potable water, low-priced medicines and rural electrification especially to the marginalized sector of our society. The Arroyo administration has identified tourism development as a major component in the over-all strategy to alleviate poverty.

A good measure of success has indeed been attained during the last three years. The Philippine economy has steadily improved registering a 6% growth during the first quarter of this year. The prospects for sustained growth were enhanced by the Presidents victory in the May 10 elections although she still has to be officially

---

[9] H.E. Roberto M. Pagdanganan, Secretary of Tourism

proclaimed by the Congress of the Philippines. We have had to contend not just with the manual counting of votes but the tedious constitutional process in our democratic system as well. We are confident though that our Congress shall complete the canvassing of votes and proclaim the President before the deadline set by our constitution on June 30. President Arroyo and the Vice-President elect shall take their oath of office at noon of the same date. Even in electoral processes, we certainly have a lot to learn from our neighboring countries like India which despite its being the second most populous country in the world took only about three days to know their election results.

Let me point out however that the slow pace of our electoral process is not an indication of the rate of tourism development in the Philippines. In fact, international tourist arrivals in the Philippines as of June 9, 2004 have registered an increase of 32% over the same period last year. Barring unforeseen circumstances, we project that tourist arrivals in the Philippines shall reach a record high of 2.4 million in 2004 exceeding the 2.22 million attained in 1997. This is estimated to generate as much as $2 billion in tourism receipts and as many as half a million additional jobs.

A number of community-based programs are being undertaken by the Department of Tourism in coordination with other stakeholders. This is to ensure that tourism development shall also benefit the marginalized sector. Let me cite some of these programs.

> A Marine Life Tour Program was recently developed by the Department of Tourism in a village in Bohol, located very close to Cebu which is one of the country's major tourism hubs. Community organizing, training and continuing dialogues with the community were undertaken by the Department of Tourism with the support of the local government. The program has resulted in providing jobs to the poor fishermen who once destroyed the environment by catching and butchering whales and dolphins as a means of livelihood.

> In El Nido, Palawan which is considered one of the high-end resorts in the country, El Nido Foundation was set up by the resort owner, the Ten Knots Development Corporation as a way of manifesting its corporate social responsibility. The foundation provides financing for small cooperatives and micro-entrepreneurs through a series of "lending windows" directed to individuals, groups and association in the community. It therefore is able to help improve the quality of life of the local community while at the same time promoting environmental protection and cultural preservation.

> Another pro-poor program of the Department of Tourism is the Entrepreneurial Development for Rural Tourism which aims to provide knowledge and skills on craft-making and instill the spirit of entrepreneurship among local communities. The program has four components, namely: (a) product assessment, (b) training, (c) business management, and (d) networking. The program runs over a nine (9) week period.

The foregoing and other similar undertakings are part and parcel of our over-all tourism strategy whose main components are as follows:

> Strong partnership with the private sector, including media, local government units, and other national government agencies.

> Balanced and focused marketing and product development program. The key is to develop new product packages to meet demands of specific market segments. Existing and planned infrastructure development should also be market driven.

> Instilling a culture of tourism among our people. Tourism creates jobs; tourism means business; therefore it should be everybody's business.

It is evident from available data that many of our ASEAN neighbors have adopted their own strategies and have achieved even greater progress. For instance, international tourist arrivals this year are projected to exceed 10 million in Thailand, 14 million in Malaysia, 8 million in Singapore, 5 million in Indonesia and 3 million in Vietnam. As of May 2004, international tourist arrivals in Cambodia and Vietnam have registered 20% growth over the same period last year.

This brings me to my next point. We should be able to achieve greater successes individually and collectively by ensuring stronger and sustained cooperation in intra-regional tourism development among Asian countries. This could include information and technology sharing, regular consultations and twinning arrangements to complement each other. We do not have to keep on reinventing the wheel. Our countries have their own distinctive tourism attractions and products to offer. Therefore, while we engage in healthy competition we should also promote positive complementation. This should ultimately prove to be mutually beneficial to all of us.

For instance, tourists who go to Cambodia or Vietnam to satisfy their cultural interest will probably want to go to Hong Kong for shopping and to the Philippines or Indonesia for diving and beach activities. There are of course many other possibilities depending on the tourists preference. Tourists have varied interest which they would like to satisfy at the least cost and the shortest possible time. They would certainly like to maximize such opportunities while touring the region.

Asia constitutes two-thirds of the worlds' total population and is the fastest growing economy. As the disposable income of Asians improve, their desire to travel increases, as well. Asia will most certainly be the biggest source market for international tourism in the foreseeable future. In fact, China alone is projected to be the biggest source market by the year 2020 if not earlier. These developments should naturally benefit the Asians first. What a great way to alleviate poverty in the region! The more prosperous helping the less fortunate ones.

Perhaps, it is worthwhile to point out that Europe accounted for 400 million out of 703 million international tourist arrival in 2002. And most of such tourist arrivals were Europeans themselves. A similar situation can and should arise in Asia as more Asians progress. But we should not just wait and watch. We should make this happen. And the way to do it is through intra-regional cooperation and coordination.

I submit that tourism ministers in Asia not just ASEAN meet regularly at least once a year to discuss and debate matters of common interest and establish appropriate policies. Technical meetings and workshops at lower levels should also be undertaken as often as necessary to take appropriate actions following such policy decisions.

Through stronger and sustained regional interaction we will be able to more effectively address our common concerns. One very good example is the issuance of travel advisories which are sometimes abused by certain governments. Together, we should be able to successfully advocate for more transparent, accurate and fair travel advisories for both developed and developing countries.

Intra-regional tourism will promote not just more equitable progress but also closer fellowship and better understanding among our peoples in the region. As Prime Minister Hun Sen of Cambodia said in his keynote speech on June 8, 2004 at the at Siem Reap conference, "let us promote peace through tourism." Now, I am sure you will agree that if there is peace, prosperity cannot be far behind.

In closing let me congratulate the WTO and the Government of the Socialist Republic of Vietnam for hosting this conference. Let me also congratulate all the participants and wish you a most successful conference. I believe that this shall go a long way in pursuing our common quest to alleviate poverty. I will even hasten to add that this is a great step in our peoples' march towards prosperity.

Mabuhay at maraming salamat po.

MINISTERIAL STATEMENT OF THE
ROYAL GOVERNMENT OF CAMBODIA[10]

Secretary General Francesco Frangialli of the World Tourism Organization,
Excellencies,
Ladies and Gentlemen,

I have great pleasure to be part of this Ministerial Conference on Cultural Tourism and Poverty Alleviation in the ancient imperial capital of Hue, the most significant world heritage site in Vietnam. I wish to express my gratitude to the World Tourism Organization and the Vietnam National Administration of Tourism for jointly organizing this Ministerial Conference.

This significant gathering follows the 41st Meeting of the WTO Commission for East Asia and the Pacific and the Technical Seminar on Cultural Tourism and Poverty Alleviation in Siem Reap, Cambodia which many delegates here attended earlier this week.

The Seminar in Siem Reap examined the ways in which cultural tourism can be channeled effectively to achieve poverty alleviation in our region. It also identified policies that governments could adopt to increase their share of the cultural tourism market and increase the contribution to poverty alleviation. In addition we explored the roles that local authorities can play in cultural tourism management to ensure that socioeconomic benefits are fairly distributed among the local poor.

Excellencies,
Distinguished delegates,
Ladies and Gentlemen,

Tourism provides a significant potential for poverty reduction, economic growth and development. For many developing countries, and in particular Least Developed Countries (LDCs), tourism is literally one of the important economic sector that provides concrete opportunities for economic growth. Sustainable tourism not only provides material benefits but also generates cultural pride.

The asset of cultural wealth is of particular relevance to the global economy and conducive to international tourism activities. In this regard, Cambodia found a dominant source of growth in this sector of activities and demonstrated significant potential to accelerate development. For Cambodia tourism has become a prominent export sector and it is one of the major export receipts earner.

Developing linkages is key to poverty reduction through tourism. The poverty reduction effect of international tourism is expected to take place through the wide income-multiplying impact of tourist's expenditure.

The need for competitive, steady local supplies to the hospitality industry, for example supplies of food and beverages, is a vital linkage; offering a wide range of economic opportunities to local enterprises and households, and much scope for poverty reduction

---

[10] H.E. Mr. Veng Sereyvuth, Minister of Tourism

through sustainable activity in rural areas. Encouraging and promoting linkages between the tourism industry and the sphere of local suppliers, particularly those in the farming and small manufacturing sectors, is of paramount importance for a successful impact on poverty reduction from tourism.

There are practical limitations to the income-multiplying impact of tourism development. These limitations are usually analyzed in terms of "leakages" from the tourism economy. They are inevitable at the beginning of the development process. What matters is to aim at reducing them over time through appropriate policies.

The national policy is aimed at promoting a competitive and sustainable development of tourism and is founded on the recognition of poverty reduction in this sector. Relevant international organizations can assist in strengthening the institutional capacity to increase the local input to the tourism economy in a poverty-reduction perspective. The policies are generally geared toward encouraging the local economic actor in the development of tourism products. This requires effort to develop human resources and encourage tourism-specific entrepreneurship and financial and technical support, in particular for small enterprise development.

May I take this opportunity to emphasize that to prove and accomplish the commitment to the declaration of the UN Millennium Development Goals, the Royal Government of Cambodia has launched its 2003-2005 Cambodia National Poverty Reduction Strategy (NPRS) and set up the Tourism Poverty Alleviation Working Group in which the Ministry of Tourism acts as Chairman and its members are the decision-makers from other relevant Ministries and Authorities. In this way we can ensure that the Poverty Reduction Policy of the Royal Government is undertaken effectively and visibly.

To encourage and support the involvement of poverty-stricken local communities in tourism projects, the Ministry of Tourism of Cambodia has the National Development Plan, which will be adopted by the government. The Plan includes pro-poor tourism policies; these policies must be brought to the attention of planners across various sectors, such is in environmental and cultural tourism.

The adoption of pro-poor tourism will ensure that tourism development projects are incorporated into development plans for regional and community groups. The key aspects of the relationship between tourism and poverty alleviation include:

1- Initiatives and actions of the government to encourage and support the local community in tourism for poverty alleviation.

- The government can obviously assist by building infrastructure. An example is the roads to rural areas thereby facilitating tourism activity, such as in Sambo Preykuh, the cultural and historical site in Kompong Thom province.
- The committee and inter-ministerial high-level working group has set up for the support of, and to ensure, poverty alleviation policies which are applied consistently across ministries with the common objective for poverty alleviation.
- Community groups were established in rural areas that feature tourist sites, such as in Rattanakiri Province, or Kompong Speu province. The community is encouraged to provide services for tourism development such as a tour guide,

accommodation and restaurants. When locals manage tourism ventures then there is increased opportunity for direct re-investment into the project.

- Public awareness programmes through National TV, workshops designed to make decision-makers as well as the general public aware of the key role that sustainable tourism development can play in alleviating poverty.

2- The private sector plays an important role by developing initiative to ensure that the benefits of tourism trickle down to the poor. Such initiatives include:

- Diversify and develop tourism products, contribute to Master Plans, investment in facilities and services and preservation of the environment and culture. Examples include Kirirom National Park, Rattanakiri and fresh water dolphins in Kratie province.
- Selection of private and international tourism investor to conduct tourism development of village based tourism, tourism product, training, small medium enterprises (SMEs).
- Marketing and promotion, transportation facility. In the age of the internet the private sector has more ability than ever to develop niche networks for marketing special interest tourism activity. There is a growing percentage of travelers who are looking for experiential tourism, away from normal paths. It is important that marketing efforts for models such as community based tourism activities are absolutely clear in expounding the benefits they generate. In Cambodia we have seen the development of the Cambodia Community-Based Eco-tourism Network (CCBEN), a network of organizations, educational institutes and projects that are involved in community-based eco-tourism.
- Encourage the private sector and communities to use local agricultural product.
- Ensure that success and sustainable development includes the participation of local communities and also that these communities benefit from their participation. Domestic tourists are particularly important for local sellers and owners of small enterprises. Therefore, it is important that tourism promotion also focuses on the domestic market.

3- The most important condition for tourism project to be more responsive to the need of the poor are:

- Small Medium Enterprises (SMEs) in transportation, food supply and so on
- Local participation and understanding of the benefits from the sector.
- Hearing and acceptance of the recommendation and initiatives from the local people as to what they need.
- Partnership between government, the private sector, NGOs, and the local community.

4- For small tourism projects involving the poor, especially poor rural people, to be commercially successful there are some condition required:

- Respect and protect the environment, culture and traditions
- Regulation and planning of land use must be carried out equitably and effectively.

5- International agencies as well as NGOs play an important role in turning tourism into a more effective tool to combat poverty by actions such as:

- Funding support to SME's for product development
- Promoting local products for export
- Initiating and implementing public awareness programmes
- Monitoring and evaluation of the role and activities
- Develop policy and responsiveness to local needs
- Consider social, economic and cultural impacts to the host community

Donor facilitated investment by international agencies and NGOs is vital for the development of tourism in LDC's whose governments have limited funding capacity. Often the local population will not have the resources or capacity to develop tourism opportunities and the role of agencies and NGOs assumes additional importance.

Excellencies,
Distinguished delegates,
Ladies and Gentlemen,

By coming together at this conference, we are affirming our intentions to strengthen our responsiveness to support for the effective application of tourism programmes oriented towards poverty reduction. I look forward with enthusiasm to the outcomes from this conference.

Thank you.

MINISTERIAL STATEMENT OF INDONESIA[11]

H.E. Mr. Francesco Frangialli, the Secretary-General WTO,
H.E. Mdm. Vo Thi Tang, Chairperson of the Vietnam National Administration of Tourism,
Distinguished delegates,
Ladies and gentlemen
First of all I would like to congratulate on the initiative of this important meeting. Attending this kind of meeting is very significant for us to discuss issues, exchanging views, information, and experiences of common interest. I am pleased to present a statement on behalf of the Government of Indonesia. In this context, I also would like to express our great gratitude and deep appreciation for WTO and the government of Vietnam for inviting us in this famous city of its rich of heritage cites and its beauty and also for the warmest welcomes and hospitality extended to us.

Distinguished delegates,
Ladies and gentlemen,
Tourism has been recognized as a powerful instrument for the socio-economic development especially, for the developing countries. This is because it can create job opportunities which bring economic benefits to host communities. With properly planned and managed, tourism also serves as a tool for poverty alleviation, conservation of natural and cultural assets and other benefits.

As we understand, the meaning of cultural tourism has changed over the last two centuries, from the practice of traveling around Europe to study the fine arts, traveling to develop "class", and then it also can be interpreted as an educational tour or tour with cultural performance.

Regardless the definition of cultural tourism, it is a matter of fact that tourism cannot invariably be isolated form many other aspects of culture, and this is particularly true of places like in Indonesia.
Indonesia has been well known as an archipelago tropical country scattered over 17,000 islands with a population of 200 million people which consist of 300 major ethnic groups and an even larger numbers of language sub-groups. As a pluralistic society, we can say with strong confidence, that Indonesia's particular strengths in tourism, are in its cultural richness and variety as well as in the diversity of its attractions, its varied and dramatic scenery, extensive wildlife, numerous beach resorts and diving locations.

Distinguished delegates,
Poverty alleviation is now becoming the top priority on the international agenda for the 21st Century set out in the United Nation's Millennium Development Goals endorsed by the Heads of State and representatives in the year 2000. However, the context of poverty today conceives a bundle of indicators which tends to be more heavily economic parameters primarily describing among others: (1) the level of income per capita, (2) the grade of health, and (3) the level of education. Such indicators reflect the human development index to measure the quality of community focus particularly on material needs.
In the case of Indonesia, poverty is defined as a situation where people are not in a well being condition, economically as well as socio-culturally. This relates to Indonesia's

---

[11] Mr. Thamrin B. Bachri, Deputy Minister For Capacity Building And International Relations

philosophy on tourism development is that tourism is viewed as the Balance of Life Concept. It literally means harmonious relationships between man with God, with fellows and with the environment. In its implementation, the Balance of Life concept requires a balance between exploiting and preserving the environment. This concept also puts human beings in the centre of the balance, not being the object of development but the subject as seen in Diagram 1.

Diagram 1 : THE HUMAN BALANCE OF LIFE CONCEPT

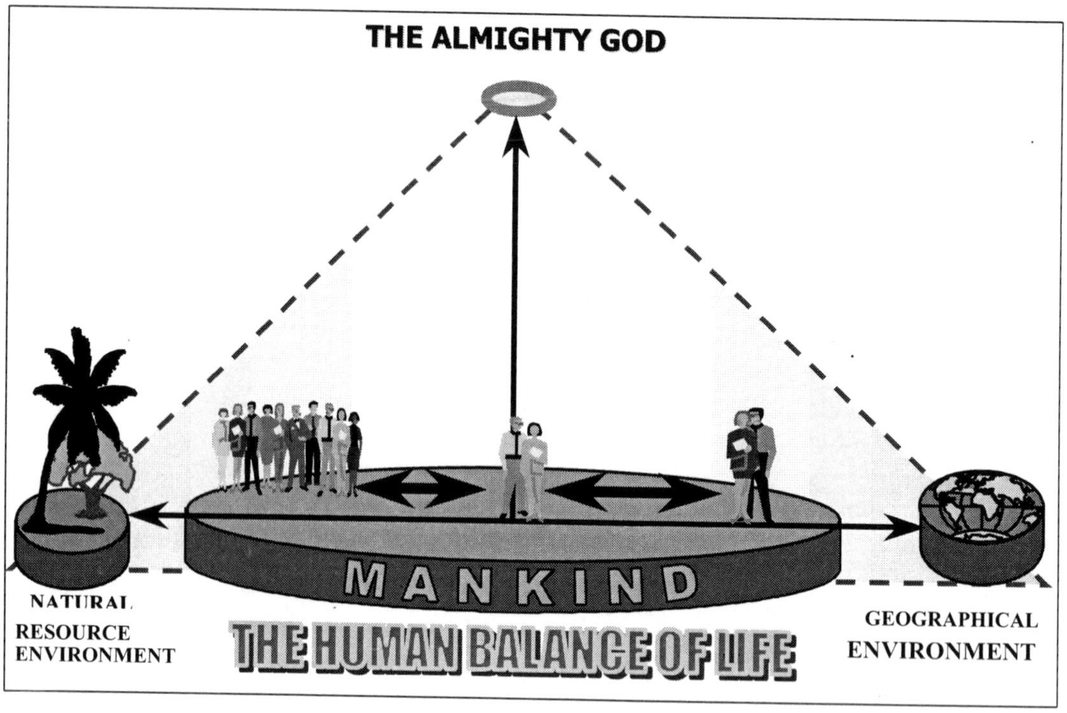

Ladies and gentlemen,

The policy of tourism development in Indonesia cannot be isolated form cultural policies. It is clearly set out in the national strategic plan that the treatment of cultural aspects (both tangible including traditional village, temple; as well as intangible such as: folklore, arts, festivals) as tourist attractions should be viewed as responsible tourism directed to revive and preserve its existence in order to stimulate the friendship among nations. The government puts emphasis on the empowerment of community level in the development of national culture and tourism. Culture and tourism are also viewed as a forum which is able to serve to ensure community benefits in terms of economical aspects, to create job opportunities, especially for micro, small and medium enterprises. It means that tourism development should be community-based.

Therefore, Indonesia's commitment to the improvement of poor communities and their environment is clearly seen from the Government's policy in relation to the tourism sector which is directed towards achieving sustainable development particularly at the grass root level. In line with this, the continuing process of government decentralization has implied a greater involvement of districts and local communities in planning, development, promotion, and management of the tourism sector, so that it is appropriate that local communities be fully involved in planning for sustainable tourism development.

It is understandable that linkage between cultural tourism and poverty alleviation in Indonesia can be seen in the development of community-based tourism. As the tourism sector tends to be relatively labour-intensive meaning it emphasis on community empowerment, therefore it is an effective means of distributing wealth. While the community takes more control over its development and becomes fully involved in decision-making concerning its development and future, therefore tourism can be a means to build community pride, to enhance the sense of community identity, to promote inter-cultural and to encourage the revival of traditional crafts and the preservation of environment.

Distinguished delegates,
We acknowledge and support all the initiatives carried out by the WTO including the initiative on poverty alleviation. We also have learned each other that each nation is rich with cultural aspects. In this connection, there are several conclusions and recommendations that I would like to propose here.

1. Cultural tourism development policies, strategies and guidelines both at national and regional level which are incorporated with sustainability principles, have certainly supported the UN millennium goals, especially poverty alleviation.
2. Poverty alleviation in tourism should not be viewed from economic point of view only, but it has to be balancè with other aspects so it allows the communities to preserve and develop their culture and their traditional values.
3. Cultural tourism should also be viewed as the right for people to see the other parts of the world and better understand of the diverse culture which brings peaceful life all over the world.
4. The involvement of the community in tourism development is able to enhance their pride of their local culture and to improve their understanding of the importance to preserve their culture as their identity.
5. To enhance the improved participation of the community, government intervention is needed in planning, business undertaking for a better access to financial support, training programs and facilitating the establishment of micro and small enterprises as well as a better access to various related information.
6. There should be a formal regulation to enforce the tourism industry to contribute to the development and preservation of local culture which is the main attraction or the core product of tourist consumption.
7. The local government should urge the big enterprises to always have partnership with the local community to enhance maximum participation of the community in most stages of their operation.

Thank you.

MINISTERIAL STATEMENT
OF THE ISLAMIC REPUBLIC OF IRAN[12]

Excellency Mr. Vu Khoan the Deputy Prime Minister of the Socialist Republic of Vietnam;
Excellency Mr.Francesco Frangialli , the secretary General of World Tourism Organization;
Excellencies;
Distinguished Delegates;
Ladies and Gentlemen;

At the outset , on behalf of the Islamic Republic of Iran ,I wish to thank the organizers of the ongoing conference and the government of Socialist Republic of Vietnam for holding this important event in the beautiful land of Vietnam. I also take this opportunity to thank the authorities of WTO for bearing the responsibilities to develop the tourism industry in the world as well as their endeavors to distribute properly the wealth to alleviate poverty from the human societies through promotion of tourism.

The world today in the light of information and technology revolution has been changed into global village.

At the beginning of the third Millennium which on the initiative of H.E. Katami ,the president of I.R. of Iran is designated by the United Nations " the year of Dialogue among Civilizations", the world is facing two major problems ; unemployment and poverty.

The reason for gathering here is to create general determination for increasing employment, elimination of poverty and its ugly features from human societies. This strive must be sanctified. Obviously, the world is suffering from class divide as well as the existence of widespread poverty in various societies and countries. The status quo is by no means appropriate for the modern world. Poverty is challenging positive human achievements and has depicted a dismal future outlook for the whole world.

The Islamic Republic of Iran is a culturally diverse country and in fact is a minimized world in which all cultures has peacefully coexisted for many centuries. This culture comprises of ethnic and local subcultures which its manifestations can be seen in music ,art , poetry ,literature and architecture . What we, as the supporter of peace and Dialogue among Civilizations in the world are proposing is based on this historical background. In fact ,what we are looking for is to prepare the ground for encouraging the people to travel to Iran and get familiar the culture and civilization which not only belong to Iranian but also, is part of human civilizations.

In order to achieve this goal, we establish a new Organization called " Iran Cultural Heritage & Tourism Organization" at the level of Vice- President and a member of the Cabinet to indicate our serious determination for safeguard, revival and introduction historical relics as well as development of Tourism industry.

---

[12] H.E. Seyed Hossein Marashi, Vice President of I.R. of Iran, and President of the Cultural Heritage and Tourism Organization

Undoubtedly, tourism advancement of my country will increase Iran 'share in the tourism global markets and strengthen the industry throughout the world, specifically in Asia continent. Moreover, it will expand human relations in a wide range.

To get the predicted goals , Islamic Republic of Iran warmly welcomes all tourists to the country.

In addition ,we support foreign investment and cooperation of the other nations in order to take advantages of their experiences and enhancement bilateral ties for the exchange of information.

Advertising Iran 's potentials in target and international markets to increase awareness of tourists about unique capacities of this historical land, facilitating tourist visa on arrival are some of the our measures .

To give you a good example ,we have provided a 14-day tourist visa on entrance for the citizens of a few countries such as ; Malaysia and Singapore which is a successful action.

Besides, in accordance of the programs provided with the effective cooperation of WTO,20 year outlook of tourism development of Iran ,predicts 20 millions tourist arrivals annually by 2024.

We admit that sustainable development of tourism industry will be impossible without serious support from governments and international bodies to protect environment and safeguard historical buildings, cultural remains, as well as religious, moral and cultural values.

Excellencies,
We propose that:
* Tourism and cultural heritage friendship associations should be established through intergovernmental agreements to identify and introduce such capacities;

* To transfer experiences from countries successful in the field of cultural tourism and poverty elimination, a special committee should be established under the supervision of Secretary General of WTO . Islamic Republic of Iran announces its readiness to cooperate in this regard.

* The year 2006 should be designated as the year of cultural tourism to draw more attention from policymakers and macroeconomic planners;

* Attention must be paid to bolstering and developing rural tourism in countries to fight poverty and take advantage of many capacities for promotion of cultural goals of nations.

Excellencies,
Honorable Secretary General,
We suggest on the second anniversary of the incidence of catastrophic earthquake in the historical & cultural city of Bam (in Kerman Province ,I.R, of Iran) in 2006 to hold an international tourist gathering with the cooperation of WTO ,UNESCO and I.R.of Iran

in Bam city in order to the world which unprecedently sympathized with the people and government of Iran after earthquake ,to play historical and constructive role in revival of tourism in Bam.

At the end ,I would like once again to thank the warm hospitalities of the government of Socialist Republic of Vietnam and WTO extended to us and also for the proper organizing of this conference in the city of Hue .

Thank you.

MINISTERIAL STATEMENT OF LAO PDR[13]

H.E. Mrs. Vo Thi Thang Chairperson of Vietnam National Administration of Tourism
H.E. Mr. Francesco Frangialli, General Secretary of WTO
Honorable Tourism Ministers
Distinguished delegates
Ladies & Gentlemen,

It is a great honor and pleasure for the Lao PDR delegation to be invited to attend the Ministerial Conference on Cultural Tourism and Poverty Alleviation, held in Hue the world culture heritage city of Vietnam , at the moment when Hue is launching its prestigious festival for 2004. On behalf of The Lao National Tourism Authority, we would like to take this auspicious opportunity to express our sincere thanks to Vietnam National Administration of Tourism and the World Tourism Organization, for inviting us and for the warm hospitality and excellent arrangements made for our delegation.

As we are aware , tourism is a powerful instrument to push and enhance the socio-economic development, especially for the developing and least developed countries as it helps to creating job and generating income to the whole community. The government of Lao PDR has identified tourism as one of the priority sectors in the national socio-economic development program. The government policy is to promote natural, cultural and historical tourism to attract international tourists to the country and contribute to poverty alleviation.

Laos has two world heritage sites namely the 14th Century Luang Prabang City and Wat Phu in Champasak province. Other key resources and attractions are the enigmatic Plain of Jars in Xieng Khouang province, which is also under consideration for World Heritage status, the Nam Ha Eco-tourism Project in Luang Nam Tha province, the Hoprakeo, That Luang and Sisaket temples in Vientiane, That Ing Hang temple in Savannakhet province ,Khonphapheng waterfall on the Mekong river in Champasack province. On the other hand, Laos is a very peaceful society with 49 different ethnic groups living together in harmony and sharing a common national and cultural identity. Their smiles and kindness represent the warm welcome and hospitality extended to all guests visiting the country.

Since the Lao government's decision to open the country to international tourists in 1990's there has been rapid growth in the sector. The number of tourist arrivals has gradually increased over the years, ranging from 14,400 visitors in 1990 to 735,660 in 2002, thus generating US$ 113,8 million, and ranking as the number 1 income for the country.

Lao PDR is eager to share its experience with our friends and colleagues present here on how tourism is being used as a vehicle for sustainable development and poverty alleviation of the population.

In recent years my government has invested heavily in the development of infrastructure to support the tourism industry such as roads, electricity, airports and

---

[13] H.E. Mr. Somphong Mongkhonvilay, Minister to the Prime Minister's Office of Lao PDR Tourism, Chairman of Lao National Tourism Authority

other necessary systems. Infrastructure improvements around cultural, natural and historical sites are being made with consideration that the local people can also benefit from and be part of these ventures . At the same time, in cooperation with our neighboring countries of the of the Great Mekong Sub-region (GMS), we are working together to develop the so called triangle or quadrangle economic cooperation, thus including the tourist promotion and development cooperation. To date through out the country, we have opened more than ten international border checkpoints and three international airports to facilitate the flow of population and goods. Yet our government has also decided to extend the tourist visa for foreign tourists from 15 to 30 days and by 2005 Laos will exempt the entry visas for all citizens of the ten ASEAN countries.

The Lao Government has still placed tourism among 8 priority sectors for poverty alleviation and socio-economic development. I also would like to inform the conference that the Lao National Tourism Authority has just completed the formulation of the Natural and Eco-tourism Strategy and Action Plan, which strongly focuses on of poverty alleviation, sustainable development and environment conservation.

Tourism is still at its early stages in my country, but we realize that tourism can really provide the ample opportunity for the population to alleviate its hard workship and poverty. Tourism is really a vital vehicle to boost cultural and natural protection and finally it can strongly support the socio-economic development.

On behalf of the Lao National Tourism Authority, I would like to welcome all friends to visit Laos to enjoy our rich natural and cultural heritages.

I wish the conference great success and all delegations happiness.

Thank you

MINISTERIAL STATEMENT OF MALAYSIA[14]

H.E. Madam Vo Thi Thang
Hon. Chairperson of the Vietnam national administration of tourism (VNAT)

H.E. Mr. Francesco Frangialli
Secretary general of world tourism organisation (WTO)

Excellencies,

Ladies and gentlemen,

Allow me, first of all, to convey to our host country, Vietnam, greetings and good wishes from the people of Malaysia. On behalf of my delegation and myself, I would like to express my sincere appreciation and gratitude to the government of Vietnam for the warm hospitality and the excellent arrangements made in hosting this important ministerial conference. My thanks are also extended to the secretary general of the world tourism organisation and his dedicated staff for coordinating in the hosting of this conference.

I am indeed pleased and honoured to address this August meeting of very distinguished delegates on the subject of **Cultural Tourism and Poverty Alleviation**. Interest in cultural tourism has always been alluring to tourist and it is increasingly becoming an important form of tourism throughout the world. In fact, cultural tourism forms an important component of international travel and tourism industry of the world today. But cultural tourism is not just confined to tangible aspects of cultural heritages like historical sites and monuments. It also includes festivals, performing arts, cultural events, as well as travel for pilgrimages as important components of cultural tourism. I certainly agree with WTO's view that cultural tourism is also about immersion and enjoyment of the lifestyle of the local people, the local area and what constitutes its identity and character.

The Asia-pacific is endowed with world's outstanding cultural assets, both tangible and intangible. It is currently contributing as the main source of tourist attractions. With WTO's forecast of international tourist arrivals to reach 1 billion in 2010, cultural tourism certainly stands as an important segment in attracting tourists to this part of the region. Special attention must therefore be accorded to its sustainable development in order to ensure that its contributions are fairly distributed among the local community.

Ladies and gentlemen,

Let me at this juncture share Malaysia's experience in the development of its tourism industry. Tourism industry is a very important sector to the Malaysian economy. It is currently the **second largest foreign exchange earner** and employs a significant level of the **country's total work force**. So far we have made great achievements in maintaining a sustainable development in the tourism sector despite the few setbacks which are beyond our control, such as the financial crisis that we experienced in 1997/98, the impact of the September 11 event and the war in Iraq as well as the spread

---

[14] H.E. Datuk Dr. Leo Michael Toyad, Minister of Culture, Arts and Tourism

of SARS. Nevertheless, tourist arrivals reached a new record of **13.3 million** in year **2002** with **USD 6.8 billion** in tourism receipts. In 2003, though the tourist arrivals dropped to **10.6 million,** we did well considering the circumstances. The government of Malaysia is fully committed to the sustainable development of the tourism industry making it as a catalyst for **social and economic development** for the nation and the wellbeing of its people.

Cultural tourism in Malaysia has been an important component of our tourism promotion. The historical cities of Malacca and Penang, the multi racial mix, festivals, performing arts and cultural events are our cultural heritages which have offered many attractions, making **Malaysia** as one of the ideal tourist destinations. In fact the tag line *Malaysia Truly Asia* speaks for itself the cultural dimension as one of the Malaysia's main tourism product - the people and the culture, ethnicity, diversity in heritage.

Ladies and gentlemen,

Tourism certainly can contribute to poverty alleviation through the creation of employment and income. In this regard, cultural and rural tourism in particular, has been an important vehicle in the creation of employment and income distribution to the local communities in Malaysia. The Malaysian government's initiatives to promote tourism including **cultural and rural tourism** are part and parcel of its efforts in the **social and economic** wellbeing of its people, particularly the rural communities. The government of Malaysia has always focused in its tourism development plans, the well being of the local community, to benefits from its growth. In fact, the government has encouraged local communities to participate in tourism related activities such as the *homestay* and *handicraft* activities including agro-based industries, and small / medium food industries . The main idea is to help supplement the household income of the local communities especially those located in rural areas so that they can enjoy a better standard of living. Through the efforts of the ministry of tourism, and other agencies such as the agriculture and rural development, there are now more than 65 registered homestay enterprises undertaken by the local communities involving more than 1,000 families throughout the country, thereby providing opportunities to participate in tourism activities beside giving opportunities to tourist to experience the traditional Malaysian lifestyle.

Similarly, there are 13 handicraft centres providing employment and income to more than 1,853 people throughout the country. Besides, under the rural tourism thrust to alleviate poverty, the local communities are encouraged to grow fruit trees to supplement their income through fruit festivals held annually. Thus, it can be said that the cultural and rural tourism have been the two most important thrust by the ministry of tourism to help local communities to benefit from the growth of the tourism industry in Malaysia.

Ladies and gentlemen,

The issue of poverty alleviation in Malaysia has received special attention and is addressed directly in its development plans. Poverty in Malaysia is conceptualized in both absolute and relative terms. Absolute poverty is measured in terms of the **Poverty Line Income** (PLI) which is USD 139 (RM 529) whilst relative poverty is defined in terms of inequality between ethnic urban and rural. Households whose gross monthly incomes were below half the **PLI** were classified as hardcore poor. Most of the poorest groups are in villages, settlement plantation and in the urban sector.

Malaysia's efforts to eradicate hardcore poverty were spearheaded by a special programme known as the **Development Programme For The Poorest**. In addition, the government also implemented various programmes and projects aimed at rural and agricultural households. Among others, the poor participated and benefited from projects such as the *integrated agricultural development projects, the provision of agriculture infrastructure, replanting schemes, land consolidation and rehabilitation, and support services. In addition, greater employment opportunities from off-farm and non-farm activities helped to increase income of poor households.*

While attention will continue to be given to direct welfare assistance, attitudinal change and the provision of basic amenities, poverty eradication programmes will place primary emphasis on income-generating projects. Among others, the income-generating projects include cash crop cultivation, livestock rearing, aquaculture, **petty trading and cottage industries.**

The above government initiatives have resulted in the overall incidence of poverty to decline from 52.4 % in 1970 to 5.1% in 2002. The total number of poor households fell from one million to 198,300 over the same period.

The overall poverty alleviation strategies planned by Malaysia for the new millennium incorporates elements of good governance and social development. The thrust of poverty alleviation will be directed at reducing the incidence of poverty among Malaysians.

Ladies and gentlemen,

In the efforts to alleviate poverty, i am pleased to note of WTO's initiatives in introducing the **step** (*sustainable tourism -eliminating poverty*) programme which provides guidelines for successful and sustainable cultural tourism development at national and local levels and as a tool for poverty alleviation in member countries. Malaysia fully supports this initiative and stand ready to further explore the possibilities of using cultural tourism as potential tool for reducing poverty levels among such communities.

Malaysia is serious in ensuring that its development efforts are in line with the concept of sustainable development. It has taken various steps in safeguarding its natural as well as its cultural heritages through institutional responsibilities and establishing regulatory frameworks in the conservation and preservation of natural and cultural heritages.

In conclusion, i would like to take this opportunity, once again, to thank the host government and the secretary general for organizing this conference. It is hoped that with the concerted efforts by all parties concerned, poverty alleviation can be a reality. Malaysia stands ready to extend its fullest cooperation to make tourism the nucleus for socio-economic development and well being of nation and community at large.

Thank you.

MINISTERIAL STATEMENT OF THE REPUBLIC OF KOREA[15]

Honorable Mr. Francesco Frangialli,
Madam Vo Thi Thang, Chairwoman of the Vietnam National Tourism Authority,
Distinguished Ministers and Representatives of WTO Member States,
Ladies and Gentlemen!

First of all, I wish to express my sincere appreciation to Mr. Frangialli, Secretary General of the WTO, and Madam Vo Thi Thang, Chairwoman of the Vietnam National Tourism Authority, for their tremendous efforts in organizing and hosting the Ministerial Conference on Cultural Tourism and Poverty Alleviation.

It is my distinct honor and privilege to be here with all of you today and give a presentation on ST-EP, the project being carried forward by the WTO and Korea, which is sure to contribute to empowering us to tackle a longstanding and compelling issue.

On the outset, I would like to express my deep appreciation to all of you for making such grave efforts to promote the development of the international tourism industry. I am sure that the inspirational presentations we make today will be truly helpful for us in proceeding with our efforts.

As you are aware, Korea is devoted to spurring sustainable tourism as a crucial tool for alleviating poverty. As part of this effort, Korea has embarked on the ST-EP Project with the World Tourism Organization.

Now, I would like to start my presentation on ST-EP and I hope you will be able to grasp what ST-EP is about and come to realize its significance.

Let me begin by explaining the background of the ST-EP Foundation and the developments that have taken place until now.

As you can see in the first box on the slide, sustainable tourism is significant in the fact that it is closely related with environmental, social, and cultural resources. It can bring about conducive economic benefits and create a climate where the interests of tourists, local residents, and the environment can all be achieved. The urgency of sustainable tourism was proposed at the United Nations Conference on Environment and Development (UNCED) in 1992. At the UN Assembly in 1987, it was stated that sustainable development should be at the heart of policies and cooperation. Also at the World Summit on Sustainable Development (WSSD) in 2002, it was noted that a new concept should be proposed to link sustainable tourism with poverty elimination.

The WTO has been continuously making efforts for ST-EP and increasingly more and more countries have shown interest in it. Korea was also greatly interested in ST-EP and consequently decided to actively contribute to the initiative. The latest ongoing work is the establishment of the headquarters of the ST-EP Foundation in Korea, and to this end, the WTO and the Korean Government signed a memorandum regarding the matter. The next slide shows the major features of the ST-EP Foundation and what it sets out to achieve in the end. Further consultations will take place with the WTO.

---

[15] Mr. Jee-chul Oh, Vice-Minister of Culture and Tourism

The main mission of the ST-EP Foundation is to eliminate poverty through sustainable tourism, which is the fundamental meaning that comprises the word "ST-EP". To achieve this goal, the ST-EP Foundation will strive to strengthen international cooperation, provide tourism development roadmaps to target countries, and conduct researches on ST-EP.

The three functions, as seen on the top level of the diagram, will result in the implementation and management of sustainable tourism project, creation of jobs, and increase of income in developing countries.

As you are aware, although Korea was a least developed country only four decades ago, it has achieved rapid economic development. To some extent, this is attributable to the help from the international community. Korea would like to give back the assistance we received to developing countries and share our experience and know-how with them.

The following slide displays the areas that ST-EP will target to eliminate poverty through sustainable tourism

Now I would like to move on to go over the main strategies of the ST-EP Foundation. There are four strategies that the ST-EP Foundation can undertake to eliminate poverty.

First, the ST-EP Foundation will strengthen international cooperation and forge new relations. To this end, ST-EP will designate a council to interact with governments, international organizations, NGOs, Corporations/Donors, etc. An Advisory Group will provide professional knowledge and the demand and needs of the beneficiaries to the ST-EP Foundation.

Second, the ST-EP Foundation will implement and develop ST-EP projects.

The ST-EP Foundation will conduct research on ST-EP and foster high quality tourism human resource to operate and manage a ST-EP Project. The ST-EP Foundation will provide support to help developing countries establish a tourism development plan. Korea's tourism experts can assist research and development, and the Ministry of Culture and Tourism's education and training programs can be helpful in human resource development. Furthermore, trained professionals can map out tourism development plans based on research and development results.

Third, the ST-EP Foundation will conduct branding of ST-EP.

Promotion will be a critical factor, because an exposed and noticeable brand will help other organizations or NGOs to take on a part in the ST-EP Foundation's poverty elimination projects. (Branding) Defining the brand of the ST-EP Foundation is needed to raise the awareness on the ST-EP Foundation. (Events) Holding various promotional events and campaigns will enforce the ST-EP brand. Organizing ST-EP award ceremonies will further expose the ST-EP brand, helping it garner attention from the world. (Brand Council) Lastly, international leaders and celebrities will be invited to join the ST-EP Council.
Korea can further contribute through its highly advanced e-promotion technology.

The last one is securing funds for the ST-EP Foundation. In the initial stage, the WTO, Korea, and other interested countries can contribute and then corporations and individual donors may follow suit. Korea and the WTO are planning to provide 5 million US dollars and 500 thousand US dollars respectively, in total 5.5 million US dollars. ST-EP will use the money to conduct research on the ST-EP Project. We look forward to ST-EP becoming a self-sufficient foundation by taking advantage of promotional events and branding to receive the returning funds resulting from them.

It is our goal that ST-EP's patrimony stands at 100 million US dollars by 2015. Korea has abundant experience in holding large-scale events like the Olympics, the World Cup, and various international conferences. Based on our experience, we will be able to significantly contribute to organizing a wide variety of events.

Finally, I would like to outline the results expected from the ST-EP Foundation. First, worldwide interest and awareness in ST-EP will be increased through promotion and branding. Second, keen interests by countries and organizations around the world will help establishing a worldwide network for ST-EP. Third, ST-EP will promote research and development projects on ST-EP to support target countries. Active research will help us explore effective ways to provide assistance to countries in need. Fourth, ST-EP will support developing countries with strategies that I have explained previously, which is the ultimate role of ST-EP.

I would like to wrap up my presentation by saying that although we still have a long way to go to achieve the goals, I am confident that this is a good start. I firmly believe that ST-EP is a great chance that we just cannot afford to miss. If we all join hands and embark on the journey together, anything can be possible. I would like to take this chance to kindly ask for your active support and cooperation.

Thank you for your kind attention.

MINISTERIAL STATEMENT OF SRI LANKA[16]

It is both a pleasure and a privilege to address this august gathering as the Minister for Industry, Tourism and Investment promotion in Sri Lanka on a theme which is very relevant and important to countries like ours. At the outset I would like to thank the organizers for availing this opportunity.

The theme of the seminar underlines two specific dimensions, namely poverty and cultural Tourism that itself in my opinion is a combination of a problem and the optimal solution to the problem. Poverty is a lingering problem to most of our developing countries in South Asia.

Madam Chairperson, Sri Lanka is a small island destination of 64,610 sq km strategically located in the Indian Ocean. However, as Anton Chekhov the Russia's greatest dramatist and writer having visited Sri Lanka, then Ceylon, as a tourist on the 12th November 1890 flashed in his records," It is a paradise on earth" in terms of the salubrious weather, natural scenic beauty, highest bio diversity, rich flora and fauna, sandy beaches and it's talented people. Sri Lanka's population today is nearly 20 mn which is growing annually at the rate of 1.2%. One fifth to one third of the population (around 3 - 5 million) is categorized as poor, based on a lower poverty line of US$ 12 and a higher poverty line of US$ 15 per person per month. According to the findings of the ADB, over 85% of the poor live in rural areas while 7% in urban areas and 6% in the state sectors. Consumption poverty has been estimated to be over 33% in rural and estate sectors where agriculture is the primary means of living.

Since independence, reducing poverty has been a singular challenge facing successive Governments in Sri Lanka. Immediately after the Second World War as far back as in 1944, a rice ration had been placed in operation in support of the barest minimum consumption requirements of every citizen in the country. In 1985 a revised food ration was introduced under the "food stamp" scheme on a more structured basis aiming at only the households living in poverty. The Government policy right through out has been to provide cost subsidized transport services both railway and road and free health and education services benefiting every body in general and poorer sections in particular. Poverty alleviation efforts initiated up to 1985 proved the premise that affording the selected households living in poverty a certain amount of food ration periodically can do very little to elevate them beyond poverty levels in a sustainable manner.

In 1989 the "janasaviya Programme" (people empowerment) introduced by the then United National Party Government was aimed at people empowerment with the former playing only the role of a catalyst or a facilitator. However, in the implementation gradually politics crept into the system and the distribution of janasaviya benefits was restricted mostly to party supporters of the Government in power.

Taking a constructive step forward, the Peoples Alliance Government in 1994 established the " Samurdhi" (prosperity) movement with a huge financial base and several novel administrative structures to effectively manage the poverty alleviation

---

[16] H.E. Mr. Anura Priadarsi Solomon Dias Bandaranaike, Minister of Industries, Tourism and Investment Promotion

programme. Samurdhi Banks were established in all Divisional Secretary divisions for recipient households to obtain small scale loans. The Department of Poor Relief and the Samurdhi Commissioner General's Department were set up to implement the Samurdhi stamp distribution.

Samurdhi Authority was set up in 1996 to manage the "Samurdhi Task Force" comprising young unemployed graduates who were supposed to ensure implementation of the village level development projects with the involvement of the community which was considered as the prime concern.

War affected poverty has added another dimension to poverty in Sri Lanka. Due to the protracted civil conflict it is estimated that at least half the population in the Northern and Eastern provinces are affected by poverty.

The conflict situation has declined local and foreign investment to the country and retarded tourism and other dynamic industries substantially shutting off massive economic benefits to the people living in poverty. With a view to realize the poverty alleviation objectives constructively in the future, the Government that assumed office in April this year, which I represent, created a separate Ministry with the portfolio of "Samurdhi & Poverty Alleviation". All policies and programmes in relation to poverty reduction will be formulated and implemented by the new Ministry and its agency network.

Madam Chairperson, in our quest for ways and means of effectively reducing poverty we have at least now been convinced that tourism can intervene as an appropriate partner to provide enormous economic opportunities to the people living in remote villages in our less developing countries. Among the various facets of tourism "cultural tourism" has the highest potential to reach the poor quite speedily and to benefit them in numerous ways.

Using culture as a vehicle for sustainable tourism development is now becoming an important item in the priorities of many public policy planners. It is about immersion in and enjoyment of lifestyle of the local people, the local area and what constitutes its identity and character. Through cultural tourism it is hoped that economic growth, investment and employment will be generated which will consequently, make an important contribution towards poverty reduction in our country.

Sri Lanka is very proud and fortunate to inherit a diverse cultural heritage dating back to more than 2500 years. Kandy which lies on the Central highlands is considered to be the most thriving cultural centre in the country today. Its famous ancient temple housing the tooth relic, and its annual cultural pageant the Asela Perahera has contributed much towards cultural tourism in the island.

There are also at present seven world heritage sites in Sri Lanka including the first two capitals of Anuradapura and Pollonnaruwa in the Northern part of the country. Sigiriya, the rock fortress is also among them built on a natural rock between 477-495 AD which has become known as the palace in the sky among tourists world over. Together with these heritage sites several Dagabas, Buddhist temples, Buddha statues and a gamut of irrigation reservoirs still remain well preserved as archeological attractions which are amazing and popular among both local and foreign tourists. The tradition of dance, drumming and acrobatics had been closely linked with the community since good old days. Colombo or Ambalangoda are the places to witness the ritualistic exorcism of 'devil dancing and folk theatre which combines dance, masked drama, drumming and exorcism rituals to vividly recreate Sri Lankan folklore. Several hotels in various parts of the country organize these traditional dancing performances in their hotels as a tourist attraction, which creates a substantial income to the poor communities involving in these performances.

The woodcarvings have a history of more than 1500 years. Most spectacular ancient woodcarvings are found well preserved even today. These traditional talents are being used by some sections of the rural community to produce an array of souvenirs for tourists to purchase which ensures substantial income to them. Pottery manufactured with clay is ancient as the Sri Lankan history.

Batik production although comparatively a recent development originated from Indonesia is now well established among Sri Lankan industrialists along the coastal line in the South West Coast where Tourism is highly developed. German, UK and Italian tourists mostly buy these very popular souvenir items. The production process employs rural women in large numbers resulting several employment opportunities for them to earn a living.

Special reference needs to be made of Sri Lankan cuisine which is closely linked with the food habits of the three nationals namely Singhala, Tamil & Muslim living together. One of the main features of Sri Lankan cuisine is it's amazing taste mixed with several spices and chilies which are locally grown and historically known.

Among the array of cultural elements indigenous medicine known in the whole of South Asia as Ayurveda has taken a prime place as a precious legacy of Sri Lankan culture creating for itself a huge demand from hotels where exclusive medical services and accommodation facilities are maintained. Ayurvedic medical profession involving several types of treatment methods such as therapeutic steam baths, oil massage, medicinal drinks, etc. has created several job opportunities for the native unemployed youth both male and female to find jobs in Ayurvedic resorts.

Madam Chairperson, this brief description amply manifests the window of opportunity cultural Tourism has opened up in support of our poverty alleviation efforts. However to position and market cultural tourism in its proper perspective Government policy need to be re-directed towards educating specially the rural poor on the grave necessity to preserve the culture in it's original fascination if they are to benefit from the cultural heritage since it is very sensitive to the external forces arising out of tourism itself.

Mostly the rural poor are the custodians of the native culture with immense talents to produce what the tourists demand. Therefore the Government must play a pioneering role in protecting their interests without allowing them to be exploited by the possible middle men may be brokers, tour guides etc.

Such factors considerably prevent the trickle down effects of tourism to rural community. A good example is the group tour package tourism promoted by the International tour operators which leaves very little freedom for their tourists to choose the preferred product while in the host destination. Their interests are covered by the package price paid by them in advance. Unfortunately in the past Sri Lanka has not been able to invigorate more of independent high-end travelers who usually have extended holidays to associate with the local community creating more economic benefits to them such as eco-tourists. Our Government has several plans aiming at creating more and more economic opportunities for the rural sector community to benefit from cultural tourism so that in an overall sense Tourism can ensure over and above other industries a greater contribution towards the Government's poverty alleviation endeavors.

Thank you for your kind attention.

MINISTERIAL STATEMENT OF THAILAND[17]

Mr. Chairman,
Secretary-General of the World Tourism Organization,
Excellencies,
Distinguished Delegates,
Ladies and Gentlemen,

On behalf of His Excellency Mr. Sontaya Kunplome, the Minister of Tourism and Sports of Thailand, I wish to congratulate and express appreciation for the Government of the Socialist Republic of Vietnam and the City of Hue for hosting this very important meeting. I also wish to inform the meeting that due to his prior engagement, Minister of Tourism and Sports of Thailand regrets for not being able to attend this meeting and wishes to extend his best wishes for a very successful meeting.

In view of the theme of this Ministerial Conference, "Cultural Tourism and Poverty Alleviation", Hue is one of the most appropriate venue for the meeting for Hue is one of the most important cultural and historical tourist destinations in Southeast Asia, particularly in the Mekong Region, having the East-West Economic Corridor (EWEC) and other transportation network development projects under the GMS cooperation framework as the important infrastructures for promoting regional tourism. Apart from her famous historical heritage, the Imperial City of Hue also has long and close historical ties with Bangkok and now enjoys close cooperation with Ayudhya Province, her sister city. Between Thailand and Vietnam, the EWEC also leads to Thailand-Vietnam Friendship Village at Baan Najok, Nakorn Phanom Province, where the late President Ho Chi Minh used to reside for some time, which also contributes to the promotion of historical and cultural tourism between Vietnam and Thailand.

I am confident that, with the support of World Tourism Organization and all related development organizations and agencies, the EWEC and other GMS transport linkage projects will contribute to the increase of tourism in this developing region. In this regard, Thailand has actively supported cooperation efforts in promoting cultural tourism with Vietnam on bilateral and regional basis, including ASEAN, GMS, ACMECS, ACD and APEC.

In addition to historical sites, Vietnam and all countries in this region is home to various ethnic groups that are rich in cultural diversity which I believe, is a valuable resource for the promotion of cultural tourism. In this regard, the World Tourism Organization and all related development agencies can help promote cooperation among the governments concerned in the projects or programs to support responsible cultural tourism to help contribute to the sustainable social and economic development and poverty reduction of the ethnic people living in this region, which Thailand stands ready to support and share experiences.

The problem of poverty in Asia has been generally known. Using tourism for poverty alleviation by the World Tourism Organization is an essential policy that Thailand has also given importance to this issue.

---

[17] H.E. Mr. Krit Kraichitti, Ambassador of Thailand to Vietnam, on behalf of H.E. Mr. Sontaya Kunplome, Minister of Tourism and Sports

At present, we are linking One Village One Product or OTOP Tourism Villages with main tourism sites in order to attract tourists to pay in the areas where communities are located and strengthened. This is a means of community – based tourism.

In the period of 5 months, since January 2004, the project has been implemented in two provinces in the northern part of Thailand, Chiang Mai and Chiang Rai. It can be found that people have earned 10 % more and tourists have spent more one or two hours in the villages.

I am, therefore, pleased that representative of Thailand had an opportunity to present the OTOP Tourism Villages initiative in the Seminar on Cultural Tourism and Poverty Alleviation in Siem Reap on 8 June.

Thailand adheres to the principle of sustainable tourism development that alleviates poverty, thus accepted to chair the World Tourism Organization Committee on Sustainable Development of Tourism. Therefore, the fourth meeting of this Committee was held in Chiang Mai, Thailand, in March 2004.

Our commitment makes us to initiate the Five Countries One Destination Project known as *Heritage Necklace* under the framework of ACMECS which has been presented and approved during the 41st Meeting of the World Tourism Organization Commission for East Asia and the Pacific in Siem Reap, Cambodia. The five cities in five countries are: Bagan in Myanmar, Luang Prabang in Lao PDR, Siem Reap in Cambodia, Nan in Thailand, and of course, Hue in Vietnam.

The five cultural heritages will be treated on equity basis, linked as one destination, standardized in services and management, in collaboration with the World Tourism Organization. This single destination of the five countries forming the *Heritage Necklace* reflects the development of cultural tourism in our region. May I take this opportunity to thank the Governments of the four countries for the cooperation and thank the World Tourism Organization for the recognition of our region.

Finally, I would like to express our appreciation to the Vietnam National Administration of Tourism for the wonderful arrangement of the Ministerial Conference on Cultural Tourism and Poverty Alleviation.

MINISTERIAL STATEMENT
OF HONG KONG, CHINA[18]

I am pleased to have this opportunity to speak on behalf of the Hong Kong Special Administrative Region (SAR) Government on this important topic.

Tourism is a key driver for economic growth, a significant earner of foreign exchange, a major source of tax revenue for governments, and an important generator of business opportunities for enterprises of large and small. More importantly, tourism straddles many sectors and is a labour intensive industry and hence a major employer at all economic levels. Undoubtedly, it is an effective force to combat poverty.

Hong Kong is a rather developed and generally affluent economy. Despite this, the role of tourism in Hong Kong follows the logic of tourism everywhere: it is important for the job opportunities it brings for local residents and for enhancing their quality of life. By creating job opportunities at different levels, the tourism industry in Hong Kong helps absorb relatively low-skilled labourers who would otherwise become unemployed due to the restructuring of our economy. Tourism is helping in our efforts to grow the economy and alleviate the conditions of certain population segments in Hong Kong.

Building on our convenient location and good connections to the rest of the world, and capitalising on our rich tourism resources, the Hong Kong Government has designated tourism as one of four pillar industries for Hong Kong and is committed to fostering the development of the tourism industry of Hong Kong. We showcase in particular the diverse attractions, the cosmopolitan lifestyles, the unique "East meets West" culture, the rich inventory of both modern and traditional architectures and artistic performances.

Travelers are looking for a variety of travel experiences in the countries and cities they visit: different cultures, different traditions, different heritage and different lifestyles. Opportunities exist for us to build on these expectations to enrich the attractiveness of destinations. To continue to maintain and enhance Hong Kong's status as the most popular city destination in Asia, we adopt a multi-faceted strategy – the aim is to enhance the diversity of tourism by building new attractions and enhancing existing facilities. To take this forward, we recognize that cultural tourism is one of the key tourism resources and that careful planning and development in this field will bring about economic benefits and opportunities.

To enhance the development of cultural tourism for economic development, we are actively pursuing cultural projects with an emphasis on sustainable development for the benefit of the local community. We have an appropriate planning mechanism that takes into account the technical, financial, transportation and conservation aspects of each project.

We will strive to promote local tourism to support the growth of small businesses and employment by taking appropriate initiatives to attract wide participation from the private sector and local community in the development of cultural products and the provision of tourism services. We believe the enhancement of tourism products in the

---

[18] Mr. Duncan Pescod, Deputy Commissioner for Tourism

local community will improve quality of life, especially in rural areas, which are characterized in Hong Kong by population decline, unemployment and environmental problems.

To ensure the benefits to the local community, we will give actively support the participation by local residents and operators in taking forward local cultural initiatives. We will strive to incorporate in the planning of local cultural projects practical means whereby tourism spending will benefit the lower-income groups.

Effective collaboration is necessary to ensure the presentation of tourism product to our visitors. We will continue to enhance communication and liaison between different stakeholders for the development of cultural tourism by building effective and efficient partnerships between all parties concerned.

We will also strive to raise the awareness in the tourism industry of the importance of cultural tourism for economic development. In addition, we will also endeavor to raise the community's awareness of tourism benefits.

Recognizing the importance of the sustainable growth of the sector, we believe there is a need to strike a balance between cultural and heritage conservation and the continual modernization and development of the tourism sector. Challenges exist as increased visitation to historical cultural and heritage sites will stress these often fragile sites. To ensure cultural assets are viably used for sustainable poverty alleviation, it is necessary to protect and manage our assets properly.

We recognize the critical importance of accessibility to our attractions. Improvements in transportation links and hardware infrastructure will continue to be pursued under existing policy initiatives in order to facilitate visitors to enter into and move around Hong Kong.

Tourism is a fast growing industry with few boundaries. Intra-regional travel is becoming a worldwide trend. Under increasingly tight time constraints for traveling, visitors are looking for multi-destination itineraries to experience different cultures in one single trip. The Hong Kong SAR Government and the Hong Kong Tourism Board are committed to develop partnerships with countries in the region and we will continue to identify new opportunities for the development of suitable partnerships.

We recognize and support the effective work carried out by the World Tourism Organization (WTO) in promoting cultural tourism for poverty alleviation. The Hong Kong SAR Government pledges its continued support to the WTO's initiatives in this field.

MINISTERIAL STATEMENT OF BHUTAN[19]

His Excellency The Honorable Chairman
Their Excellencies
Ladies and Gentlemen

There is no doubt that tourism offers an enormous potential to create employment, generate wealth, earn foreign exchange and enhance people to people relations for global peace and harmony. The benefits of a properly managed tourism to the rural poor cannot be overlooked as it offers plenty of opportunities for the economically disadvantaged to supplement their income as well as provide them with employment. Cultural resources are something that the poorer nations are rich in. The fact that people are willing to travel extensively to discover and experience the rich cultural resources of another country is a positive indication and an opportunity that countries can maximize on without causing adverse effects.

Cultural tourism offers an individual the opportunity to participate in and learn about another culture. This could result in better understanding and appreciation of each other's beliefs, culture and way of life, thereby enhancing and promoting a situation where everyone can live in peaceful co-existence. I commend the effort of the World Tourism Organization in trying to provide platforms such as this for decision makers to come together in making collective efforts towards eradicating poverty and promoting peace and harmony in the world.

In Bhutan the development of tourism is still in its early stages and the number of tourists visiting Bhutan is very small even today. While being aware of the benefits of earning more income, the Royal Government pursued a cautious policy to ensure that the delicate cultural and environmental balance is not adversely affected. This has been done deliberately to ensure that the negative effects of tourism are avoided to the extent possible and to learn from the mistakes of those who tread the path before us. This is an advantage that a late starter has!

Bhutan will be moving forward in ensuring that the socio-economic benefits from tourism become more meaningful by encouraging more visitors and establishing more facilities. The Kingdom of Bhutan is fully committed to supporting sustainable tourism and in encouraging this industry to provide more socio-economic benefits to its people as well as employment opportunities.

With the majority of our people living on subsistence farming the Royal Government of Bhutan's pro-poor focus is evident in its approach to integrated rural development that encompasses the provision of free water supply, rural credit systems, infrastructure, telecommunication systems, electricity, free education and free medical facilities. Simultaneously, various income-generating programs have also been initiated with the government providing subsidized inputs. Various public policies, aimed at poverty reduction and equitable development, have been formulated including the highly progressive personal income taxation and electricity tariff system that reduces the burden on the poor.

---

[19] Mr. Lhatu Wangchuk, Director General, Department of Tourism, Ministry of Trade and Industry

Therefore, with regard to political commitment and the creation of an enabling environment for development of tourism as poverty alleviation tool, Bhutan is fortunate that we have a government fully committed to providing the development of tourism a high priority in its hierarchy of plans and programmes as spelt out in various policy documents such as the 9th Plan and the Vision of 2020. However, this move will not be made at the risk of harming all that we have treasured so far nor will we be encouraging mass tourism. For us the physical and spiritual well being of an individual is more important than economic or material gain. Thus, the underlying principle of development in any area has been that material benefit should not be gained at the expense of our culture, environment and tradition – which is what makes Bhutan what it is today. This vision that has emanated from the throne is at the heart of all our development activities. Therefore, tourism will be promoted in a manner that will reinforce our culture and environment – in consistence with the philosophy of Gross National Happiness (GNH). In other words – tourism will be promoted in a manner that is sustainable and responsible that will be of benefit to both the visitor as well as the host.

Within this paradigm we will be working towards ensuring that the benefits from tourism are as equally spread as possible with participation from all concerned. With an enlightened vision of empowering the people to participate in all spheres of development activities through the decentralization process the development of tourism too will be no different. Any pro-poor tourism development will be done so in consultation with and participation of the local communities concerned. For we know that without the full hearted participation and agreement of the main stakeholders any activity, howsoever noble the intention, will not bear fruit. In this context we are presently in the process of introducing community-based tourism on an experimental basis while at the same time being very conscious that this should not substitute for any other economic activity that they have been engaging in. Only upon the assessment and evaluation of these pilot areas will we proceed further in our plans of expanding this nationally if the results are positive.

The success story of the GMS has inspired the South Asian nations to also work together in promoting tourism at a sub-regional level. A combined effort will be more effective and it is hoped that cooperation and goodwill be promoted among neighbours. This alliance will not only be targeting visitors from outside the region but will also be promoting tourism within the sub-region. Through this collaboration we hope to not only generate employment and support alleviation of poverty but also help promote people to people contact and mutual goodwill amongst the neighbours – an important factor for friendly coexistence.

Like many other countries in South Asia the living and vibrant cultural heritage of Bhutan and its pristine environment are its USP. We hope to keep this culture alive and the environment unspoilt by preserving them while at the same time promoting their various facets, the benefits from which will eventually lead towards an enhanced livelihood for our people.

Thank you and Tashi Delek!

Presentation by UNESCO

DEVELOPING LOCAL CAPACITIES FOR CONSERVING HERITAGE RESOURCE AND MANAGING TOURISM AT HERITAGE SITES[20]

1. Tourism Development and Local Heritage

As the fastest growing and one of the most profitable industries in the world, tourism offers unparalleled opportunities for the economic development of local communities living in or near heritage sites in Asia and the Pacific. Properly managed tourism development can help to stem the out-migration of youth and other marginally-employed members of the community, alleviate poverty by providing new employment opportunities, revitalise traditional building and craft industries, enhance both the physical and the intangible heritage and offer a positive, peaceful way for communities to express pride in their cultural identity.

Painful experience in many areas of the world however, has shown that unplanned tourism development, although it may be profitable in the short term, can do irreversible damage to humankind's most precious heritage sites. Tourism can undermine the heritage value of these sites, despoiling them for future generations of inhabitants, students and visitors. The tourism juggernaut has the power to destroy the landscape with inappropriate infrastructure, force the out-migration of indigenous populations and cause over-exploitation and deterioration of the fragile cultural and natural resources. This vicious downward spiral also undermines heritage tourism by degrading and devaluing the very resources on which the tourism is based.

Local communities, heritage conservationists and tourism industry professionals operating in this region are acutely aware of the problems confronting them, and in particular that the development of tourism as an economic sector is being threatened by the lack of articulation of interests and cooperation between the parties involved. These groups sought assistance from UNESCO as well as other bodies, to provide workable solutions to find common ground between stakeholders and to help develop models for mechanisms that will create a sustainable cultural tourism industry that is beneficial to all and preserves the heritage resources of the community.

2. UNESCO Project on "Culture Heritage Management and Tourism: Models For Co-operation Among Stakeholders"

The UNESCO Project on **"Culture Heritage Management And Tourism: Models For Co-operation Among Stakeholders"** (1998-2003) addressed these concerns directly and brought into play action plans for the sustainable management of heritage and tourism which have been built up from the community level. The project provided all stakeholders -- and in particular women and youth - the opportunity to represent their own interests and play an important role in the development of sustainable tourism industries. Coming from a variety of circumstances and areas of expertise, partners - especially those in weaker positions, with less power - had the opportunity to learn from each other and develop ideas and opportunities.

---

[20] Mr. Richard Engelhardt, Regional Advisor for Culture in Asia and the Pacific, UNESCO Bangkok

2.1 Objective

The project aimed to open and structure avenues of communication between the tourism industry and those responsible for the conservation and maintenance of cultural heritage properties. By developing and testing models for the preservation of heritage and development of tourism as a local resource, the aim is to form mutually-beneficial alliances that will be both economically profitable and socially acceptable to local inhabitants and other stakeholders.

2.2 Implementation strategy

The project fostered the creation of key networks within heritage and tourism sectors, utilising in particular UNESCO's LEAP ('Integrated Community Development and Cultural Heritage Site Preservation in Asia and the Pacific Through Local Effort') network of heritage site managers, and heritage experts from the private and public sectors. The project developed closer networking ties with the tourism industry through industry bodies and national tourism organisations.

The project was implemented in five phases:
- **Phase I**: Case studies to evaluate tourism potential
- **Phase II**: Workshop to formulate action plans
- **Phase III**: Action plan implementation period
- **Phase IV**: Workshop to construct and test models
- **Phase V**: Evaluation and mainstreaming workshop

2.2.1. Phase I: Preparation of case studies

Eight historic heritage towns were selected for pilot project implementation. They are: Bhaktapur (Nepal), Melaka (Malaysia), Lijiang (China), Levuka (Fiji), Luang Prabang (Lao PDR), Hoi An (Viet Nam), Vigan (Philippines) and Kandy (Sri Lanka) - sites located in developing countries where cultural tourism development is a development priority by policy and by practice.

In each of these pilot sites, a team of local experts and/or stakeholders prepared an in-depth case study on the impact of tourism on heritage preservation, analyzing the following components:
> heritage resources
> tourism infrastructure
> econometric statistical analysis
> management, staffing and employment
> revenue capture and reinvestment

2.2.2. Phase II: Workshop to formulate action plans

Following the elaboration of the case studies, a regional workshop was organised in Bhaktapur, Nepal in April 2000 where teams from pilot sites presented their case studies to an audience of stakeholders from a wide selection of communities throughout the region. The workshop was facilitated by experts in heritage conservation, tourism economics and community development.

During the workshop, the expert resource persons provided guidance to pilot site team members in formulating site-specific action plans to address the problematic issues of communication and coordination between the tourism and heritage sectors identified during the Phase I studies. Components of the action plan were as follows:

re-direct investment from infrastructure development into meeting the increased maintenance costs of cultural sites, in order that they are not degraded by expanding tourist flows

put into place mechanisms and indicators which would give warning in advance when a cultural resource is approaching its carrying capacity, so that preventive action can be taken

establish and enforce professional standards of renovation and interpretation, in order to preserve the authenticity of cultural sites

measure the economic success of actions not on the basis of capital accumulation or international capital flow, but on the basis of local employment and job creation

2.2.3. Phase III: Action plan implementation period

The pilot sites implemented their action plans for a period of eighteen months from April 2000 to October 2001. Towards the end of this period, the pilot sites were requested to prepare their report on the implementation of their action plans, highlighting stakeholders involvement, sourcing and nature of funding, and evaluation of outcomes.

2.2.4. Phase IV: Workshop to construct and test models for co-operation among stakeholders

A workshop was organized in Lijiang, China in October 2001 to evaluate and reformulate site action plans and to construct replicable models for co-operation among stakeholders, based on the outcome and analysis of the test applications of these models in the pilot sites over the course of the previous 18 months. The resultant models were intended to: secure conservation and management of the cultural heritage in a sustainable way; respect the living traditional ways of life; include the local population and promote competence building, employment and other benefits especially among the poor part of the population; and induce tourism industry to compensate the heritage by increased revenues.

2.2.5. Phase V: Evaluation and mainstreaming workshop

A final project evaluation and mainstreaming workshop was organized in Penang, Malaysia from 15-18 January 2003 to: (1) evaluate the impact in the eight pilot sites of their participation in the project, in order to understand and make explicit the benefits of the process; (2) refine the Lijiang Models of Cooperation; and (3) to mainstream the lessons learnt from the pilot site activities into government policy at local, provincial and national level, thus transforming the Lijiang Models into action across the board.

The pilot site self-evaluations included the mapping of inputs which have resulted in the most significant and sustained results, the identification of indicators which most reliably measure their successes, and documentation of their 'wise practice' case studies for other sites to emulate.

2.3 The Lijiang Models of Cooperation Among Stakeholders

The outputs of the UNESCO project on "Culture Heritage Management And Tourism: Models For Co-operation Among Stakeholders" are currently being compiled into a user-friendly "Manual for Tourism Management in Heritage Cities and Towns in Asia and the Pacific", which will be distributed in the region. They are currently available online at http://www.unescobkk.org/culture/ norad-tourism/index.html

The key outputs are the models for cooperation among heritage tourism stakeholders in the region, which were developed on the basis of the locally developed plans by the participating sites. The models provide an operational strategy for sustainably developing tourism, especially with long-term local involvement and benefits. The models are as follows:

2.3.1 Models for fiscal management of heritage conservation, maintenance and development at the municipal level achieved through: review of the impact of income generating mechanisms; and identification and implementation of new income generating mechanisms.

(Refer to Annex I: Flowchart of the Model for Fiscal Management)

Mainstreaming into government policy would entail the following:
- comprehensive financial planning based on an agreed conservation management plan, considering environmental and social carrying capacity, risk management, preparedness and assessment, public-private partnerships, conservation incentives and financial support systems for private conservation efforts, and restructuring of tourism revenue collection for conservation and maintenance
- support heritage management programme with legal, administrative and institutional framework
- financial support for core programme from internal and external sources, external debt and revenue capture from special events and innovative activities

2.3.2 Model for investment by the tourism industry in the sustainability of the cultural resource base and supporting infrastructure achieved through: education of tourism operators on the value and conservation needs of the heritage; and formulating mechanisms by which the tourism industry can contribute financially and in other ways to preservation activities.

(Refer to Annex II: Flowchart of the Model for Investment by the Tourism Industry)

Mainstreaming into government policy would entail the following:
- identify and implement tourism revenue-capture schemes to finance 'material goods' and services, such as: heritage capital to restore built heritage and improve site presentation; tourism capital to enable community provide more convenient parking spaces, public toilets, food and accommodation facilities; 'carrying capacity' capital for tourism support services like electricity, water and waste management.
- Increase cultural awareness level and understanding among policy makers and community stakeholders on culture resource base and its economic potentials

236

Establishment of interpretation and tourist information centers to educate tourists and tourism operators on the value and conservation needs of the heritage

2.3.3 Model for community education and skills training leading to employment in the heritage conservation and culture tourism sectors, with emphasis on opportunities for women and youth, *achieved through: identifying new businesses and employment opportunities which can be made available locally; and designing programmes of skills training plus financial incentives to turn these potential opportunities into reality at the local level.*

(Refer to Annex III: Flowchart of the Model for Community Education and Skills Training)

Mainstreaming into government policy would entail the following:
strong political will and commitment among policy makers
formulate human resource development plan based on the demand of the tourism industry
preparation and implementation of educational and training programmes
local government to facilitate the establishment of partnerships in education and training with prival tourism industry
allocate public funds for tourism promotion and skills training programmes

2.3.4 Models for conflict resolution and consensus building among tourism promoters, property developers, local residents and heritage conservationists *achieved by: providing a structured venue where all stakeholders can raise and discuss situations and concerns, as well as receive education and information about heritage conservation needs and tourism development activities; and empowerment of local stakeholders through joint participation and implementation of both heritage conservation projects and culture tourism activities*

(Refer to Annex IV: Flowchart of the Model for Community Education and Skills Training)

Mainstreaming into government policy would entail the following:
community empowerment through education and awareness
early stakeholders' involvement in planning and strategizing
consensus building through equal access to information and respect for every stakeholder idea
form community committees to monitor activities and to report back findings to the community

3. Regional Application of the UNESCO Tourism Project: Linking Tourism Development To Preserving Cultural Heritage In The Buddhist Circuit

The Buddhist temples and the associated knowledge and traditions found in Southeast and South Asia represent a unique and representative heritage, not only to Asia and the six percent of the world's population who are Buddhist, but to mankind at large. A large number of these sites are found in what is becoming one of the world's most successful tourism growth areas. However, the traditional heritage at the Buddhist sites faces great pressures from international tourism which too often promotes superficial, non-authentic cultural products, and the rise in global construction materials and techniques. These factors have led to the degradation of traditional practices which define Buddhist communities, including unique building crafts and decorative arts.

3.2 Developing the Buddhist Circuit

As a precursor to further developing the Buddhist Circuit as part of the Asian Development Bank (ADB) South Asia Sub-regional Economic Cooperation (SASEC) Tourism Working Group (TWG) project, attention must be paid to strengthening the conservation of Buddhist heritage in these sites - both in terms of the built monuments as well as the living traditions. The tourism strategy which will be implemented in Bhutan, Bangladesh, India and Nepal for promoting these sites should take into account the need to build capacity among care takers of the heritage, so as to promote long-term sustainable development of the sites, while maintaining their cultural authenticity intact.

During the ADB SASEC Fourth Tourism Working Group (TWG) Meeting in Thimphu, Bhutan from 26-28 May 2004, UNESCO has been designated as the lead agency in the formulation of the conceptual framework for the development of Buddhist circuits under the following themes:
> Living Buddhism in the Himalayas
> Buddhist Art and Archaeology in South Asia

A third sub-theme on Footsteps of the Lord Buddha is currently the subject of on-going cooperation with JBIC and the Government of India.

3.2 UNESCO Project on "Cultural Survival and Revival in the Buddhist Sangha"

In this context, UNESCO seeks to strengthen the on-going Buddhist traditions within the framework of the Buddhist community itself through the on-going 3-year project **"Cultural Survival and Revival in the Buddhist Sangha".** The project is implemented in co-operation with the Nordic World Heritage Foundation with funding from the Government of Norway. The sub-regional implementation of the project is a continuation of a successful pilot project in Luang Prabang, Lao PDR. The following countries are included in the co-operation: Cambodia, China (Yunnan Province and Tibet), Lao PDR, Myanmar, Sri Lanka and Thailand. Additional implementation sites are situated in Bhutan, India, Nepal and Mongolia. The total budget for the three-year project period (2004-6) is approximately US $1,800,000.

3.3.1 Objectives

The project aims to build traditional local capacity in heritage conservation in Buddhist sites by reviving traditional decorative arts and building crafts, and developing preventative conservation skills among local caretakers of heritage, in particular amongst religious communities, such as the Buddhist *sangha*.

The project was developed in response to requests from monks and communities that see their heritage threatened by the disappearance of traditional skills and knowledge, and the tear and wear of tourists. Only if local traditions are preserved in a way that strengthens local people's identity, will local communities be prepared for handling increased tourism in a responsible manner.

Most of the selected sites are situated in poor areas with great development needs. Without mobilisation of necessary resources needed to preserve the authenticity and integrity of this unique heritage, these sites and communities run the risk of gradually being destroyed as a tourist attraction.

At the same time, many sites are inscribed on the UNESCO World Heritage List or are on the countries' Tentative List. The national responsibility and the priority accorded to the conservation of the tangible as well as the intangible heritage of these sites by both national authorities will facilitate the successful implementation of the project.

Partnerships and networks will be built by engaging actors form multiple sectors in the project in order to put into place innovative mechanisms which will guarantee the project's long-term sustainability with support from local communities and authorities at all levels. Moreover, the project will strengthen the social cohesion of local communities by reaffirming values implicit in their heritage and identity, while supporting sustainable production and consumption systems.

The recent Information and Strategy Development workshop for launching the expansion of this project, held in Luang Prabang, Lao PDR from 10-14 May 2004, provided a forum for representatives from Buddhist sites throughout the Mekong sub-region as well as the South Asia region to identify their needs and resources in conserving their living Buddhist traditions.

The situational reports presented by the site teams indicated that the living traditions of Buddhism in the region are a vibrant, integral part of the local identity and cultural resources. At the same time, they are under threat from development pressures; shifting socio-cultural tastes which privilege modern ways; and discontinuities in transmission of traditions and skills to the younger generation, brought about by political changes or lack of qualified trainers and interested trainees.

3.3.2 Implementation strategy

In response to these issues, site representatives identified modalities of project implementation as follows: awareness-raising amongst Buddhist *sangha*, community members and key decision makers about the conservation of Buddhist heritage; documentation and practical training in reviving dying or lost crafts associated with Buddhist practices; development of curricula concerning heritage conservation and management targeting the secondary and tertiary educational institutions for monks; training of monks and decision makers in preventative conservation, especially of key Buddhist landmarks. The overall output as a result of these project streams is to revive the living Buddhist practices in these sites.

In addition to local-level implementation, a sub-regional strategy for sharing resources and addressing linked concerns was developed. Sub-regional caucuses will provide the forum for sub-regional strategies for creating a network for training and technical mentoring, as well as monitoring and creating key partnerships with other initiatives, such as the ADB SASEC TWG. In the case of the South Asian sites, a sub-regional caucus to be spearheaded by the Indian National Trust for Art and Cultural Heritage (INTACH), will be convened in the third quarter of 2004.

In the context of the future influx of tourism along the Buddhist Circuit, the proposed site projects must be explicitly linked to the development of the cultural infrastructure which is needed to maintain, manage, and in some cases, revive the authentic practices of these communities. From the demand side of the equation, the visitors to the Buddhism sites will be drawn by reasons of religious pilgrimage or educational interest in Buddhist traditions. This demand will be translated into a desire to interact with genuine Buddhist heritage at these sites. The challenge is then to preserve the heritage while also facilitating increased tourism flow.

As such, the projects will be undertaken in a framework which offers three benefits:

Reinvigoration of traditional Buddhist practices, including ritualistic or devotional crafts central to the on-going practice and transmission of Buddhist heritage, such as production and caretaking of "thanka" paintings, palm-leaf manuscripts, among others.

Development of knowledge resources within existing Buddhist institutions, which will serve as a repository for local cultural resources, as teaching resources for future transmission among the local community, as well as educational tools for outside visitors. For instance, the establishment of monastery-based museums will develop a much-needed inventory of Buddhist artifacts, while serving as best-practice teaching models for undertaking such crafts in the present-day. At the same time, the museums will serve an important function in educating visitors about the broader historical and social context of the living traditions which they will experience on-site.

The strengthening of socio-economic opportunities for Buddhist communities, including linking the crafts revival to poverty alleviation as well as education, particularly within the traditional modes of Buddhist temple-based community capacity building.

Given this, an approach which heavily emphasizes the development of visitor amenities over the maintenance of authentic local heritage will likely deliver the pitfalls of mass-market tourism, leading to the dilution of the local heritage in the service of the lowest common denominator.

However, if the planned tourism strategy respects this framework, the visitors will serve as a catalyst for raising the awareness of the significance of these sites, even amongst local or national stakeholders. This will allow for a respectful approach to socio-economic development which will enhance the sites both in the short-term as well as the long-term.

3.4 Future steps

The ADB initiatives to strengthen tourism development in the Greater Mekong Sub-region and in the South Asian "Buddhist Circuit" provide a timely opportunity to cooperate with UNESCO in jointly developing a strategy for conserving and developing the cultural heritage resources of the region. A holistic approach to managing these local resources should bring together concerned stakeholders from the tourism as well as culture sectors. In particular, the application of the tourism development models developed through the UNESCO Project on "Culture Heritage Management and Tourism: Models For Co-operation Among Stakeholders" will provide the modalities to ensure the sustainable development of the Buddhist sites.

CONFERENCE PROGRAMME

Hue, Vietnam, 11-12 June 2004

Friday, 11 June

08:00 - 08:45	Registration
08:45 - 08:55	All delegates to be seated in the Conference Hall for the Opening Ceremony
09:00 – 09:30	Opening Ceremony - Inauguration Declaration by the Deputy Prime Minister of the Socialist Republic of Vietnam, H.E. Mr. Vu Khoan - Speech by the Chairperson of the Vietnam National Administration of Tourism (VNAT), H.E. Mdm. Vo Thi Thang - Speech by the Secretary General of the World Tourism Organization, Mr. Francesco Frangialli
09:30 – 09:45	Photo session for Heads of Delegation with H.E. the Deputy Prime Minister of the Socialist Republic of Vietnam in the gardens of the Saigon Morin Hotel
09:45 - 09:50	Presentation of gifts to Heads of Delegation by the Chairman of the People's Committee of Hue, H.E. Mr. Nguyen Xuan Ly
09:50 – 10:10	Coffee/tea break
10:10 – 10:20	Introduction by WTO
10:20 – 11:00	Presentation by Mr. Eugenio Yunis, WTO Chief for Sustainable Development for Tourism "Contribution of Cultural Tourism to Poverty Alleviation"
11:00 – 11:15	Presentation by the Deputy Head of Advisory Unit of Industry Development, VNAT, Dr. Pham Trung Luong
11:15 – 11:45	Presentation by the Chairman of the People's Committee of Hue, H.E. Mr. Nguyen Xuan Ly
11:45 - 12:15	Ministerial Statements[*] India: Minister of Tourism, H.E. Mrs. Renuka Choudhury Philippines: Secretary of Tourism, H.E. Mr. Roberto M. Pagdanganan
12:15 – 13:15	Lunch hosted by VNAT at the Morin Restaurant

---

[*] Ministers or heads of delegations are invited to make a 15-minute statement on the subject of the Conference, the content of which will be incorporated into the final Declaration of the Conference.

13:15 – 15:00	Ministerial Statements continued	
	Cambodia:	Senior Minister and Minister of Tourism, H.E. Mr. Veng Sereyvuth
	Indonesia:	Deputy Minister for Capacity Building and International Relations, Mr. Thamrin Bachri
	I.R. of Iran:	Vice-President of the Islamic Republic of Iran, and the President of the Iran Cultural Heritage and Tourism Organization, H.E. Mr. Seyed Hossein Maraashi
	Lao PDR:	Minister of the National Tourism Authority, H.E. Mr. Somphong Mongkhonvilay
	Malaysia:	Minister of Culture, Arts and Tourism, Datuk Dr. Leo Michael Toyad
	Rep.of Korea:	Vice-Minister of Culture and Tourism, Mr. Jee-chul Oh
	Sri Lanka:	Minister of Industries, Tourism and Investment Promotion, H.E. Mr. Anura Priadarsi Solomon Dias Bandaranaike
15:00 – 15:15	Coffee/tea break	
15:15 – 16:00	Ministerial Statements continued	
	Thailand:	Ambassador of Thailand to Vietnam, H.E. Mr. Krit Kraichitti, , on behalf of H.E. Mr. Sontaya Kunplome, Minister of Tourism and Sports
	Hong Kong SAR:	Deputy Commissioner for Tourism, Mr. Duncan Pescod
	Bhutan:	Director General, Department of Tourism, Ministry of Trade and Industry, Mr. Lhatu Wangchuk
16:00 - 16:15	Presentation by Mr. Richard Engelhardt, Regional Advisor for Culture in Asia and the Pacific, UNESCO Bangkok	
16:15 - 17:00	Questions and answers session	
18:15	Delegates to assemble in lobby of Saigon Morin Hotel for departure for dinner	

| 18:30 | Welcome dinner reception hosted by VNAT and the People's Committee of Hue at the Century Hotel |

Saturday, 12 June

09:00 – 10:15	Panel discussion
	Dr. Wienndu Nuryanti, Secretary-General, International Centre for Culture and Tourism, Indonesia
	Mr. S.K. Misra, Chairman of the Indian National Trust for Art and Cultural Heritage (INTACH), India
	Mr. Pradech Phayakvichien, Advisor to the Tourism Authority of Thailand
10:15 – 11:00	Reading of the Draft Hue Declaration on Cultural Tourism and Poverty Alleviation and questions and answers
11:00 – 11:15	Coffee/tea break
11:15 – 12:00	Adoption of the Hue Declaration on Cultural Tourism and Poverty Alleviation
	Closing Statements
12:00	Lunch hosted by VNAT at the Morin Restaurant
13:30	Delegates assemble in the lobby of Saigon Morin Hotel for departure on Technical Tour of Hue
15:00	Return to Saigon Morin Hotel
17:00	Delegates assemble in the lobby of Saigon Morin Hotel
18:30 - 20:30	Grand Opening Ceremony of the Hue Festival 2004
20:30 - 22:00	Dinner hosted by the Organizing Committee of the Hue Festival 2004

List of Participants

AUSTRALIA

Mr. Russell MILES
Second Secretary (Development Cooperation)
Australia Embassy
8 Dao Tan, Ba Dinh
HANOI
Tel: 844-831 7754/5
Fax: 844-831 7706
email: russell.miles@dfat.gov.au

BHUTAN

Mr. Lhatu WANGCHUK
Director-General
Department of Tourism
DOT, Ministry of Trade & Industry
THIMPHU
Tel. 975 2 325 225
Fax. 975 2 323 695
e-mail: lwangchuk@tourism.gov.bt

CAMBODIA

H.E. Mr.Veng SEREYVUTH
Senior Minister and Minister of Tourism
Ministry of Tourism
3 Preah Monivong Blvd.
PHNOM PENH
Tel. 855 12 811 100
Fax. 855 23 426 877
e-mail: veng@camnet.com.kh

Mr. Saroeuth KOUSOUM
Director General
Ministry of Tourism
3 Preah Monivong Blvd.
PHNOM PENH
Tel. 855 16 631 803
Fax. 855 23 426 107
e-mail: kousoum@mot.gov.kh

Mr. In THOEUN
Director of ASEAN and International Cooperation
Ministry of Tourism
3 Preah Monivong Blvd.
PHNOM PENH
Tel. 855 12 821 114
Fax. 855 23 426 107
e-mail: asean@mot.gov.kh

Ms. Sim PONNARATTANIN
Personal Assistant to the Minister
Ministry of Tourism
3 Preah Monivong Blvd.
PHNOM PENH
Tel. 855 12 711 028
Fax. 855 23 426 877
e-mail: Rattanin@mot.gov.kh

HONG KONG (SAR)

Mr. Duncan PESCOD
Deputy Commissioner for Tourism
Tourism Commission, Economic Development & Labour Bureau
2/F., East Wing, Central Government Offices
Lower Albert Road, Central
HONG KONG
Tel. 852 2810 3249
Fax 852 2801 5792
e-mail duncanpescod@edlb.gov.hk

INDIA

H.E. Mrs. Renuka CHOWDHURY
Minister of Tourism
Ministry of Tourism
Transport Bhavan, 1 Sansad marg
NEW DELHI 110001
Tel. 91 11 2371 8310
Fax 91 11 2373 1506

H.E. Mr. Ravi NEELAKANTAN
Ambassador
Embassy of India in Hanoi
58-60 Tran Hun Dao Str.
HANOI
Tel: 844 824 4990

Mr. Amitabh KANT
Joint Secretary
Ministry of Tourism
Transport Bhavan, 1 Sansad marg
NEW DELHI 110001
Tel. 91 11 2371 5084
Fax 91 11 2371 5084

Mr. Sudhir KUMAR
First Secretary
Embassy of India in Hanoi
58-60 Tran Hun Dao Str.
HANOI
Tel: 844 824 4990

Shri Dinesh BHATIA
Private Secretary to the Minister
Ministry of Tourism
Transport Bhavan, 1 Sansad Marg
New Delhi 110001
Tel: 91 11 2371 8310
Fax: 91 11 2373 1506
E-mail: dineshbhatia@tourism.nic.in

Mr. DO Van Hai
Clerk
Embassy of India in Hanoi
58-60 Tran Hun Dao Str.
HANOI
Tel: 844 824 4990

INDONESIA

H.E. Mr Thamrin Bhiwana BACHRI
Deputy Minister for Capacity Building
and International Relations
Ministry of Culture and Tourism
Jalan Medan Merdeka Barat 17
YAKARTA, 10110
Tel. 62 21 383 8413
Fax 62 21 348 33601
e-mail: bhiwana@budpar.go.id

H.E. Mrs. Artalili R.M.P TOBING
Ambassador of the Republic of
Indonesia to the Socialist Republic of
Vietnam.
Embassy of the Republic of Indonesia
50 Ngo Quyen Street, Hanoi
Tel: 84-4-8253353
Fax: 84-4-8259274
e-mail: dubes@indonesia-hanoi.vn

Mr. Rachmat RANUDIWIJAYA
Ambassador Extraordinary &
Plenipotenciary
Embassy of Republic of Indonesia in
Spain
Agastia, 65
28043, MADRID
Tel. 34 91 413 0292
Fax 34 91 413 8994
e-mail: kbri@embajadadeindonesia.es

Mr. Sutjipto DONOKUSUMO
Indonesian Consulate General in Ho
Chi Minh City, Vietnam

Mrs. Ni Wayan Giri ADNYANI
Deputy Director for Multilateral
Cooperation
Ministry of Culture and Tourism
Jalan Medan Merdeka Barat 17
YAKARTA, 10110
Tel. 62 21 383 8413
Fax 62 21 348 33601
e-mail: nwgia@budpar.go.id

Mr. Tangkuman ALEXANDER
Second Secretary
Embassy of the Republic of Indonesia
50 Ngo Quyen Street, Hanoi
Tel: 84-4-8253353
Fax: 84-4-8259274
Email:
alexander-tangkuman@yahoo.com

Mrs. Andalusia TRIBUANA
Third Secretary
Embassy of Indonesia
Agastia, 65
28043, MADRID
Tel. 34 91 413 0292
Fax 34 91 413 8994
e-mail kbri@embajadadeindonesia.es

ISLAMIC REPUBLIC OF IRAN

H.E. Mr. S. H. MARAASHI
Vice President of I. R. of Iran &
President of
Iran Cultural Heritage & Tourism Org.
(ICHTO), N°. 238 Sindokht Crossroad
West Fatemi Ave.
TEHRAN
Tel: 98 21 601 34 83
Fax: 98 21 601 34 98
Email: info@ichto.org

H.E. Mr. Hossein Molla ABDOLLAHI
Ambassador of I. R. of Iran to the
Socialist Republic of Vietnam

Mr. Morteza TALE
Former Director, Planning and Standard
(ITTO)
N°. 238 Sindokht Crossroad
West Fatemi Ave.
TEHRAN
Tel: 98 21 643 56 61
Fax: 98 21 643 53 95

Mr. Seyed M. K. KHOLDINASAB
Office of President
Iran Cultural Heritage & Tourism Org.
N°. 238 Sindokht Crossroad
West Fatemi Ave.
TEHRAN
Tel: 98 21 69 444 87
Fax: 98 21 643 53 95
e-mail: kholdinasab@asia.com;
m_kholdinasab@hotmail.com

LAOS

Mr. Somphong MONGKHONVILAY
Minister
Lao National Tourism Authority
Lane Xang Avenue
PO Box 3556
VIENTIANE
Tel. 856 21 21 2251
Fax. 856 21 21 2769

Mr. Ounethouang KHAOPHANH
Director
Management Control on Tourism
Industry and Law Division
Lane Xang Avenue
P.O Box: 3556
Vientiane, Lao PDR
Tel: 856-21 212251 - 212961
Fax: 856 21 212679
Email: Laonta@Laotel.com

Mr. Khom DOUANG CHANTHA
Deputy Director
Lao National Tourism Authority
Lane Xang Avenue
PO Box 3556
VIENTIANE
Tel. 856 21 21 2251
Fax. 856 21 21 2769

Mr. Silipanya VONG PHACHANH
Officer
Lao National Tourism Authority
Lane Xang Avenue, PO Box 3556
VIENTIANE
Tel. 856 21 21 2251
Fax. 856 21 21 2769

MALAYSIA

Hon. Datuk Dr. Leo Michael TOYAD
Minister
Ministry of Tourism
Floor 27, Menara Dato 'Onn
Pusat Dagangan Dunia Putra (PWTC)
46 Jalan Tun Ismail
Tel. 856 21 21 2251
Fax. 856 21 21 2769

Mr. Alex Rajakumar PONNIAH
Principal Assistant Secretary
Ministry of Tourism
33rd Floor, Menara Dato 'Onn
Pusat Dagangan Dunia Putra (PWTC)
46 Jalan Tun Ismail
50694 KUALA LUMPUR
Tel: 603 2696 3288
Fax: 603 2693 7111
Email: alex@mocat.gov.my

Mr. M. MUKUNDAN
1st Secretary
Embassy of Malaysia to the Socialist
Republic of Vietnam
Embassy of Malaysia
16th Floor, Fortuna Tower
6B Lang Ha, Hanoi
VIETNAM
Tel: 84-4-831 3400
Fax: 84-4-831 3402

MALDIVES

H.E. Mr. Hassan SOBIR
Minister of Tourism
Ministry of Tourism, Male', Republic of
Maldives
Tel: 960-325027
Fax: 960-322512
Email: hsobir@visitmaldives.com

PAKISTAN

Mr. Mohammad Yousaf ALI
Ambassador of Pakistan to the Socialist
Republic of Viet Nam
Embassy of Pakistan
8th Floor, Daeha Bussiness Center, Kim
Ma District, HA NOI, VIETNAM
Tel: 84-4-7716420-21
Fax: 84-4-7716418
Email: parep-hanoi@hn.vnn.vn

PHILIPPINES

HE. Mr. Roberto M. PAGDANGANAN
Minister
Department of Tourism
DOT BLDG., T.M KALAW AVE
MANILA
Tel. 63 2 524 1751
Fax 63 2 521 7374
E-mail: otdp@tourism.gov.ph

Mr. Phineas ALBURO
Action Officer, International Coop.
Dept., Department of Tourism
DOT BLDG., T.M KALAW AVE
MANILA
Tel. 63 2 524 1751
Fax 63 2 521 7374
e-mail: otdp@tourism.gov.ph

Ms. Josefina Leona RIEL
Chief of the State, Office of the
Secretary
Department of Tourism
DOT BLDG., T.M KALAW AVE
MANILA
Tel. 63 2 536 3154
Fax 63 2 521 7374
E-mail: uriel501@yahoo.com

Mr. Ivan Anthony HENARES
Senior Tourism Operations Officer
City Government of San Fernando,
PAMPANGA
A. Consunji Street, Santo Rosario, City
of San Fernando
Pampanga 2000 PHILIPPINES
Tel: 63 45 9612872
Fax: 63 45 9615022
Email:
tourism@cityofsanfernando.gov.ph

REPUBLIC OF KOREA

Mr. Jee-Chul OH
Vice Minister of Culture and Tourism
Ministry of Culture and Tourism
82-1 Sejong-no, Jongno-Gu
SEOUL 110703
Tel. 822 3704 9010
Fax 822 3704 9019
E-mail: jcoh@mct.go.kr

Mr. Beong-heok YOO
Director
Ministry of Culture and Tourism
82-1 Sejong-no, Jongno-Gu
SEOUL 110703
Tel. 822 3704 9780
Fax 822 3704 9789
E-mail: bhyoo@mct.go.kr

Ms. Soo-Hyun MYUNG
Deputy Director
Ministry of Culture and Tourism
82-1 Sejong-no, Jongno-Gu
SEOUL 110703
Tel. 822 3704 9780
Fax 822 3704 9789
E-mail: myung22@mct.go.kr

Mr. Han-hee SONG
Assistant Director
Ministry of Foreign Affairs and Trade
95-1 Do-ryom Dong, Jongno-gu
SEOUL 110 787
Tel. 822 2100 7557
Fax 822 3704 7970
E-mail: culturepr@mofat.go.kr

SRI LANKA

Mr. Anura Priadarsi Solomon Dias
BANDARANAIKE
Hon. Minister
Ministry of Industries, Tourism &
Investment Promotion
No. 64, Galle Road
COLOMBO 03
Tel. 94 11 244 1464
Fax 94 11 244 1501

Dr. Upananda VIDANAPATHIRANA
Secretary
Ministry of Industries, Tourism &
Investment Promotion
No. 64, Galle Road
COLOMBO 03
Tel. 94 11 244 1464
Fax 94 11 244 1501
e-mail mindsec@sltnet.lk

Mr. Abdul Hafeel Mohamed ONAIS
Private Secretary to the Minister
Ministry of Industries, Tourism &
Investment Promotion
No. 64, Galle Road
COLOMBO 03
Tel. 94 11 244 1464
Fax 94 11 244 1501

Mr. Weragoda Arachchilage
GAMANEE GUNARATHNA
Personal Security Officer to the
Minister
Ministry of Industries, Tourism &
Investment Promotion
No. 64, Galle Road
COLOMBO 03
Tel. 94 11 244 1464
Fax 94 11 244 1501

THAILAND

H.E. Mr. Krit KRAICHITTI
Ambassador
Embassy of Thailand to Vietnam

Dr. Sasithara PICHAICHANNARONG
Director-General
Office of Tourism Development
Ministry of Tourism and Sports
National Stadium, Rama I Road
Pathumwan
BANGKOK, 10330
Tel. 662 215 3788
Fax. 662 214 1491
e-mail: sasitharap@yahoo.com

Ms. Pannipa CHAYASOMBAT
Policy & Plan Analyst
Office of Tourism Development
Ministry of Tourism and Sports
National Stadium, Rama I Road
Pathumwan
BANGKOK, 10330
Tel. 662 612 4024
Fax. 662 216 6658
e-mail: talumpuk@yahoo.co.uk

Ms. Prapa TANTASUPARUK
Tourism Development Officer
Office of Tourism Development
Ministry of Tourism and Sports
National Stadium, Rama I Road
Pathumwan
BANGKOK, 10330
Tel. 662 612 4024
Fax. 662 216 6658
e-mail: prapatanta@yahoo.com

Ms. Ubolwan PRADABSOOK
Official
Tourism Authority of Thailand
1600 New Pechaburi Road
Makkasan
BANGKOK, 10400
Tel. 662 652 8203
Fax. 662 685 8204
e-mail: Ubolwan.pradabsook@tat.or.th

Mr. Paradech PHAYAKVICHIEN
Tourism Authority of Thailand
1600 New Pechabñi Road, Makkasan,
Bangkok 14000
Tel: 662 6528203
Fax: 662 6528204
Email: paradech@tat.or.th

Ms. Tida SUKEEPLAP
First Secretary
Royal Thai Embassy
63-65 Hoang Dieu Street
HANOI
Tel: 84-4-8235092/4
Fax: 84-4-8235088
Email: tida@fpt.vn

VIETNAM

H.E. Ms. Vo Thi Thang
Chairperson
Vietnam National Administration of
Tourism
80, Quan Su Street
HANOI
Tel: (84-4) 942 1063
Fax: (84-4) 942 4115
email: icdvnat@vietnamtourism.com

Mr. PHAM Tu
Vice Chairman
Vietnam National Administration of
Tourism
80, Quan Su Street
HANOI
Tel: (84-4) 942 1063
Fax: (84-4) 942 4115
email: icdvnat@vietnamtourism.com

Mr. PHAM Quang Hung
Director - International Coop. Dept.
Vietnam National Administration of
Tourism
80, Quan Su Street
HANOI
Tel: (84-4) 942 1063
Fax: (84-4) 942 4115
email: hung65icd@yahoo.com

Mrs. CHU Ha Lan
Acting Director - Administrative Office
Vietnam National Administration of
Tourism
80, Quan Su Street
HANOI
Tel: (84-4) 942 3314
Fax: (84-4) 942 4115

Mr. NGUYEN Quy Phuong
Deputy Director - Tourism Promotion
Department
Vietnam National Administration of
Tourism
80, Quan Su Street
HANOI
Tel: (84-4) 942 2280
Fax: (84-4) 942 4115

Mr. PHAM Trung Luong
Deputy head - Advisory Unit for
Industry Development
Vietnam National Administration of
Tourism
80, Quan Su Street
HANOI
Tel: (84-4) 942 5912
Fax: (84-4) 942 4115

Mr. LE Minh Duc
Staff - Tourism Promotion Department
Vietnam National Administration of
Tourism
80, Quan Su Street
HANOI
Tel: (84-4) 942 2280
Fax: (84-4) 942 4115

Mr. TRAN Phu Cuong
Staff - International Cooperation
Department
Vietnam National Administration of
Tourism
80, Quan Su Street
HANOI
Tel: (84-4) 942 1061
Fax: (84-4) 942 4115
e-mail: cuongtp70@yahoo.com

Mr. DINH Ngoc Duc
Staff - International Cooperation
Department
Vietnam National Administration of
Tourism
80, Quan Su Street
HANOI
Tel: (84-4) 942 1061
Fax: (84-4) 942 4115
e-mail:
dinhngocduc@vietnamtourism.com

Ms. PHAM Ngoc Diep
Staff - International Cooperation
Department
Vietnam National Administration of
Tourism
80, Quan Su Street
HANOI
Tel: (84-4) 942 1061
Fax: (84-4) 942 4115
e-mail: pndiep@yahoo.com

Ms. TRAN Thi Phuong Nhung
Staff - International Cooperation
Department
Vietnam National Administration of
Tourism
80, Quan Su Street
HANOI
Tel: (84-4) 942 1061
Fax: (84-4) 942 4115
e-mail:
nhung_vnat@vietnamtourism.com

AFFILIATE MEMBERS

Mr. Young-uk LEE
President
Korea Culture & Tourism Policy
Institute
827 Bangwha -3 dong
Gangseo-gu
SEOUL 157 857
Tel. 82 2 2669 9801
Fax 82 2 2669 9881
e-mail: presi@kctpi.re.kr

Mr. Kwang Hoon RYU
Director of Research Planning Team
Korea Culture & Tourism Policy
Institute
827 Bangwha -3 dong
Gangseo-gu
SEOUL 157 857
Tel. 82 2 2669 9838
Fax 82 2 2669 9880
e-mail: hmyang@kctpi.re.kr

Mr. Won Hee LEE
Senior Researcher
Korea Culture & Tourism Policy
Institute
827 Bangwha -3 dong
Gangseo-gu
SEOUL 157 857
Tel. 82 2 2669 9801
Fax 82 2 2669 9881
e-mail: whlee@kctpi.re.kr

INTERNATIONAL ORGANIZATIONS

SNV NETHERLANDS DEVELOPMENT ORGANISATION

Mr. Marcel LEIJZER
Private Sector Development Officer
Bezuidenhoutseweg 161
2594 AG DEN HAAG
Tel. 31 70 344 0218
Fax 31 70 385 5531
E-mail: mleijzer@snv.nl

Mr. Luuk BOON
Director of SNV
HANOI
Vietnam

Mr. Douglas HAINSWORTH
Advisor of SNV
Vietnam

UNITED NATIONS EDUCATIONAL, SCIENTIFIC, & CULTURAL ORGANIZATION (UNESCO)

Mr. Richard ENGELHARDT
Regional Advisor for Culture in Asia
and the Pacific
UNESCO BANGKOK
920 Sukhumvit Road
10110 BANGKOK
Tel. 66 2 391 0577
Fax. 66 2 391 0688
e-mail: culture@unescobkk.org

Mr. Ricardo FAVIS
Consultant for Culture
UNESCO Bangkok Office
5th Floor M.L. Pin Malakul Centennial
Building
920 Sukhumvit Road
BANGKOK 10110
Tel. 66 2 391 0577
Fax. 66 2 391 0866
e-mail: r.favis@unescobkk.org

UN – ESCAP

Mr. Ryuji YAMAKAWA
Chief – Tourism Unit
Transport Policy & Tourism Section
UN – ESCAP
United Nations Building
Rajdamnern Ave.
BANGKOK 10200
Tel. 66 2 288 1426
Fax. 66 2 288 1067
e-mail: yamakawa.unescap@un.org

OTHER PARTICIPANTS

Mr. Sheldon Albert Daniel SANTWAN
Editor
Indian Express Newspapers Ltd.
Express Towers, 1st Floor
Nariman Point
MUMBAI-21
Tel. 91 22 2204 0109
Fax 91 22 5630 1007
e-mail ehc@vsnl.com

Mr. Mark MENDES
Editorial Consultant
Indian Express Newspapers Ltd.
Express Towers, 1st Floor
Nariman Point
MUMBAI-21
Tel. 91 22 2204 0109
Fax 91 22 5630 1007
e-mail ehc@vsnl.com

Mr. Christopher EDMONDS
Research Department
THE ECONOMIST
1001 East-West Center
HONOLULU, HI 96848-1601
Tel. 1 808 944 7362
Fax. 1 808 944 7399
e-mail: Edmondsc@eastwestcenter.org

Dr. Rowan MACTAGGART
G.R.M Sustainable Tourism
Development Consortium, Australia.
Level 29, Lennons Commercial Tower,
Brisbang, QLD 4000, AUSTRALIA
Tel: +61-7-3025-8500
Fax: +61-7-3025-8555
Email: rowanm@grm.com.au

Mr. Moo-Jin CHUN
President
CI Communication
752-2 Gong-Duk Dong
Mapo-ku
SEOUL
Tel. 822 757 2572
Fax 822 318 8834
E-mail: coo@cicomm.co.kr

Mr. Hyeok Juv KWAN
Manager
CI Communication
752-2 Gong-Duk Dong
Mapo-ku
SEOUL
Tel. 822 757 2572
Fax 822 318 8834

Mr. Jin Young JUNG
Assistant Manager
CI Communications Co. Ltd.
752-2 Gong-Duk Dong
Mapo-ku
SEOUL
Tel. 822 757 2572
Fax 822 318 8834
E-mail: smus78@cicomm.co.kr

WTO SPEAKERS

Mr. S.K. MISRA
Chairman
Indian National Trust for Art & Cultural
Heritage (INTACH)
71, Lodhi Estate
NEW DELHI
Tel. 91 11 2465 4090
Fax 91 11 2461 1290
e-mail intach@del3@vsnl.net.i

Dr. Wiendu NURYANTI
Secretary-General
International Centre for Culture and
Tourism
Jalan Lingkar Utara, 234
YOGYAKARTA 55281
Tel. 62 274 520 907
Fax 62 274 583 783
e-mail stuppa@yoyga.wasantara.net.id

Mr. Pradech PHAYAKVICHIEN
Advisor, Tourism Authority of Thailand
1600 New Pechaburi Road
Makkasan
BANGKOK, 10400
Tel. 662 652 8203
Fax. 662 685 8204
e-mail: Pradech@tat.or.th

WTO DELEGATION

Mr. Francesco FRANGIALLI
Secretary-General
World Tourism Organization
Capitán Haya, 42
28020, MADRID
Tel. 34 91 567 8100
Fax. 34 91 571 3733
e-mail: omt@world-tourism.org

Dr. Dawid de VILLIERS
Deputy Secretary-General
World Tourism Organization
Capitán Haya, 42
28020, MADRID
Tel. 34 91 567 8100
Fax. 34 91 571 3733
e-mail: omt@world-tourism.org

Dr. Harsh VARMA
Chief – Technical Cooperation
World Tourism Organization
Capitán Haya, 42
28020, MADRID
Tel. 34 91 567 8100
Fax. 34 91 571 3733
Email: omt@world-tourism.org

Mr. Eugenio YUNIS
Chief – Sustainable Development of
Tourism
World Tourism Organization
Capitán Haya, 42
28020, MADRID
Tel. 34 91 567 8100
Fax. 34 91 571 3733
Email: omt@world-tourism.org

Mr. XU Jing
Regional Representative for Asia and
the Pacific
World Tourism Organization
Capitán Haya, 42
28020, MADRID
Tel. 34 91 567 8100
Fax. 34 91 571 3733
Email: omt@world-tourism.org

Ms. Vanessa SATUR
Assistant – Technical Cooperation
World Tourism Organization
Capitán Haya, 42
28020, MADRID
Tel. 34 91 567 8100
Fax. 34 91 571 3733
Email: omt@world-tourism.org

Ms. Christine BREW
Assistant - Regional Representation for
Asia and the Pacific
World Tourism Organization
Capitán Haya, 42
28020, MADRID
Tel. 34 91 567 8100
Fax. 34 91 571 3733
Email: omt@world-tourism.org

Mr. Ruud KLEP
Consultant
World Tourism Organization
Capitán Haya, 42
28020, MADRID
Tel. 34 91 567 8100
Fax. 34 91 571 3733
Email: omt@world-tourism.org

**HOST ORGANIZING
COMMITTEE**

Mr. CHAU Dinh Nguyen
Director of the Department of Foreign
Affairs of Thua Thien Hue Province
24 Ly Thuong Kiet Street, Hue City,
Vietnam
Tel: 84-84-822005
Fax: 84-54-833639
Email: dfat.thue@dng.vnn.vn

Mr. DO Bien Thuy
Deputy Director of the Department of
Foreign Affairs of Thua Thien Hue
Province
24 Ly Thuong Kiet Street, Hue City,
Vietnam
Tel: 84-84-822005
Fax: 84-54-833639
Email: dfat.thue@dng.vnn.vn

Mr. HUYNH Tien Dat
Head of the International Cooperation
Division
Thua Thien Hue Department of Foreign
Affairs
24 Ly Thuong Kiet Street, Hue City,
Vietnam
Tel: 84-84-822005
Fax: 84-54-833639
Email: dfat.thue@dng.vnn.vn